OLD TESTAMENT HISTORY

III

FROM THE BIRTH OF SAMUEL

TO THE DEATH OF DAVID

OLD TESTAMENT HISTORY SERIES

Each Volume is intended to provide material for one term's work. The following are some of the chief features of the scenes:

i. The Narrative is given for the most part in the words of the Authorized Version.

ii. Brief Historical explanations and general commentary are inserted in their proper places.

iii. The chronological order of events has been followed.

iv. Each period is illustrated by reference to contemporary literature (e.g. Prophets and Psalms) and monuments.

v. Footnotes are added, but only where difficulties of thought or language seem to demand explanation.

Vol. 1 FROM THE CREATION TO THE CROSSING OF THE RED SEA

Vol. 2 FROM THE CROSSING OF THE RED SEA TO RUTH

Vol. 3 FROM THE BIRTH OF SAMUEL TO THE DEATH OF DAVID

Vol. 4 FROM THE ACCESSION OF SOLOMON TO THE FALL OF THE NORTHERN KINGDOM

Vol. 5 FROM HEZEKIAH TO THE END OF THE CANON

OLD TESTAMENT

HISTORY

FROM THE BIRTH OF SAMUEL

TO THE DEATH OF DAVID

BY THE REV.

J. M. HARDWICH, M.A.

LATE SCHOLAR OF ST. JOHN'S COLLEGE, CAMBRIDGE
AND BELL UNIVERSITY SCHOLAR;
ASSISTANT MASTER AT RUGBY SCHOOL

AND THE REV.

H. COSTLEY-WHITE, M.A.

LATE SCHOLAR OF BALLIOL COLLEGE, OXFORD;
HEADMASTER OF BRADFIELD COLLEGE;
LATE ASSISTANT MASTER AT RUGBY SCHOOL

PERIOD III

Originally published by JOHN MURRAY, LONDON, 1913

This edition published by

Living Library Press, Bristol TN, USA, © 2024

PREFACE

THE aim of this series may be stated briefly. It is an attempt to combine the advantages of a general history with those of the ordinary commentary: the former is open to the charge that it does not make the reader familiar with the language of the Bible; while the latter is too often overloaded with notes and does not cover sufficient ground. In these volumes the Bible is left to tell its own story, after difficulties of arrangement and language which exist in it have been removed or explained.

Practical experience has shown that the Old Testament may conveniently be divided into five periods, each containing enough matter to occupy one school term. Without laying claim to any credit for originality, the editors have tried to keep certain definite aims in view—the chronological sequence of events, the historical setting of the narrative, and (in the later volumes) illustrations from the Prophets and other portions of the Scriptures.

It has been impossible in the commentary altogether to avoid the use of technical terms and other words which may be unfamiliar to the youngest reader. These have, however, in many cases been explained where they occur.

Frequent reference should be made by tile reader to good maps of Palestine and the surrounding countries.

PREFACE

The editors particularly recommend Murray's Handy Classical Maps, Palestine, from which they venture to differ, in the present volume, only in the location of Gibeah of Saul and Rachel's Tomb (pp. 28, 32).

This volume, like its predecessor, has had the advantage of being submitted in manuscript to the patient criticism of Mr. C. E. M. Hawkesworth.

To him, as to the authors of those standard works on the period mentioned on page ix, their obligations to whom will be evident on nearly every page, the editors offer their sincere thanks.

CONTENTS

PART I. SAMUEL THE JUDGE

PART II. SAUL THE KING

CONTENTS

PART III. DAVID THE KING

APPENDIX

PRINCIPAL ABBREVIATIONS EMPLOYED IN THIS VOLUME

Dr. L.O.T.	Dr. Driver's *INTRODUCTION to the Literature of the Old Testament*, 1891 Edition.
H.D.B.	Hastings' *Dictionary of the Bible in one Volume* (1909).
H.G.H.L.	*Historical Geography of the Holy Land,* by G. Adam Smith, 6th ed. (1898).
Kenn.	*Samuel,* Edited by Dr. Kennedy (The Century Bible, 1905).
Kent.	*Israel's Historical and Biographical: Narratives,* by Dr. Kent (1905).
LXX	The Septuagint: the Greek version of the Hebrew Scriptures, begun in the third cent. B.C.
Ott.	Canon Ottley's *History of the Hebrews* (1901).
Rel. Sem.	*The Religion of the Semites,* by W. Robertson Smith.
Sl.	The tenth cent. document, *Life of Saul and David,* see p. xiv.
Sm.	The Deuteronomic document, *Life of Samuel,* see p. xv.
Smith	Dr. H. P. Smith's *Commentary on the Books of Samuel*: International Critical Commentary (1904).
Vol. 1, 2, 5	Refer to other volumes of the present series (1908-10).
Well.	Wellhausen's *History of Israel and Judah,* 3rd ed. (English, 1891).

E. THE CALENDER OF THE JEWISH YEAR

ORDER IN THE		MONTH	ENGLISH EQUIVALENT, APPROXIMATELY
SACRED YEAR*	CIVIL YEAR*		
i	7	Abib or Nisan	April
ii	8	Ziv or Iyyar	May
iii	9	Sivan	June
iv	10	Tammuz	July
v	11	Ab	August
vi	12	Elul	September
vii	1	Ethanim or Tishri	October
viii	2	Bul or Marcheshvan	November
ix	3	Chisleu	December
x	4	Tebeth	January
xi	5	Shebat	February
xii	6	Adar	March

*The "civil" year is the older Hebrew year, which began in autumn. But in early days, before the Exile, the Babylonian calendar, by which the year began in spring, was also in use in Palestine. This latter calendar was adopted for ritual purposes, and the festivals

INTRODUCTION

(a) Character of the Period

The period embraced in this volume was one of the most important in Hebrew history. It covers a space of a little over a century, from about 1090 to 970 B.C. During that century there occurred a great constitutional change: the several tribes, with their local interests and dangers, their separate organizations for judicial, administrative, and military purposes, and their mutual jealousies, were united under a monarch. From this point the real *national* history of Israel began. At the close of the period of their Military Dictators, the Judges, the Hebrews were left with certain elements which made for unity—identity of race, religion, and law, and the memory of the past. But as yet this capacity for union had not been appreciated. Hence it was that external enemies had taken advantage of the internal disorganization of the country to establish an overlordship over it. Spasmodically the Judges had made efforts to liberate the several districts from foreign domination. But at the opening of the period before us the failure of these attempts is painfully evident. The Philistines were masters of the land. At its close the Philistines had been reduced to the dependence upon the king of a united Israel, and Israel was in Hebrew history mistress of an empire extending from Hamath on Orontes in the far north, to the Gulf of Akaba in the south, and from the Mediterranean to the heart of the Desert beyond the Syrian and Ammonite principalities.

INTRODUCTION

Moreover, with the establishment of the Monarchy the literary history of Israel also began. Henceforth there was a nation to write about, historians to write, and the necessary inspiration and facilities for writing. And in the religious sphere it was from this date that there originated that peculiar development of the gift of prophecy, the influence of which upon the religion of Israel and the world cannot be over-estimated.

(b) Authorities for the Period

Our knowledge of the history of these years is derived from:
1. The two books of Samuel and 1 Kings 1 and 2.

2. 1 Chron. 10-29.

3. Occasional references and allusions in the Psalms, Prophets, and New Testament.

It will be necessary to consider for a moment the origin and nature of these documents in order that the reader may clearly understand how far the Bible narrative supplies us with an accurate record of (i) the history of the people, (ii) the history of the religion of those times.

(c) Nature and Authorship of the Books of Samuel [1]

The books of Samuel are not the work of a single historian. They are a composite structure. They consist of long and short extracts from the works of writers of varying authority and different date. These extracts

---

1. It is assumed that the reader is already familiar with the elementary principles of Historical Criticism, an outline of which was sketched in the INTRODUCTION to vols. 1 and 2 of this series.

have been combined into a whole by a compiler, editor, or redactor. This is proved by examining the contents of *Samuel*. (a) The *literary and linguistic test*. Some parts of *Samuel* are written in a style and with a vocabulary which are quite different from those employed in other parts. This suggests that more than one writer has been at work. For the same writer could hardly adopt one style and vocabulary at one moment and others at another. Browning does not write at times like Pope, nor Macaulay like Bacon. (b) The *historical test*. There are in *Samuel* several instances of the same event being recorded twice. The two records often contradict each other in certain details This is just what happens when two independent writers set out to describe the same event. There are, e.g. two accounts of the denunciation of Eli's house, two of Saul's rejection, two of David's introductions to court, and so on. Again, in some cases the same event is described from two entirely different points of view. In one place Samuel is regarded as the great theocratic ruler of Israel: in another he is a local seer, known only in his own district, but not to Israel at large. In one place the writer is hostile to the monarchy; he views it as being regarded with disfavor by God, and therefore by Samuel: in another Samuel is depicted as being eager for it, and God Himself suggests it. In one place the historian simply and vividly narrates the facts, without comment. In another he is of the *didactic type*. He uses the facts and traditions[1] in order to teach (*didaskein*) a moral

---

[1] The word "tradition" merely means that the account of a given event has been handed down by one or more of various methods of transmission. It does not imply that the story "thus designated is necessarily untrustworthy and unhistorical" (Kent, quoted by Kennedy, from whom much of this section is derived).

lesson. His aim is not to hand down a narrative of events, but "to interpret to his contemporaries God's discipline of His people in their history." For example, he uses the historical fact of Saul's rejection from the throne to enforce the lesson that "obedience is better than sacrifice." By arguments such as these we saw, in treating of the Pentateuch, that the four main sources of that narrative, which are known as J, E, D and P, could be distinguished. The same is the case with Samuel, though here there is not such entire unanimity among critics as to the precise origin and date of the different parts. However, the conclusions generally agreed upon are roughly these.

1. An historian of marked literary ability who lived not long after Solomon's time, about 920 B.C., wrote a history of the rise of the monarchy in Israel. The parts of his history with which we have to deal concern themselves with Saul and David. Hence, adopting H. P. Smith's denotation, we call this writer and his work *Sl* (= Saul). He had at his command—

a. Certain court records made and kept in the royal palace.

b. Certain annals made by Samuel, Nathan, and Gad, originating in the training-schools of the prophets.

c. Certain collections of ballads and other poetry.

d. And for the latter part of his history he could have consulted old men who had actually witnessed the events he describes.

He had therefore ample materials for producing an authentic history of the time. His success as a writer and his trustworthiness as an authority are acknowledged on all hands. Here, for the first time in the history of Israel, we have a first-class historian. His narrative is the oldest that exists in the Bible; for we saw that the writers of the Pentateuch, though drawing from ancient materials, themselves lived and wrote at a later date than this. To this writer belong a large proportion of the chapters dealing with Saul and David, and particularly the long section, 2 Sam. 9-20, which constitutes "the finest, as it is the earliest, specimen of continuous prose narrative in the Old Testament." 1 Kings 1, and part of 2 are also from this author.

2. Another historian, of the didactic type, being "dissatisfied with the worldly view" of the early kings presented by *Sl*, set out to rewrite the history, utilizing the work of *Sl* and certain other sources of information. His main idea was to write a life of Samuel, and to show how "Samuel was ruler by divine right until the choice of David" (Smith). Hence, he shows hostility to Saul, and to the monarchy until it justified its existence under David, the most popular of Israelite heroes. This author is probably post-Deuteronomic; that is, he lived after the publication, in 621 B.C., of Deuteronomy, with the religious ideas of which he is deeply imbued. His work is distinguished by the symbol *Sm* (= Samuel).

3. Besides these two main sources there are discernible some minor extracts of varying date. The story of the Ark, for example, is probably from a very early source (10th cent.), as are also several features in the story of Samuel.

4. These materials were subsequently pieced together to form a continuous narrative of the early monarchy by a post-Deuteronomic editor, probably after the Exile, that is, after the fifth century. The result of his work is the books of Samuel as we now have them.

INTRODUCTION

(d) Nature and Authorship of the Books of Chronicles

The compiler of the Ecclesiastical Chronicles was a Levite or a scribe of the fourth century B.C. A scribe means one of those Professional students of the Jewish legal and other sacred documents who, together with the priests and Levites, occupied themselves with literary research and editorial reproduction after the return from the Exile. This compiler had before him our present books of Samuel and Kings. These he partly reproduced in his own book, with slight alterations, and partly supplemented with lists, genealogies, and scraps of information from other sources. As a trustworthy historical guide Chronicles cannot be relied on, unless it is corroborated by other information—as it is, in this case, by Samuel. Where it differs from Samuel the authority of Samuel is always to be preferred. But the book is a valuable authority for the history of religion. It exhibits clearly the religious ideas, not of the age its author writes about, but of the age at which he wrote. Between the religion of Samuel's age and the religion of the Judaistic period, when this writer lived, with all its elaborate ritual, there is a long progress of revelation. The author tells over again the story of a long-past age as it appears in his eyes. And, perhaps in part unconsciously, in telling the tale he assigns to the early ages religious beliefs, customs, and institutions about which the original historians of that age knew nothing, and which did not come into being until a later day.

(e) Estimate of the Value of the Records

1. *Historical*—From the foregoing sections it will be apparent that, as a true record of events, the sacred narratives

of this period are of higher value in some parts than in others. The older portions are history in the strict sense; the later are rather in the nature of historical philosophy. They represent actual events but overlay them with the reflections of the author. But that they are therefore of less value as history in all cases need not be supposed; for it is the view of one school at least of modern critics that "the true scientific historian is he who most conscientiously seeks to ascertain and present the lessons which the past has to offer" (P. Hume Brown, quoted by Kennedy.)

2. *Religious*—It was in this latter sense that the Hebrew writers themselves interpreted their duty as historians. That is why Samuel and Kings were included in the second volume of their canon, the Prophetical Scriptures. [1] Their object was to portray the development of moral principle and religious belief among their people. They chowed, by taking the biographies of their past heroes for examples, how God had by degrees revealed His character and will. No other nation in the world's history was made the recipient of a revelation of this unique character. [2] The revelation was progressive. First, by the agency of their early leaders, then by the prophets, God spoke to them. The inspired teaching of the prophets revolutionized the beliefs, elevated the moral and religious sense, and consequently remolded the habits and practices of the people. Hence the ruder notions of God's Person and of the things acceptable to Him which Saul and David entertained as *Sl* shows us—e.g. David thought he "propitiated God" by giving the Gibeonites blood for blood, and executing

---

[1] See Appendix, p. 181.
[2] See further, vol. 2, pp. xx seq.

Rizpah's innocent sons [1]—were wholly repugnant to the later writer *Sm*, and still more so to the Chronicler, by whose day the old notions had given place to a more perfect knowledge of God as the Universal Spirit.

It is in this record of the progress of Divine revelation that the real value of the Old Testament Scriptures lies.

(f) The Prophets

The intimate bearing of Prophecy upon the history and the religious development of Israel will unfold itself to the reader as he pursues the narrative of the Bible text. A few words of preliminary explanation are, however, expedient. Three periods can be traced in the history of prophecy.

1. Before the age of Samuel.
2. The rise of schools of the prophets in Samuel's day.
3. The literary prophets, from about 760 B.C. onwards.

1. Later writers speak of individuals of early times as prophets: Abraham, Moses, Deborah, are thus described. The "man of God" who predicts Eli's doom is likewise regarded as a prophet. It is clear that the definition of a prophet is "one who was conscious of a message from God to His people, and who was impelled by the Spirit, sometimes unwillingly, to declare it." It is irrational to suppose that God in ancient times "left Himself without witness." In diverse parts and in diverse ways—*polumeros kai polutoros*—He revealed Himself to the world and in a unique way to the people whom He had specially selected for this purpose. Had He not guided the Hebrews

---

[1] Further instances will be observed by the reader in the text: some of them are re-marked upon in the notes.

by means of a special training such as no other nation has experienced, their actual history would seem meaning—less and even impossible. What the meaning of it was, the eventual coming of Christ made clear; and the whole history of the people is seen to have been a progressive training for that event (vol. 2, p. xxiii; G. A. Smith, *Modern Criticism and the Preaching of the O.T.*, Lect. IV). The earliest prophet, then, is one conscious of a divine inspiration, and of a mission; half blindly, perhaps, and despite all human barriers, he obeys the impulse. Modern life presents similar phenomena in every age. The enlightened leader of mankind is the counterpart of the oldest Hebrew "prophet." And the parallel is illustrated by one of the most ancient titles of the prophet—a Seer, a man who sees the right and sets about the doing of it. [1]

2. But the power of prophecy was, under the divine guidance, to be developed. In times of national stress, humiliation, or excitement, in antiquity as in modern days, in the West as in the East, large numbers of individuals tend to be "inspired" with enthusiastic, even ecstatic religious feeling. Such are the Bacchanals of Greece, the dervishes of the Egyptian and Arabian deserts, the Revivalists of modern Wales, perhaps even the "speakers with tongues" [2] of the infant Church. These movements, the power of which is contagious beyond measure, have their use. They are at bottom sincere, potent, and, in the true sense, a manifestation of the Spirit.

In Samuel's day the stress of long humiliation before the

---

[1] In its narrower sense the word "seer" denotes one who had superior powers of vision, of the fortune-telling kind.

[2] The present writers do not, forever, hold the popular view that the "speaking with tongues" was a sort of inarticulate outpouring of sound. The passages in *Acts* and the Pauline Epistles do not seem to them to necessitate this interpretation.

Philistine aggressor had led to a wide-spread exaltation of religious feeling of this kind. Bands of enthusiasts, in whom the religious spirit was identical with the patriotic, roamed the country in processions, accompanied by music and the dance. It is these whom we meet in the story of Saul (p. 33, below, etc.). Either by Samuel himself (1 Sam. 19:20), as the later Deuteronomist editor thought, or at any rate in his time, the better elements of these companies were selected and concentrated in religious training-colleges at Ramah, Bethel, Gilgal, Jericho, and elsewhere. There in the cloister (the misinterpreted *Naioth* of our texts), their religious enthusiasm was chastened and cultivated, their inspiration directed to its right ends. *The spirits of the prophets* were trained to become *subject to the prophets* (1 Cor. 14:32). They were called, as the roving bands had been, *Nebhiim*, Prophets. Not all, indeed, who were trained in the schools became ultimately prophets; nor were all the subsequent prophets trained in the schools. Students were free to come and go as they pleased, as in theological colleges today. But these colleges became a center of religious life and instruction, a divine means for the revelation of the divine will. To their influence, if not in all cases actually to their training, we owe men like Nathan and Gad, Elijah and Elisha, and subsequently the whole series of literary prophets, from Amos to the author of Daniel. For though Amos and Elijah may never have set foot inside a "school," it was the work of the schools which had produced in the nation that body of feeling to which they appealed, and thus made prophecy possible for them in Israel.

In the schools the arts of music, poetry, and literature were cultivated. To their collections of national records can be traced the beginnings of historical literature in Israel: Samuel, Nathan, and Gad each wrote a history of their times (1 Chron. 29:29). Without them we should have had no Pentateuch— no Psalms, no Books of the Prophets.[1] To the nation the two chief duties of the prophet were: (1) To maintain the religion of Jehovah intact against heathenism. (2) To expand the religious and moral ideas and practices of the nation in accordance with the progressive revelation of God to man given to individual prophets; in a word, to elevate public opinion. (3) To support the throne—with which the theocracy was now identified; and consequently, also, to denounce any backsliding on the part of its occupant. (4) In earlier times, before the development of the priesthood, to exercise priestly functions: Elijah offers sacrifices, Elisha's pupil anoints Jehu as king.

3. Since the work of the first prophet who left a written record of his message. (Amos, 760 B.C.) falls two centuries after the close of our present period (970 B.C.), a discussion of this phase of prophecy must be reserved for its proper context (vol. 4). Here it may be observed (1) That the prophetic art and the influence of prophecy in this third period owe much to the previous history of prophecy noted above. (2) The prophet was a direct instrument of divine revelation, however greatly his method of communicating his inspired message was conditioned by his own human personality and external circumstances. Indeed, the personal

---

[1] Wellhausen, however, disagrees. He says: "The rabbinical notion that these societies were schools and academies in which the study of the Torah and of sacred history-were preserved imports later ideas into an earlier time." How, then, can he explain the results of their work, which are an unquestioned fact of history?

element, the prophet's own experience and conviction strengthens rather than weakens the authority with which he speaks. A man himself convinced could convince the world. (3) His business was not only to declare, to upbraid, to encourage, but also to predict. He predicts national events and ensuing punishments upon his own and other nations. Modern criticism of the exaggerated stress formerly laid on this essential part of a prophet's functions has "led to the opposite extreme of underestimating its importance."

"A candid examination of the whole conditions of the case must lead to the admission of a supernatural power and knowledge in Hebrew prophecy... The attempts to explain this away have failed. The prophetic power was not exceptional political shrewdness, not the mere sanguine expectation of enthusiasts, or the gloomy forebodings of convinced pessimists; it was not like the second-sight of the Highlander, the effect of excitement upon a highly sensitive temperament" (W. T. Davison in *H.D.B.* p. 762). Nor yet can their power of foretelling events be explained away as if the prophets were merely what we call "wise after the event," for that is not true. In short, the prophetic messages were, in sober fact, just what they professed to be—the "Word of the LORD" sent through men to men.

(g) Chronology of the Period

There is a general agreement, on many grounds, that Solomon's accession is to be placed about 970 B.C. The notes of time given in our text, also, for David's reign, are circumstantial and trustworthy, though in the Hebrew text they are left blank for Saul's reign (1 Sam. 13:1). David's entire reign lasted forty years. This puts his accession in 1010 B.C. Saul's reign, again, was clearly a short one: the "forty years" assigned to him in Acts 13:22 does not square with the data of the historical books of the Old Testament. His son Jonathan is consistently regarded as a slightly older contemporary of David. David must have been born in 1040 B.C. (2 Sam. 5:14); and we may reasonably assign Jonathan's birth to c. 1045 B.C. He was of military age, about 18, at his father's accession (1 Sam. 13:2): so Saul's accession must be assigned to about 1027 B.C. [1] Samuel was "old" at this date; and for this and other reasons (see vol. 2, p. 135), his birth is to be dated about 1090 B.C.

Provisionally, then, our date-scheme for the period will run thus:

	B.C.
Birth of Samuel	c. 1090—1095
Battle of Aphek and death of Eli	c. 1073?
Birth of Jonathan	c. 1045
Birth of David	c. 1040
Accession of Saul	c. 1027
Accession of David	c. 1010
Assassination of Amnon by his brother Absalom	c. 983
Rebellion of Absalom	c. 974
Death of David and accession of Solomon	c. 970

[1] The scheme here suggested necessitates a slight modification of that offered for the preceding period in vol. 2, p. 135 of this series, first edition. In that place Petrie's date for Saul (1053-1040) was adopted, and David's birth placed in 1065. These two dates were probably placed some twenty-five years too early.

PART 1
SAMUEL THE JUDGE

INTRODUCTORY

THE character and history of Samuel presented in the text speak for themselves. It is only necessary here again to call attention to the feature a lready remarked upon—that the composite nature of the records has led to a double representation of Samuel's position in the State. In one record he is the accepted theocratic Judge of the whole people; in the other he is a local Seer of Ramah. His work as a prophet has been examined in the INTRODUCTION.

It is probable that the invasion of the Philistines upon which the scene opens in 1 Sam. 4 was a continuation of that in which Samson had already performed the heroic exploits recorded in *Judges*. How great a lapse of time had intervened we cannot say. Nor is it clear how old Samuel was at the time of the battle of Aphek, or how soon after this event he was established as Judge.

The Philistines were a sea-faring people of non-Semitic race. Shortly before the Hebrew occupation of Canaan they had settled on the south-west coast and gained possession of the plain. Most likely they had sailed from Crete, which seems to have been one of their chief homes, as it was for many other races at the dawn of history. From the Philistines Palestine derived its name; for later Greek and Roman invaders, landing on the coast of the Philistine country, applied to the whole land the name of that part with which they had first come into contact.[1]

It seems that the Philistines adopted in the main the religion of the Canaanites, who were Semitic by race. Politically they formed a confederacy governed by five Tyrants, or Lords, whose seats of government lay at Gaza, Gath, Ekron, Ashdod, and Ashkelon.

A. THE LAST OF THE JUDGES

THE BIRTH OF SAMUEL AN HIS DEDICATION TO JEHOVAH'S SERVICE
1 Samuel 1

Elkanah's yearly pilgrimage from Ramah to Shiloh.—1. Now there was a certain man of Ramathaim-zophim, of Mount

---

[1] *Cp.* the accidental spread of the names "Hellenes and Graeci" (Bury, *History of Greece,* p.106).

1. **Two slight difficulties confront us at the outset of the story:** (i) where was Samuel's birthplace? (ii) To what tribe did he belong?

(1) The words **Ramathaim-zophim** are grammatically impossible as a place-name. We must read: "a certain man of Ramah, a Zuphite." But which of the eight Ramahs of the O.T. is meant? and where is the "land of Zuph" (9:5)?

Samuel's **Ramah** has been identified with (a) a village in Ephraim nine miles north of Jerusalem, just north of the Benjamite border; (b) the better-known Ramah in Benjamin five miles north of Jerusalem; (c) a village about twenty miles north-west of Jerusalem on the line between Lydda and Shiloh. The general tenor of the narrative makes (a) the most likely of the three. And the land of Zuph, which has no marks of identity of its own, will therefore be somewhere in "the hill country of Ephraim" on the border of the tribal provinces of Ephraim and Benjamin.

(ii) (a) **Ephrathite** is often in O.T. equivalent to Ephraimite, and this is almost certainly the meaning here (as R.V.). (b) But the word also means a native of the Bethlehem district (as in Ruth 1:2): and in 1 Chron. 6 : 34 Samuel's family is said to belong to the tribe, not of Ephraim, but of Levi. On this theory the present verse would state that Samuel's Levite ancestor Zuph had settled in the neighborhood of Bethlehem-judah. M ost authorities, however, recognizing the late date of the *Chronicles,* hold to the other interpretation of Ephrathite here, as meaning Ephraimite. And

Ephraim, and his name was Elkanah, the son of Jeroham, the son of Elihu, the son of Tobu, the son of Zuph, an Ephrathite: 2. and he had two wives; the name of the one was Hannah, and the name of the other Peninnah: and Peninnah had children, but Hannah had no children. 3. And this man went up out of his city yearly to worship and to sacrifice unto the LORD of hosts in Shiloh. And the two sons of Eli, Hophni and Phinehas, the priests of the LORD, were there.

Hannah's distress at her childlessness—4. And once at the yearly feast it came to pass that Elkanah sacrificed (now he used to give to Peninnah his wife, and to all her sons and her daughters, portions: 5. but unto Hannah he gave

indeed, if Samuel was born a Levite, his special dedication to the ministry by his mother would have no significance—he would be already a minister of Jehovah by virtue of his birth in the priestly clan.

2. **'Hannah'** corresponds to our Grace, **'Peninnah'** to Coral, or Pearl.
Polygamy was allowed by Hebrew law (Deut. 21:15, etc.). but became rare after the Captivity.

3. The LORD thus printed in capitals in the English versions represents the Hebrew name of God, "Jehovah" or "Yahweh."
This is the first place in the O. T. where the additional title "(God) of hosts" (Sabaoth) occurs: a title which reflects the old Jewish notion that Jehovah led Israel's armies to victory over the enemy's armies, which were championed too, on their side, by their local god (see below, p. 16).

Shiloh had been the religious capital of the country ever since Joshua had set up the Tabernacle and the Ark there (Josh. 18:1, vol. 2 of this series, p. 125, etc.). We have already come across this annual festival at the sanctuary (probably the Feast of Tabernacles, *id.* p. 33) in Judg. 2 1 : 19 *(id.* p. 1 9 2), when the occasion was seized to secure wives for the Benjamites.

4. The text of these verses is corrupt: and indeed, throughout *Samuel* there is more textual corruption than in any book of the Bible except possibly *Ezekiel.* Here, as occasionally elsewhere, the editors have inserted alterations, in italics, in order to secure to the reader the right sense without excessive recourse to critical notes. These alterations represent either *(a)* a more correct rendering of the Hebrew or *(b)* the Greek (LXX) version where it is sounder or *(c)* emendations by critical scholars. There is a long parenthesis between verse 4 *a* and verse 7 *b,* not very skillfully introduced by the compiler, describing what used to take place in former years. Verse 7 *b* brings the story back to this particular year.

At a sacrifice, after Jehovah and the priests had received their portions, the head of the house distributed portions to his family to feast upon.

a worthy portion; for he loved Hannah; but the LORD had shut up her womb. 6. And her adversary also provoked her sore, for to make her fret, because the LORD had shut up her womb. *So Elkanah would do year by year, when he went up to the house of the Lord), but Hannah covered her face and wept and would not eat.* 8. Then said Elkanah her husband to her, Hannah, why weepest thou? and why eatest thou not? and why is thy heart grieved? am not I better to thee than ten sons?

Her prayer—9. So Hannah rose up after they had eaten *and presented herself before the Lord.* Now Eli the priest sat upon a seat by a post of the temple of the LORD. 10. And she was in bitterness of soul, and prayed unto the LORD, and wept sore. 11. And she vowed a Vow, and said, O LORD of hosts, if thou wilt indeed look on the affliction of thine handmaid, and remember me, and not forget thine handmaid, but wilt give unto thine handmaid a man child, then I will give him unto the LORD all the days of his life, and there shall no razor come upon his head.

Eli rebukes and then blesses her—12. And it came to pass, as she continued praying before the LORD, that Eli marked her mouth. 13. Now Hannah, she spake in her heart; only her lips moved, but her voice was not heard: therefore Eli thought she had been drunken. 14. And Eli said

temple. The Ark was enshrined apparently not in the simple Tent of Meeting (see vol. 2 *passim),* though the compiler of the book is inconsistent on this point *(e.g.* 2 : 22 of the complete text), nor in the elaborate Tabernacle described by the Priestly writer (P) of the Pentateuch (vol. 2, p. 3ff.), but in a substantial wooden building with doors and out-chambers (3:2). This "temple" was apparently destroyed by the Philistines after their victory at Aphek (below chaps. 4 and 5), and the priests migrated to Nob (21).

11. The author clearly means that Hannah promised, in addition to "giving the boy to the Lord," to make of him a lifelong Nazarite, like Samson (Judg. 13:5). The LXX has the textual addition "and wine and fermented liquor he shall not drink." Nazarites, *i.e.,* "the separated ones," undertook three vows: the growing of the hair, abstinence from all produce of the grape, avoidance of pollution by contact with the dead (Num. 6). The vow was either perpetual or for a short period. "Nazaritism seems to have been the outcome of a reaction against the disastrous influence which Canaanitish heathenism had exercised upon Hebrew religion. The Nazarites endeavoured, by an example of asceticism, to restore the austere simplicity of faith and manners which Israel had learned in the wilderness" (Ott. p. 116).

unto her How long wilt thou be drunken? put away thy wine from thee. 15. And Hannah answered and said, No, my Lord, I am a woman of a sorrowful spirit: I have drunk neither wine nor strong drink, but have poured out my soul before the LORD. 16. Count not thine handmaid for a daughter of Belial: for out of the abundance of my complaint and grief have I spoken hitherto. 17. Then Eli answered and said, Go in peace: and the God of Israel grant thee thy petition that thou hast asked of him. 18. And she said, Let thine handmaid find grace in thy sight. So the woman went her way, and did eat, and her countenance was no more sad.

A son is born to her—19. And they rose up in the morning early, and worshipped before the LORD, and returned, and came to their house to Ramah: and Elkanah knew Hannah his wife; and the LORD remembered her. 20. Wherefore it came to pass, when the time was come about after Hannah had conceived, that she bare a son, and called his name Samuel, saying, Because I have asked him of the LORD. 21. And the man Elkanah, and all his house, went up to offer unto the LORD the yearly sacrifice, and his vow. 22. But Hannah went not up; for she said unto her husband, I will not go up until the child be weaned, and then I will bring him, that he may appear before the LORD, and there abide for ever. 23. And Elkanah her husband said unto her, Do what seemeth thee good; tarry until thou have weaned him; only the LORD establish

16. **Belial)** is not a proper name: it = worthlessness; so **daughter of Belial** means "vile or worthless woman." In post-biblical Jewish literature, however, Belial is a name for Satan: so in 2 Cor. 6 : 15 (Kenn. p. 40).

20. **Samuel** (Heb. *Sheniuel)* is connected by sound with the verb *shaal,* to ask: hence the explanation in the text. Etymologically Shemuel and *shaal* have no connection: the etymological meaning of Shemuel is either " name of God" or "His name is God," *i.e.,* "Jehovah is God" (Kenn.). With fanciful derivations of proper names in the Bible compare the similar characteristics in Greek tragedy, *e.g. lone,* from *ienai, helenai* from *helene,* etc.

21. **his vow,** *i.e.,* on Hannah's behalf he meant to promise the boy to the Lord.

23. **the Lord establlsh,** *i.e.,* may God spare you and the babe to do as you propose. weaning in the East usually took place when the child was two years old: sometimes not till he was six. The later age seems more probable here, as (2:11) the child starts his

thy word. So the woman abode, and gave him son suck until she weaned him.

Samuel is "lent to Jehovah" at Shiloh for ever—24. And when she had weaned him, she took him up with her, with a three year old bullock, and one ephah of flour, and a bottle of wine, and brought him unto the house of the LORD in Shiloh: and the child was young. 25. And they slew a bullock, and brought the child to Eli. 26. And she said, Oh my Lord, as thy soul liveth, my Lord, I am the woman that stood by thee here, praying unto the LORD. 27. For this child I prayed; and the LORD hath given me my petition which I asked of him: 28. therefore also I have lent him to the LORD; as long as he liveth he shall be lent to the LORD. And he worshipped the LORD there.

HANNAH'S PSALM
1 Samuel 2:1-10

1. And Hannah prayed and said,

(i) Thanksgiving and praise— My heart rejoiceth in the LORD, mine horn is exalted in the LORD: my mouth **is** enlarged over mine enemies; because I rejoice in thy salvation.

2. There is none holy as the Lord: for there is none beside thee: neither is there any rock like our God.

---

temple ministry at once. The classical scholar will recall the similar childhood of I o n.

24. **ephah** = 6¼ gallons: or, by another system of measurement: 8½ gallons, *i.e.,* about one bushel.

28. **he worshipped,** *i.e.,* Samuel worshipped. But the text has become dislocated and corrupt through the insertion of Hannah's song by a later hand into the original story.

2:1. This psalm was inserted here by a late editor of the history, who chose this song from some collection of psalms like those gathered together in the Psalter, and placed it here as being appropriate to Hannah's circumstances. It expresses the firm trust of the pious believer in God's dealings with the destinies of men. Mary's song, the Magnificat (Luke 1:46 *seq.),* much resembles and was largely modelled upon this psalm. The song consists of four stanzas, as marked in the text.

mine horn, *i.e.,* "my head is lifted up": the metaphor is from a horned animal tossing its head proudly in exultation.

my mouth, *cf.* Isa. 57:4: "Against whom make ye a wide mouth, and draw out the tongue? " *i.e.,* make gestures of contempt.

(ii) Rejection of the great—3. Talk no more so exceeding proudly; let not arrogancy come out of your mouth: for the LORD is a God of knowledge, and by him actions are weighed.

4. The bows of the mighty men are broken, and they that stumbled are girded with strength.

5. They that were full have hired out themselves for bread; and they that were hungry ceased: so that the barren hath born seven; and she that hath many children is waxed feeble.

(iii) *Jehovah is Disposer supreme*—6. The LORD killeth, and maketh alive: he bringeth down to the grave, and bringeth up.

7. The Lord maketh poor, and maketh rich: he bringeth low, and lifteth up.

8. He raiseth up the poor out of the dust, and lifteth up the beggar from the dunghill, to set them among princes, and to make them inherit the throne of glory: for the pillars of the earth are the LORD'S, and he hath set the world upon them.

(iv) Confidence in the future—9. He will keep the feet of his saints, and the wicked shall be silent in darkness; for by strength shall no man prevail.

10. The adversaries of the LORD shall be broken to pieces; out of heaven shall he thunder upon them: the LORD shall judge the ends of the earth; and he shall give strength unto his king, and exalt the horn of his anointed.

5. **ceased** = "have ceased to be hungry." **seven**, i.e., a good large family.

6. **grave** = Heb. *Sheol*, Gk. *Hades*, the place where departed spirits live after death. The poet (unless he is using "grave" as a metaphor for "deep distress") hints at his belief in the resurrection from the dead, a belief which was not fully attained by the Jews until after the Exile.

10. The reference to a king shows that the poet was familiar with the monarchy, and therefore later than the time of Hannah: and the reference to "his anointed" (Heb. *Messiah*), *i.e.,* primarily "the king," and thus "the Messianic King," together with the figurative language about God's judgment on the wicked, betrays the writer's acquaintance with later expectations. (See vol. 5 of this series, passim.)

A DRAMATIC CONTRAST: THE INNOCENCE OF THE CHILD SAMUEL AND THE WICKEDNESS OF ELI'S SONS

1 Samuel 2: 11-26

11. And Elkanah went to Ramah to his house. And the child did minister unto the LORD before Eli the priest.

The rapacity and profanity of Eli's sons—12. Now the sons of Eli were sons of Belial; they knew not the LORD. 13. And the priests' custom with the people was, that, when any man offered sacrifice, the priest's servant came, while the flesh was in seething, with a fleshhook of three teeth in his hand; 14. and he struck it into the pan, or kettle, or caldron, or pot; all that the fleshhook brought up the priest took for himself. So they did in Shiloh unto all the Israelites that came thither. 15. Also before they burnt the fat, the priest's servant came, and said to the man that sacrificed, Give flesh to roast for the priest; for he will not have sodden flesh of thee, but raw. 16 And if any man said unto him, Let them not fail to burn the fat presently, and then take as much as thy soul desireth; then he would answer him, Nay; but thou shalt give it me now: and if not, I will take it by force. 17. whereforefore

11 ff. The compiler has conflated *(i.e.,* pieced together) two stories, one of Samuel's childhood, the other of Eli's household, in such a way as to point the moral of his tale. The Eli document is probably the older of the two.

12. **Sons of Belial** *(cf.* above, 1:16) = depraved fellows.

13. **Sodden** = boiled; **seething** = boiling. The usual ritual in those early days seems to have been this: (1) The victim was slain and its life-blood thus given back to the Giver of all life. (2) After the victim had been cut up its flesh was boiled. (3) When the boiled flesh was ready, (a) the fat was burned for God to smell its "sweet savor," and (b) simultaneously the offerers partici-pated in a table—communion with God by eating the boiled flesh while the smoke of the burning fat was ascending to Him.

The irregularity of Eli's sons was this: (1) They sent and offensively purloined with a big fork as large a portion of the boiling meat as they could, over and above their due share. (2) At other times they seized portions of raw meat before it was boiled, intending to roast it instead of eating it boiled. (3) They took their meat *before* God had re-ceived His portion by the ceremonial burning of the fat.

16. **Let them not . . .** Better: "First let them burn the fat, and then..."

the sin of the young men was very great before the LORD: for *the* men *despised* the offering of the LORD.

Samuel's piety—18. But Samuel ministered before the LORD, being a child, girded with a linen ephod. 19. More*over* his mother made him a little coat, and brought it to him from year to year, when she came up with her husband *to* offer the yearly sacrifice.
20. And Eli blessed Elkanah and his wife, and said, The LORD give thee seed of this woman for the loan which is lent to the LORD. And they went unto their own home. 21. And the LORD visited Hannah, so that she conceived, and bare three sons and two daugh- ters. And the child Samuel grew before the LORD.

Eli vainly rebukes his disobedient sons—22. Now Eli was very old, and heard all that his sons did unto all Israel; 23. and he said unto them, why do ye such things? for I hear of your evil dealings by all this people. 24. Nay, my sons; for it is no good report that I hear: ye make the LORD'S people to transgress.   25. If one man sin against another, the judge shall judge hirn: but if a man sin against the LORD, who shall intreat for him? Notwithstanding they hearkened not unto the voice of their father, because the LORD would slay them.

The obedient Samuel—26. And the child Samuel grew on, and was in favor both with the LORD,   and also with men.

17. **the men,** *i.e.,* these young priests showed contempt for the sacred ritual.
18. **ephod** has two meanings in O.T.: (1) As here, a short linen garment, sewn down the front, and put on over the head like a chasuble: it was a distinctive part of the priests' dress. Aaron wore an ephod of a more elaborate kind (vol. 2, p. 44. Exod. 28). Samuel's was apparently a simple garment of white (?) linen. (2) As often, a gold-plated image, possibly meant to represent Jehovah in early days, which was used somehow by the priest for ascertaining the divine will.
26. St. Luke imitated this in describing Jesus' childhood (Luke 2:52).

(a) First Story: by the mouth of a Nameless Prophet
1 Samuel 2:27-36

27. And there came a man of God unto Eli, and said unto him, Thus saith
the LORD, Did I plainly appear unto the house of thy father, when they
were in Egypt in Pharaoh's house? 28. And did I choose him out of all

27. Though the genealogy of Eli is nowhere given in the O.T., it isgenerally
held, on the strength of a notice in 1 Chron. 24:3, that he was descended
from Ithamar, Aaron's fourth son. The priesthood (known after the Exile as the high-priesthood; vol. 5, p. 151), had passed out of the direct line
of Eleazar after Phinehas' death—*i.e.,* shortly before Eli's own accession, if
indeed Eli did not directly succeed Phinehas, as he well may have done, for
Josephus is our only authority for the accession of Phinehas' son, Abishua, to
the office. The ejection foretold in this passage was fulfilled in Solomon's time,
when Abiathar, Eli's great-great-grandson, was deposed, and Zadok, a direct
descendant of Eleazar, was installed priest in his stead (1 Kings 2:27). In
later days those priests who could claim descent from Zadok were considered
superior to those who could only trace their ancestry to the Ithamar branch of
Aaron's house. This section (verses 27-36) is the work of a late Deuteronomic
editor of the historical records of Samuel's day. The following tree, which
is based on our incomplete, late, and unsatisfactory Biblical records, may help
to make the history clearer.

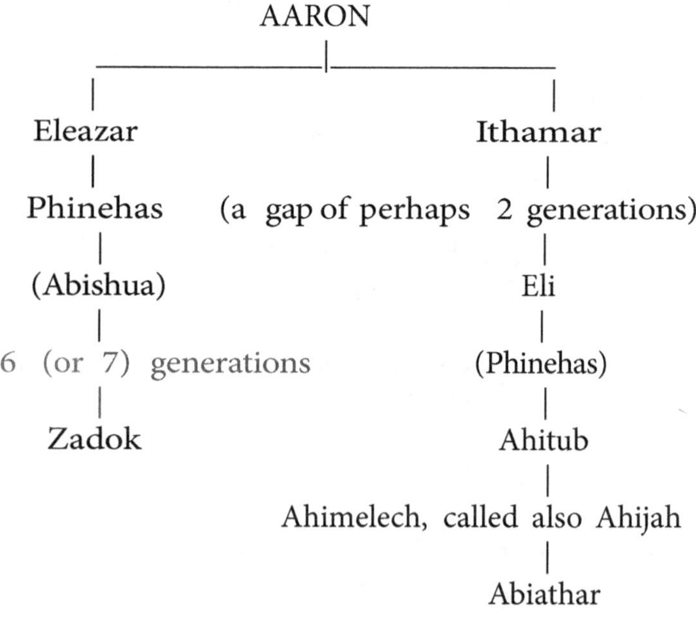

27. **Did I** has the force of "Did I not?" **house of thy father,** *i.e.,* Levi

the tribes of Israel to be my priest, to offer upon mine altar, to burn incense, to wear an ephod before me? and did I give unto the house of thy father all the offerings made by fire of the children of Israel? 29. Wherefore kick ye at my sacrifice and at mine offering, which I have commanded in my habitation; and honourest thy sons above me, to make yourselves fat with the chiefest of all the offerings of Israel my people? 30. Wherefore the LORD God of Israel saith, I said indeed that thy house, and the house of thy father, should walk before me for ever: but now the LORD saith, Be it far from me; for them that honour me I will honour, and they that despise me shall be lightly esteemed.

The doom of Eli's house is pronounced—31. Behold, the days come, that I will cut off thine arm, and the arm of thy father's house, that there shall not be an old man in thine house. 32. *And thou shalt look, being in straits and with envious eyes, upon all with which I favor Israel:* and there shall not be an old man in thine house for ever. 33. *Yet one man belonging to thee I will not cut off from my altar, but only that he may consume his eyes and cause his soul to pine away:* and all the increase of thine house shall die in the flower of their age.

And of his sons—34. And this shall be a sign unto thee, that shall come upon thy two sons, on Hophni and Phinehas; in one day they shall die both of them. 35. And I will raise me up a faithful priest, that shall do according to that which is in mine heart and in my mind: and I will build him a sure house; and he shall walk before mine anointed for ever. 36. And it shall come to pass that every one that is left in thine house shall come and crouch to him

29 a. The text is hopelessly corrupt: the attempt at translation made in the A.V. may stand as well as any other. It makes sense.

31. **arm.** The metaphor means, "I will cut off the strength and vitality of thy family: they shall all die young, prematurely."

32. Heb. text hopeless. The translation printed is H. P. Smith's conjecture.

33. The translation is Kennedy's. The allusion is to Abiathar, who alone escaped from the massacre of the priests at Nob by Saul; below, 22:20.

34. This was fulfilled at Aphek: below, 4:2.

35. **a faithful priest**. That is, Zadok; see 1 Kings 2:27, 35.
mine anointed, *i.e.,* the king: the Davidic dynasty.

36. "Eli's family shall be so reduced as to seek the menial offices

for a piece of silver and a morsel of bread, and shall say, Put me, I pray thee, into one of the priests' offices, that I may eat a piece of bread.

DENUNCIATION OF ELI'S HOUSE

(b) Second Story: by the mouth of the child Samuel

1 Samuel 3-4:1

A voice calls Samuel, just before dawn—3:1. And the child Samuel ministered unto the LORD before Eli. And the word of the LORD was precious in those days; there was no open vision. 2. And it came to pass at that time, when Eli was laid down in his place *(now his eyes had begun* to wax dim, that he could not see;) 3. and ere the lamp of God went out in the temple of the LORD, where the ark of God was, and Samuel was laid down to sleep; 4. that the LORD called Samuel: and he answered, Here am I. 5. And he ran unto Eli, and said, Here am I; for thou calledst me. And he said, I called not; lie down again. And he went and lay down. 6. And the LORD called yet again, Samuel. And Samuel arose and went to Eli, and said, Here am I; for thou didst call me. And he answered, I called not, my son; lie down again. 7. Now Samuel did not yet know the LORD, neither was the word of the LORD yet revealed unto him. 8. And the LORD

of the sanctuary for the pittance that might thus be earned" (Smith). This alludes to the straits to which the priests of the local sanctuaries were reduced when these were abolished by Josiah's reformation, 621 B.C. (2 Kings 23:5 *seq.;* vol. 5, p. 27).

1. We may imagine the "child" Samuel to be between ten and fifteen years old by now: the Heb. word, however, is applicable to a man of any age up to forty. **precious.** The meaning probably is rare—— "there was no *frequent* vision."

2. Eli apparently slept in an adjoining chamber, Samuel in the "temple"   itself. "The custom of the temple guardian sleeping within the sanctuary has its parallel in the early notice of Joshua, Samuel's p redecessor in the guardianship of the Ark, who 'departed not out of the Tent of Meeting' (Exod. 33:11)" (Kenn.). The Ark is here first called **the ark of God.**

3. The **lamp** burned by night only. In the Tabernacle, however, the lamp was kept perpetually alight according to the (later) priestly instructions of Exod. 27:20.

called Samuel again the third time. And he arose and went to Eli, and said, Here am I; for thou didst call me. And Eli perceived that the LORD had called the child. 9. Therefore Eli said unto Samuel, Go, lie down: and it shall be, if he call thee, that thou shalt say, Speak, LORD; for thy servant heareth. So Samuel went and lay down in his place. 10. And the LORD came, and stood, and called as at other times, Samuel, Samuel. Then Samuel answered, Speak;   for thy servant heareth.

God's revelation of Himself to Samuel—11. And the LORD said to Samuel, Behold, I will do a thing in Israel, at which both the ears of everyone that heareth it shall tingle. 12. In that day I will perform against Eli all things which I have spoken concerning his house: when I begin, I will also make an end. 13. *And thou shalt tell him* that I will judge his house for ever for the iniquity which he knoweth; because his sons made themselves vile, and he restrained them not. 14. And therefore I have sworn unto the house of Eli, that the iniquity of Eli's house shall not be purged with sacrifice nor offering for ever.

Results: (1) *Eli resigns himself to the divine will*—15. And Samuel lay until the morning, and opened the doors of the house of the LORD. And Samuel feared to shew Eli the vision. 16. Then Eli called Samuel, and said, Samuel, my son. And he answered, Here am I. 17. And he said, what is the thing that the LORD hath said unto thee? I pray thee hide it not from me: God do so to thee, and more also, if thou hide anything from me of all the things that he said unto thee. 18. And Samuel told him every whit and hid nothing from him. And he said, It is the LORD: let him do what seemeth him good.

11.   The author's conception of the method of divine revelation is clearly conveyed in this passage. He describes, not a dream, but the hearing of a voice enunciating a message in articulate words. We must not conclude, however, that this was the way in which the prophets and other leaders of the Hebrews became conscious of the divine will.
12. God alludes to his previous message of denunciation, above, 2 : 31 *seq.*
17. **God do so.** This adjuration originated in the ceremony of slaying a victim when a man took an oath. He prayed that the fate of the victim— viz. death—might fall on himself if he broke his oath.

(2) *Samuel's career as a prophet begins*—*19.* And Samuel grew, and the LORD was with him, and did let none of his words fall to the ground. 20. And all Israel from Dan even to Beersheba knew that Samuel was established to be a prophet of the LORD.   21. And the LORD appeared again in Shiloh: for the LORD revealed himself to Samuel in Shiloh by the word of the LORD. 4:1*a.* And the word of Samuel came to all Israel.

FULFILMENT OF THE DOOM PREDICED
AGAINST ELI'S HOUSE

1 Samuel 4

First battle: at Ebenezer—*1 b.* Now Israel went out against the Philistines to battle, and pitched beside Ebenezer: and the Philistines pitched in Aphek. 2. And the Philistines put themselves in array against Israel: and when they joined battle, Israel was smitten before the Philistines: and they slew of the army in the field about four thousand men.

Second battle: at Aphek—*3.* And when the people were come into the camp, the elders of Israel said, wherefore hath the LORD smitten us today before the Philistines? Let us fetch the ark of the covenant of

20. **Dan,** *i.e.,* from the extreme north to the extreme south boundary of Canaan. *Cf.* "From John o' Groat's to Land's E nd."

1. For the Philistines see INTRODUCTION to this section, p. 3 above. The narrative is composite (Kent, vol. 2, p. 57). Originally there were two separate accounts of the same battle, which the compiler has welded together, with the result that in our present text two battles are recorded, both fought on practically the same spot. Aphek lies in the lowland of Sharon, at the northern continuation of the Shephelah, about eight miles from the seacoast.

The object of the Philistines in the present campaign was to secure a firm footing on the high ground commanding the plain of Esdraelon, and thence to extend their dominions south over "Mount Ephraim." Hitherto their ambitions in this direction had been held in check by the "judge" Samson. By bringing the Ark into the field, as they did on other occasions, *e.g.* below, p. 141, the Hebrews deemed that they had brought Yahweh's (Jehovah's) very presence into their midst to champion them. The Ark of the early records was not the decorated symbol described in a later day by the Priestly writer, adorned with

the LORD out of Shiloh unto us, that, when it cometh among us, it may save us out of the hand of our enemies. 4. So the people sent to Shiloh, that they might bring from thence the ark of the covenant of the LORD of hosts, which dwelleth between the cherubims: and the two sons of Eli, Hophni and Phinehas, were there with the ark of the covenant of God. 5. And when the ark of the covenant of the LORD came into the camp, all Israel shouted with a great shout, so that the earth rang again. 6. And when the Philistines heard the noise of the shout, they said, What meaneth the noise of this great shout in the camp of the Hebrews? And they understood that the ark of the LORD was come into the camp. 7. And the Philistines were afraid, for they said, God is come into the camp. And they said, Woe unto us! for there hath not been such a thing heretofore. 8. Woe unto us! who shall deliver us out of the hand of these mighty Gods? these are the Gods that smote the Egyptians with *an utter overthrow* in the wilderness. 9. Be strong, and quit yourselves like men, O ye Philistines, that ye be not servants unto the Hebrews, as they have been to you: quit yourselves like men, and fight.

Capture of the Ark—10. And the Philistines fought, and Israel was smitten, and they fled every man into his tent: and there was a very great slaughter; for there fell of Israel thirty thousand footmen. 11. And the ark of God was taken; and the two sons of Eli, Hophni and Phinehas, were slain.

Death of Eli on receipt of the news—12. And there ran a man of Benjamin out of the army and came to Shiloh the same day with his clothes rent, and with earth upon his head. 13. And when he came, lo, Eli sat upon his seat by the *side of the gate, watching the road:* for his heart

---

cherubim, etc., but a simple chest of acacia-wood. It was closely connected with the idea that Jehovah was the God of the armies (hosts, Sabaoth) of Israel. The people "localized" His presence there. we too, in thought, cannot help localising the presence of God, though we know Him to be a Spirit and universal.

8. The allusion is to the overthrow of Pharaoh on the shores of the Red Sea, which are called "the wilderness" in Exod. 13:20 (Kirkpatrick.)

13, **gate,** *i.e.,* of the sanctuary at Shiloh.

trembled for the ark of God. And when the man came into the city, and told it, all the city cried out. 14. And when Eli heard the noise of the crying, he said, What meaneth the noise of this tumult? And the man came in hastily, and told Eli. 15. Now Eli as ninety and eight years old, and his eyes were dim, that he could not see.) 16. And the man said unto Eli, I am he that came out of the army, and I fled today out of the army. And he said, What is there done, my son? 17. And the messenger answered and said, Israel is fled before the Philistines, and there hath been also a great slaughter among the people, and thy two sons also, Hophni and Phinehas, are dead, and the ark *of* God is taken. 18. And it came to pass, when he made mention of, the ark of God, that he fell from off the seat backward by the side of the gate, and his neck brake, and he died: for he was an old man, and heavy. And he had judged Israel forty years.

Ichabod—19. And his daughter in law, Phinehas' wife, was with child: near to be delivered: and when she heard the tidings that the ark of God was taken, and that her father in law and her husband were dead, she bowed herself and travailed; for her pains came upon her. 20. And about the time of her death the women that stood by her said unto her, Fear not; for thou hast born a son. But she answered not, neither did she regard it. 21. And *they* named the child Ichabod, saying, The glory is departed from Israel: because the ark of God was taken, and because of her father- in- l a w and her husband.

18. **forty.** The Septuagint says twenty; but the clause, in any case, is a late insertion and untrustworthy. Eli had been a priest, not a Judge, like those of the book of Judges.

21. **Ichabod,** *i.e.,* "No glory." His mother had already become unconscious (verse 20), so the women gave the child its name.

21. Results of the battle: (1) Ephraim lost its hegemony (leadership) in Israel, together with its symbols, the camp-sanctuary at Shiloh and the Ark. (2) Benjamin, with Judah, now became the center of gravity; hence presently Saul arose *from Benjamin.* (3) The Philistines always now attacked from the north, never through Judah, w h i c h was still too strong for them. (4) People and priests fled southwards, and Nob, 2½ miles north of Jerusalem, became the religious capital. (Well., p. 44.)

THE FORTUNES OF THE ARK

1 Samuel 5-7:2 a

It is taken (1) *to Ashdod*—v. 1. And the Philistines took the ark of God and brought it from Eben-ezer unto Ashdod. 2. When the Philistines took the ark of God, they brought it into the house of Dagon, and set it by Dagon. 3. And when they of Ashdod arose early on the morrow, behold, Dagon was fallen upon his face to the earth before the ark of the LORD. And they took Dagon and set him in his place again. 4. And when they arose early on the morrow morning, behold, Dagon was fallen upon his face to the ground before the ark of the LORD; and the head of Dagon and both the palms of his hands were cut off upon the threshold; only the stump of Dagon was left to him. 5. Therefore neither the priests of Dagon, nor any that come into Dagon's house, tread on the threshold of Dagon in Ashdod unto this day. 6. But the hand of the LORD was heavy upon them of Ashdod, and he destroyed them, and smote them with emerods,

1. **Ashdod.** One of the five chief cities of the Philistines, ruled over by one of their five Tyrants (Lords).

2. **Dagon** was the national deity worshipped by all the Philistines: it was at a national feast in his honor that Samson had met his death at Gaza (Judg. 16). Nothing certain is known of his characteristics. Some theorists connect his name with a fish, some with corn, and others seek his origin in Babylonia. His temple at Ashdod continued to exist till after 160 *B.C.,* when it was destroyed by Jonathan, the second of the Maccabean princes (1 Macc. 11, vol. 5, p. 236).

3. Dagon does obeisance to Jehovah as to a superior Power.

5. The writer traces to this event the origin of a peculiar custom among the worshippers in Dagon's house. They are careful to step not—on the threshold, but over it: it must not be touched now that it had been consecrated by chance through Dagon's hands and head resting on it.

6. **emerods** means tumors or boils of a certain shape, a symptom of the Bubonic Plague. The outbreak of this was regarded, according to the prevalent notion of O.T. writers, as a direct visitation from Heaven. The bacillus of this disease is spread, as we now know, by the vermin which infest the bodies of rats and mice. Hence, we are not surprised to find that the outbreak of plague was coincident with an unusual swarming of mice over the land (6:4, 5). A probably similar epidemic in Sennacherib's army is recorded

even Ashdod and the coasts thereof. 7. And when the men of Ashdod saw that it was so, they said, The ark of the God of Israel shall not abide with us: for his hand is sore upon us, and upon Dagon our god.

(2) *To Gath*—8. They sent therefore and gathered all the Lords of the Philistines unto them, and said, What shall we do with the ark of the God of Israel? And they answered, Let the ark of the God of Israel be carried about unto Gath. And they carried the ark of the God of Israel about thither. 9. And it was so, that, after they had carried it about, the hand of the LORD was against the city with a very great destruction: and he smote the men of the city, both small and great, *and emerods brake out upon them.*

(3) *To Ekron*—10. Therefore, they sent the ark of God to Ekron. And it came to pass, as the ark of God came to Ekron, that the Ekronites cried out, saying, They have brought about the ark of the God of Israel to us, to slay us and our people. 11. So they sent and gathered together all the Lords of the Philistines, and said, Send away the ark of the God of Israel, and let it go again to *its* own place, that it slay us not, and our people: for there was a deadly destruction throughout all the city; the hand of God was very heavy there. 12. And the men that died not were smitten with the emerods: and the cry of the city went up to heaven.

(4) The Philistines decide to restore it to Israel—6:1. And the ark of the LORD was in the country of the Philistines seven months. 2. And the Philistines called for the priests and the diviners, saying, What shall we do to the ark of the LORD? tell us wherewith we shall send it

in 2 Kings 19, vol. 5, pp. 7 and 19; Herodotus, 2 : 141. Swarms of mice and similar rodents are a familiar feature in Palestine and other countries. Metal mice, which were worn as amulets or charms against their depredations, have been found in the Palestine plain." While driving over the veldt near Ladismith, in Cape Colony (not Ladysmith, Natal), the present writer came upon an army of large field-mice, so plentiful that, quick as these creatures are to avoid danger, three of them were crushed beneath his horses' feet within as many hundred yards.

6:1. The compiler has omitted to tell us what was the result of the appeal to the Tyrants in ch. 5:11. He jumps at once to the concluding chapter in the story of the Ark.

to its place. 3. And they said, If ye send away the ark. of the God of Israel, send it not empty; but in any wise return him a trespass offering: then ye shall be healed, and it shall be known to you why his hand is not removed from you.

With appropriate offerings— 4. Then said they, what shall be the trespass offering which we shall return to him? They answered, Five golden emerods, and five golden mice, according to the number of the Lords of the Philistines: for one plague was on you all, and on your Lords. 5. Wherefore ye shall make images of your emerods, and images of your mice that mar the land; and ye shall give glory unto the God of Israel: peradventure he will lighten his hand from off you, and from off your gods, and from off your land. 6. Wherefore then do ye harden your hearts, as the Egyptians and Pharaoh hardened their hearts? when he had wrought wonderfully among them, did they not let the people go, and they departed? 7. Now therefore make a new cart, and take two milch kine, on which there hath come no yoke, and tie the kine to the cart, and bring their calves home from them: 8. and take the ark of the LORD, and lay it upon the cart; and put the jewels of gold, which ye return him for a

3. **trespass offering.** The idea was that some compensation must be made to Jehovah for their having misappropriated His property, viz. the Ark. A curious modern parallel to this dedication of a golden tumor to God came beneath the writer's notice at Funchal, in Madeira. There it is a common practice among the pious who have recovered from a disease to present a wax model of the part affected to God in the Cathedral, which contains, therefore, a quaint collection of waxen arms, toes, breasts, etc.

4. **For one plague**...Philistine population was organized in a league of five cities (Pentapolis, verse 17); therefore an offering of five golden emerods and mice, one of either kind for each of the cities, would cover the ceremonial obligations of the whole people.

7. To seek an omen in the manner here proposed was a universal practice in antiquity: *cf.* below, ch. 14, Jonathan and the Philistines; 2 Sam. 5 : 24, the whispering in the tree-tops; Judg. 6, Gideon and the Midianite's dream. On this occasion, if the motherkine refused to follow their natural inclination to return to their calves, which had been separated from them, but went in the other direction towards Beth-shemesh, it would be clear that they were being specially impelled by the God of the Hebrews. And in that case it would be certain that Jehovah was the cause of the present plague among the Philistines.

trespass offering, in a coffer by the side thereof; and send it away, that it may go. 9. And see, if it goeth up by the way of *its* own coast to Beth-shemesh, then he hath done us this great evil: but if not, then we shall know that it is not his hand that smote us; it was a chance that happened *to* us.

And send it accordingly to Beth-shemesh—10. And the men did so; and took *two* milch kine, and tied them to the cart, and shut up their calves at home: 11. and they laid the ark of the LORD upon the cart, and the coffer with the mice of gold and the images of their emerods. 12. And the kine took the straight way to the way of Beth-shemesh, and went along the highway, lowing as they went, and turned *not* aside to the right hand or to the left; and the Lords of the Philistines went after them unto the border of Beth-shemesh.

Arrival of the ark a Beth-shemish—And they of Bethshemesh were reaping their wheat harvest in the valley: and they lifted up their eyes, and saw the ark, and rejoiced to see it. 14. And lhe cart came into the field of Joshua, a Beth-shemite, and stood there, where there was a great stone: and they clave the wood of the cart and offered the kine a burnt offering unto the LORD. (15. And the Levites took down the ark of the LORD, and the coffer that was with it, wherein the jewels of gold were, and put them on the great stone: and the men of Beth-shemesh offered burnt offerings and sacrificed sacrifices the same day unto the LORD.) 16. And when the five Lords of the Philistines had seen it, they returned to Ekron the same day. (17. And these are the golden emerods which the Philistines returned for a trespass offering unto the LORD; for Ashdod one, for Gaza one, for Askelon one, for Gath one, for Ekron one; 18. And the golden mice, according to the number of all the cities of the Philistines belonging to the five Lords, both of fenced cities, and of country villages.) And the great stone whereon they set down the

9. **Beth-shemesh** ("House of the Sun") was at the head of the valley of Sorek, just within the border of Judah, and the first village across the frontier from Philistia.

15. This verse (like 17 and 18a) is a later addition by a Priestly writer and interrupts the story.

ark of the LORD is a witness unto this day in the field of Joshua the Beth-shemite.

Whence it is removed, in consequence of the plague—19. And he smote the men of Beth-shemesh, because they had looked into the ark of the LORD, even he smote of the people fifty thousand and threescore and ten men: and the people lamented, because the LORD had smitten many of the people with a great slaughter. 20. And the men of Beth-shemesh said, Who is able to stand before this holy LORD God? and to whom shall he go up from us?

(5) *To Kirjath-jearim: where it stays twenty years*— 21. And they sent messengers to the inhabitants of Kirjath-jearim, saying, The Philistines have brought again the ark of the LORD; come ye down, and fetch it up to you. 7 : 1 And the men of Kirjath-jearim came, and fetched up the ark of the LORD, and brought it into the house of Abinadab in the hill, and sanctified Eleazar his son to keep the ark of the LORD. *2a.* And it came to pass, while the ark abode in Kirjath-jearim, that the time was long; for it was twenty years.

19. **fifty thousand** ... is an impossible number of men for a place like Beth-shemesh. The Greek version (LXX) probably represents the original Hebrew text. It says: "Now the sons of Jeconiah did not rejoice with the men of Beth-shemesh when they looked (with joy) upon the Ark of Jehovah; and He slew of them seventy men." This gives an intelligible sin and an intelligible punishment of it. Death comes on those who dishonor, by refusing to honor, Jehovah.

2 1 . **Kirjath-jearim** ("City of Thickets") was nine miles north-east of Beth-shemesh and nine miles west of Jerusalem. Almost certainly it was now under Philistine suzerainty, as many other Hebrew villages were. It was not until David had completely crushed the Philistine power that it was possible for Israel really to gain possession of their beloved palladium, and bring it to Jerusalem (below, 2 Sam. 6).

7:2. **twenty years.** Not much reliance can be placed upon this note of time.

No certain scheme of dates can be made out for the period before David's accession. But it is clear that the Ark remained in the obscurity of Kirjath-jearim for a g r e a t m a n y years, much more than twenty, throughout Samuel's judgeship, Saul's reign, and the early part of David's reign. Its history will be resumed below (p.120) on its recovery by David and the establishment of it at Jerusalem.

SAMUEL AS JUDGE OF THE THEOCRACY [1]
1 Samuel 7:2-17

A national confession of sin at Mizpeh—2 b. And all the house of Israel lamented after the LORD. 3. And Samuel spake unto all the house of Israel, saying, If ye do return unto the LORD with all your hearts, then put away the strange gods and Ashtaroth from among you, and prepare your hearts unto the LORD, and serve him only; and he will deliver you out of the hand of the Philistines. 4. Then the children *of* Israel did put away Baalim and Ashtaroth, and served the LORD only. 5. And Samuel said, Gather all Israel to Mizpeh, and I will pray for you unto the LORD. And they gathered together to Mizpeh, and drew water, and poured it out before the LORD, and fasted on that day,

[1]Theocracy means the rule of the nation by God Himself as its sole King. He has His mouthpiece or representative among the people, such as Moses and Samuel, but they are His viceroys, not monarchs of the nation.

3. This chapter gives us a picture of Samuel as the great theocratic leader of the people after the type of Moses *(cf.* Jer. 15:1: "Though Moses and Samuel stood before *Me,* yet My mind could not be toward this people"). His peaceful rule is represented as beginning at some time after the restoration of the Ark and as enduring for a consjderable period of time, though we cannot make any conjecture as to its exact duration. The writer of these portions of the history *(Sm)* regarded Samuel as the virtual ruler of the nation even after the constitutional upheaval which placed Saul on the throne. See pp. 3 and xiii. above. **Ashtaroth** is the plural of Ashtoreth (Astarte) the Semitic goddess of fertility, whose cult was widely distributed, and localized in various centers-hence the plural.

4. **Baalim,** plur. of **Baal,** means "Lords." The Canaanites called by this title the local gods, whom they supposed to preside over their agriculture and to confer fertility. The Hebrews at times so far conformed to this practice as even to call Jehovah by the name Baal. This was presently denounced by the prophets. Baal became so infamous a term as not even to be pronounced, and the term *bosheth* ("shame") was substituted for it wherever it occurred. Hence Ishbaal's name was changed to Ishbosheth, Meribbaal's to Mephibosheth, etc. Jerubbaal (Gideon) is likewise called Jerubbesheth in 2 Sam. 11:21. "'Baalim and Ashtaroth' may therefore be paraphrased ' the gods and goddesses of Canaan'" (Kenn.).

5. **Mizpeh**. Five miles north-west of Jerusalem.

and said there, We have sinned against the LORD. And Samuel judged the children of Israel in Mizpeh.

A Philistine onslaught—7. And when the Philistines heard that the Children of Israel were gathered together to Mizpeh, the Lords of the Philistines went up against Israel. And when the children of Israel heard it, they were afraid of the Philistines. 8. And the children of Israel said *to* Samuel, Cease not to cry unto the LORD our God for us, that he will save us out of the hand of the Philistines.

Repulsed by Samuel's mediation—9. And Samuel took a sucking lamb and offered it for a burnt offering wholly unto the LORD: and Samuel cried unto the LORD for Israel; and the Lord heard him. 10. And as Samuel was offering up the burnt offering, the Philistines drew near to battle against Israel: but the LORD thundered with a great thunder on that day upon the Philistines and discomfited them; and they were smitten before Israel. 11. And the men of Israel went out of Mizpeh, and pursued the Philistines, and smote them, until they came under Beth-car. 12.   Then Samuel took a stone, and set it between Mizpeh and Shen, and called the name of it Ebenezer, saying, *This is a witness that* the LORD helped us. 13. So the Philistines were subdued, and they came no more into the coast of Israel: and the hand of the LORD was against the Philistines all the days of Samuel. 14. And the cities which the Philistines had taken from Israel were restored to Israel, from Ekron even unto Gath; and the coasts thereof did Israel deliver out of the hands of the Philistines. And there was peace between Israel and the Amorites.

7. The Philistines were naturally suspicious that this religious gathering was in reality a military assemblage designed to throw off their yoke. The Isralites probably were unarmed at the moment.

12.   Ebenezer = "stone of help."   **Beth-car** is unknown.

13, 14. An extravagant statement, which is consistent neither with 1 4 : 52 below, " there was sore war against the Philistines all the days of Saul," nor with the general tenor of the history, which clearly gives us to understand that the Philistine oppression continued, with but slight interruptions, until David's great victories. The statement must be regarded in the same light as the similar statements in *Judges* from a similar Deuteronomic source, *e.g.* "And the land [*i.e., one district* in the land] had rest forty years."

Amorites (vol. 2, p. 103) is used as a general name for the pre Israelite natives of Canaan.

His administration of Justice—15. And Samuel judged Israel all the days of his life. 16. And he went from year to year in circuit to Beth-el, and Gilgal, and Mizpeh, and judged Israel in all those places. 17. And his return was to Ramah; for there was his house; and there he judged Israel; and there he built an altar unto the LORD.

B. THE FOUNDATION OF THE MONARCHY

This most important step in the development of the nation was viewed in different lights by different minds. *(a)* To the older of the two chief writers upon whose work the compiler of *Samuel* has drawn the creation of a monarch was a national necessity and a universal desire. It was spontaneously suggested to Samuel by God Himself. By no other means could the disunion of the tribes, so eloquently illustrated in the history of the Judges, be overcome. It was essential to cement the peoples into one nation in order to present a united opposition to the oppression of the Philistines on the west and the other aggressors on the east from whom Israel had so long suffered. That this ambition was right was proved by the results. (b) On the other hand, the Deuteronomic historian of a later day, whose work is also laid under contribution by the compiler, regarded the institution of a monarch as a revolt against God and a betrayal of the principles of the theocracy. He assigned as the motives for this revolution: (1) An unreasonable disgust at the misrule of Samuel's sons, to whom he had delegated his authority. (2) A sinful desire to imitate the institutions of other and heathen

16. There were many Gilgals in Palestine, but probably the well-known town near Jericho is meant.

nations. Hence, we have in our text *two* accounts of this event representing opposite attitudes of mind. In the Hebrew text the t w o have been fairly happily welded together. It has seemed to the present editors more instructive to disengage them and present them separately.

To the modern mind the institution of monarchy at this period in the history of the Hebrews would seem a natural sequence in their historical development. It bears an interesting parallel to a similar evolution observable in the history of other nations of antiquity and of the early Middle Age. Nor could one see any m ore obvious method by which the chosen people could have performed the unique function among the nations of the world for which the Divine will had selected them. If they were to preserve intact against all external influences their racial characteristics, to foster that genius for religion which was their peculiar gift, to develop the knowledge of God which they of all the nations *oi* the earth possessed, to continue to be the instrument of His special inspiration and teaching, unification under a king was essentially desirable for them. History and science and the religious sense alike teach us that God works by natural methods, nature itself being His creation. The natural issue of a prolonged disunion in Israel would have been her extermination; the natural benefit of cohesion under a king was the continuation of her ability to fulfil her purpose in the world.

Constitutional position of the king—Then the duties of the king in the Hebrew polity had developed—i.e., by David's time—it is seen that he held the position of:

    1. Leader and head of the army.
    2. Ultimate judicial and administrative authority. In

the period of the Judges the elders or princes of the tribes and heads of families had carried on the government locally. The king now superseded them, delegating authority when necessary to royal officials appointed by himself.

3. Head of the national religion. He sacrificed, blessed the people, appointed and dismissed priests. Later on however, as the more highly specialized ritual described in the Priestly portions of the Pentateuch grew, the religious functions of the king tended to pass into the hands of the priest and ultimately to *the* high priest. (But it is doubtful, as was seen in vol. 2, how far the whole priestly system so minutely detailed and idealized by the Exilic and postExilic writers could have actually been in force in pre Exilic times.)

4. He had no legislative power. "The Law"—a sketch of the expansion of which was given in vol. 2—developed independently of the monarch. He, in general, was kept in restraint by its precepts and by public opinion. Occasionally, however, high-handed acts of despotic violence are recorded of the kings, and the books of *Kings* are replete with denunciations of the monarchs for their lapses from the moral and religious principles embodied in their Codes.

THE ELECTION OF A KING

(A) OLDER NARRATIVE: THE SECRET ANOINTING

1 Samuel 9 and 10:1-16, 26-27

Saul's parentage—9:1. Now there was a man of Benjamin, whose name was Kish, the son of Abiel, the son of Zeror,

9:1. Saul's home was Gibeah, four miles north of Jerusalem, the road to Ramah. *He* is described as a " young man," i.e., a

the son of Bechorath, the son of Aphiah, a Benjamite, a mighty man of power. 2. And he had a son, whose name was Saul, a choice young man, and goodly: and there was not among the children of Israel a goodlier person than he; from his shoulders and upward he was higher than any of the people.

The quest of the asses—3. And the asses of Kish Saul's father were lost. And Kish said to Saul his son, Take now one of the servants with thee, and arise, go seek the asses. 4. And he passed through mount Ephraim, and passed through the land of Shalisha, but they found them not: then they passed through the land of Shalim, and there they were not: and he passed t h rough the land of the Benjamites, but they found them not. 5. And when they were come to the land of Zuph, Saul said to his servant that was w ith him, Come, and let us return; lest my father leave caring for the asses, and take thought for us.

They decide to enquire of Samuel—6. And he said unto him, Behold now, there is in this city a man of God, and he is an honorable man; all that he saith cometh surely to pass: now let us go thither; peradventure he can show us our way that we should go. 7. Then said Saul to his servant, But behold, if we go, what shall we bring the man? for the bread is spent in our vessels, and there is not a present to bring to the man of God: what have we? 8. And the servant answered Saul again, and said, Behold, I have here at hand the fourth part of a shekel of silver: that will I give to the man of God, to tell us our way. 9. (Before time in Israel, when a man went to enquire of

man in the prime of life: he had a son old enough to serve with the field force, say about eighteen (13:2). His father was a wealthy and influential person (a mighty man of "power"). The name Saul means " Asked" (of God).

4. Their route lay apparently north-west from Gibeah, down the valley of Ajalon, thence north-east, and finally south again down to Ramah, Samuel's home.

6. **this,** *i.e.,* yonder city, Ramah: they have not yet reached it.

8. **fourth part.** Not a stamped coin, but a bit of silver worth about *8d.*, though of greater purchasing power than *8d.* is in modern days.

9. This verse was originally a marginal explanation, or "gloss," placed by a later hand in the margin of the original text, and subsequently thrust into the text itself by an editor. The chapter

God, thus he spake, Corne and let us go to the seer: for he that is now called a prophet was beforetime called a Seer.) 10. Then said Saul to his servant, Well said; come, let us go. So, they went unto the city where the man of God was.

Arrival at Ramah—11. And as they went up the hill to the city they found young maidens going out to draw water, and said unto them, Is the seer here? 12. And they answered them, and said, He is; behold, he is before you: make haste now, for he came to day to the city; for there is a sacrifice of the people to day in the high place: 13. as soon as ye be come into the city, ye shall straightway find him, before he go up to the high place to eat: for the people will not eat until he come, because he doth bless the sacrifice; and afterwards they eat that be bidden. Now therefore get you up; for about this. time ye shall find him. 14. And they went up into the city: and when they were come into the city, behold, Samuel came out against them, for to go up to the high place.

God's message to Samuel—15. Now the LORD had told Samuel in his ear a day before Saul came, saying, 16. Tomorrow about this time I, will send thee a man out of the land of Benjamin, and thou shalt anoint him to be captain over my people Israel, that he may save my people out of the hand of the Philistines: for I have looked upon *the affliction of* my people, because their cry is come unto me.

The meeting of the prophet and the future king—17. And when Samuel saw Saul, the LORD said unto him, Behold the

itself belongs to an original "Life of Saul," one of the oldest documents in the whole of the O.T. (tenth cent. B.C.). In it Samuel was called a *Roeh* (Seer). The gloss-writer explained that the term Roeh had fallen out of use by his time, and *Nabki* (Prophet) was used instead. On these *Nebhiim* and Samuel's organization of them see p. xx.

Observe that Samuel is here referred to as a comparatively obscure local seer, quite inferior to the theocratic ruler of chaps. 7, 8, etc., which come from a later historical document, a "Life of Samuel."

12. high place, *i.e.,* an altar and sanctuary on the top of the hill on the lower slope of which the village, and at the foot of which the well lay. Until the publication of the Deuteronomic law by Josiah in 621 B.C. it was lawful to sacrifice at these local shrines: at that date all local sanctuaries were abolished in favor of the one central altar at Jerusalem (vol., 2 pp. xvii., 25).

man whom I spake to thee of! this same shall reign over my people. 18. Then Saul drew near to Samuel in the gate, and said, Tell me, I pray thee, where the seer's house is. 19. And Samuel answered Saul, and said, I am the seer: go up before me unto the high place; for ye shall eat with me today, and tomorrow I will let thee go, and will tell thee all that is in thine heart. 20. And as for thine asses that were lost three days ago, set not thy mind on them; for they are found. And on whom is all the desire of Israel? Is it not on thee, and on all thy father's house? 21. And Saul answered and said, Am not I a Benjamite, of the smallest of the tribes of Israel? and my family the least of all the families of the tribe of Benjamin? wherefore then speakest thou so to me? *22.* And Samuel took Saul and his servant and brought them into the parlor and made them sit in the chiefest place among them that were bidden, which were about thirty persons. 23. And Samuel said unto the cook, Bring the portion which I gave thee, of which I said unto thee, Set it by thee. 24. And the cook took up the *thigh and the fat tail* and set it before Saul. And Samuel said, Behold *the meal is served. Eat! For to the appointed time we have waited for thee to eat with the guests.* So, Saul did eat with Samuel that day.

Samuel accompanies his parting guest—25. And when they were come down from the high place into the city, Samuel communed with Saul upon the top of the house. 26. And they arose early: and it came to pass about the spring of the day, that Samuel called Saul to the top of the house, saying, Up, that I may send thee away. And Saul arose, and they went out both of them, he and Samuel, abroad. 27. And as they were going down *to* the end of the city, Samuel said to Saul, Bid the servant pass on before us, (and he passed on) but stand thou still a while, that I may shew thee the word of God.

19. **all ...heart** suggests that Saul had already been chafing at the Philistine oppression and was ambitious to take a lead in ending it. His ambition was approved by God and was now to be realized.

20. "For whom are all the desirable things of Israel—power and even royalty? Are they not destined for thee?" *Cf.* Hagg.. 2:7, "the desire of all nations," vol. 5 . p. 144.

Samuel anoints Israel's first king—10:1. Then Samuel took a vial of oil, and poured it upon his head, and kissed him, and said, Is it not because the LORD hath anointed thee to be *prince over his people Israel?* And thou shalt reign over the people of the Lord and shalt save them from the hand of their enemies round about. And this shall be the sign that the Lord hath anointed thee to be prince over his inheritance.

Samuel predicts the signs of God's approval of Saul—2. When thou art departed from me toda y , then thou shalt find two men by Rachel's sepulchre in the border of Benjamin at Zelzah; and they will say unto thee, The asses which thou wentest to seek are found: and, lo, thy father hath left the care of the asses, and sorroweth for you, saying, What shall I do for my son? 3. Then shalt thou go on forward from thence, and thou shalt come to the oak of Tabor, and there shall meet thee three men going up to God to Beth-el, one carrying three kids, and another carrying three loaves of bread, and another carrying a bottle of wine: 4. and they will salute thee, and give thee two loaves of bread; which thou shalt receive of their hands. 5. After that thou shalt come to the hill of God, where is the garrison of the Philistines: and it shall come to pass, when thou art come thither to the city, that thou shalt

10:1. The insertion in italics is from the Greek and Latin versions **of** the original Hebrew. The copyist of our Hebrew text has made **a** serious omission, by the familiar mistake of haplography: *i.e.,* his eye wandered direct from the first "anointed thee" to the second and failed to observe the highly important words in between. **this** . . . **sign** is explained by the following verses.

2. Saul is to go south to his home at Gibeah, five miles away. He will pass Rachel's tomb. The traditional site of this is near Bethlehem, four miles *south* of Jerusalem. This identification is per haps wrong: it may be due to an erroneous gloss on Gen. 35:19, which falsely identifies the Ephrath there mentioned with Bethlehem. "As Jeremiah hears *Rachel weeping for her children* in Ramah (Jer. 31:15), and as her children are Joseph and Benjamin, we naturally suppose her tomb located in the boundary of their respective territories," *i.e., north* of Jerusalem (H. P. Smith).

4. The salutation and gift, due to the impression made on the wayfarers by Saul's bearing, will be his first "tribute of royalty."

5. **hill of God,** *i.e.,* Gibeah itself-occupied by a Philistine Governor, or Resident, with his garrison! The Hebrew of the word rendered "garrison" in A.V. means "Resident."

meet a company of prophets coming down from the high place with a psaltery, and a tabret, and a pipe, and a harp, before them; and they shall prophesy: 6. and the spirit of the LORD will come upon thee, and thou shalt prophesy with them, and shalt be turned into another man. 7. And let it be, when these signs are come unto thee, that thou do as occasion serve thee; for God is with thee.

The signs are fulfilled—9. And it was so, that when he had turned his back to go from Samuel, God gave him another heart: and all those signs came to pass that day. 10. And when they came thither to the hill, behold, a company of prophets met him; and the spirit of God came upon him, and he prophesied among them. 11. And it came to pass, when all that knew him before time saw that, behold, he prophesied among the prophets, then the people said one to another, What is this that is come unto the son of Kish? Is Saul also among the prophets? 12. And one of the same place answered and said, But who is their father? Therefore, it became a proverb, Is Saul also among the prophets? 13. And when he had made an end of prophesying, he came to *the house.*

Saul's prudent reply to an inquisitive uncle—14. And Saul's uncle said unto him and to his servant, Whither went ye? And he said, To seek the asses: and when we saw that they were no where, we came to. Samuel. And Saul's uncle said unto him, and to his servant, Tell me, I pray thee, what Samuel said unto you, 16. And Saul said unto his uncle, He told us plainly that

prophets, see pp. xix, xx.

psaltery is a small portable harp; **tabret** is a small drum.

11. His friends are astonished at his sudden conversion (verse 9). in chap. 19 —from a later authority—the origin of this proverb is referred to another, though similar, occasion.   .

12. **who is their father?** Two explanations are possible: (1) "Is Saul among the prophets?" "Yes. Why should he not he? Prophetic inspiration does not depend on parentage. Kish's son may as naturally turn prophet as any other man's." The emphasis is on *their,* as opposed to *his,* Saul's. (2) "Is not the great Kish's son degrading himself and his family by associating with a band ot fanatics who have no father worth speaking of? These prophets are nobodies." The tone is contemptuous and snobbish.

III-3

the asses were found. But of the matter of the kingdom, whereof Samuel spake, he told him not.

A bodyguard spontaneously attaches itself to him—26. And Saul also went home to Gibeah; and there went with him a band of men, whose hearts God had touched. 27. But the children of Belial said, How shall this man save us? And they despised him and brought him no presents. But he held his peace.

THE ELECTION OF A KING

(B) LATER NARRATIVE: THE PUBLIC PROCLAMATION

1 Samuel 8 and 10:17-25

The unpopularity of Samuel's sons leads to a demand for a king— 8:1.   And it came to pass, when Samuel was old, that he made his sons judges over Israel. 2. Now the name of his first born was Joel; and the name of his second, Abiah: they were judges in Beer-sheba. 3. And his sons walked not in his, ways, but turned aside after lucre, and took bribes, and perverted judgment. 4. Then all the elders of Israel gathered themselves together, and came to Samuel unto Ramah, 5. and said unto him, Behold, thou art old, and thy sons walk not in thy ways: now make us a king to judge us like all the nations.

God reassures Samuel, though the demand is sinful—6. But the thing displeased Samuel, when they said, Give us a king to judge us. And Samuel prayed unto the LORD. 7. And the LORD said unto Samuel, Hearken unto the voice of the people in all that they say unto thee: for they have not rejected thee, but they have rejected me, that I should not reign over them. 8. According to all the works which they have done since the day that I brought them up out of Egypt even unto this day, wherewith they have forsaken me, and served other gods, so do they also unto thee. 9. Now therefore hearken unto their voice: howbeit yet protest solemnly unto them and shew them the manner of the

---

26. **And Saul ...Gibeah.** This repetition is due to the INTRODUCTION (in the full Bible text) of matter from another source (verses 17-25, from *Sm)* which is given in its proper context below, p. 35.

king that shall reign over them.

The royal prerogatives—10. And Samuel told all the words of the LORD unto the people that asked of him a king. 11. And he said, This will be the manner of the king that shall reign over you: He will take your sons, and appoint them for himself, for his chariots, and to be his horsemen; and some shall run before his chariots. 12. And he will appoint him captains over thousands, and captains over fifties; and will set them to ear his ground, and to reap his harvest, and to make his instruments of war, and instruments of his chariots. 13. And he will take your daughters to be confectionaries, and to be cooks, and to be bakers. 14. And he will take your fields, and your vineyards, and your olive yards, even the best of them, and give them to his servants. 15. And he will take the tenth of your seed, and of your vineyards, and give to his officers, and to his servants. 16. And he will take your menservants, and your maidservants, and your goodliest young men, and your asses, and put them to his work. 17. He will take the tenth of your sheep: and ye shall be his servants. 18. And ye shall cry out in that day because of your king which ye shall have chosen you, and the LORD will not hear you in that day.

The popular clamor proves irresistible—19. Nevertheless, the people refused to obey the voice of Samuel; and they said, Nay: but we will have a king over us; 20. That we also may be like all the nations, and that our king may judge us, and go out before us, and fight our battles. 21. And Samuel heard all the words of the people, and he rehearsed them in the ears of the LORD. 22. And the LORD said to Samuel, Hearken unto their voice, and make them a king. And Samuel said unto the men of Israel, Go ye every man unto his city.

Saul is chosen by lot—10:17. And Samuel called the people together unto the LORD to Mizpeh; 18. and said unto the children of Israel, Thus saith the LORD God of Israel, I brought up Israel out of Egypt, and delivered you out of the

11. With this passage compare the instructions to behave himself moderately which are given to the king in Deut. 17:16 *seq.*

12. **ear,** *i.e.,* to plough; Lat. *arare.*

hand of the Egyptians, and out of the hand of all kingdoms, and of them that oppressed you: 19. And ye have this day rejected your God, who himself saved you out of all your adversities and your tribulations; and ye have said unto him, Nay, but set a king over us. Now, therefore, present yourselves before the LORD by your tribes, and by your thousands. 20. And when Samuel had caused all the tribes of Israel to come near, the tribe of Benjamin was taken. 21. When he had caused the tribe of Benjamin to come near by their families, the family of Matri was taken, and Saul the son of Kish was taken: and when they sought him, he could not be found. 22. Therefore they enquired of the LORD further, Is the man yet come hither? And the LORD answered, Behold, he hath hid himself among the stuff. 23. And they ran and fetched him thence: and when he stood among the people, he was higher than any of the people from his shoulders and upward.

And presented to the people as their king—24. And Samuel said to all the people, See ye him whom the LORD hath chosen, that there is none like him among all the people? And-all the people shouted, and said, God save the king. 25, Then Samuel told the people the manner of the kingdom, and wrote it in a book, and laid it up before the LORD. And Samuel sent all the people away, every man to his. house.

CONFIRMATION OF THE NATION'S CHOICE

1 Samuel 11

An Ammonite attack on Jabesh—1. Then Nabash the Ammonite came up, and encamped against Jabesh-gilead:

20. **taken**, i.e., by means of the sacred lot, the method of applying which is unknown.

22. Saul, out of modesty, had hidden behind the baggage.

25. **manner of the kingdom**. This refers to the enumeration of kingly rights already given, 8:11-17. Samuel wrote this list down and had it preserved, so that the people should have no excuse hereafter to complain of unexpected tyranny on the part of the king.

11:1. This passage is a sequel to 10:27, where Saul, having been only secretly anointed, was left still sustaining the role of a private citizen. He is now to "do as the occasion serves, for God is with him" (10:7).

Jabesh-gilead was about seven miles east of Jordan, in Gad. For

And all the men of Jabesh said unto Nahash, Make a covenant with us, and we will serve thee. 2. And Nahash the Ammonite answered them, On this condition will I make a covenant with you, that I may thrust out all your right eyes, and lay it for a reproach upon all Israel. And the elders of Jabesh said unto him, Give us seven days' respite, that we may send messengers unto all the coasts of Israel: and then, if there be no man to save us, we will come out to thee.

Saul justifies his election by his kingly qualities—2. Then came the messengers to Gibeah of Saul, and told the tidings in the ears of the people: and all the people lifted up their voices, and wept. 5. And, behold, Saul came after the herd out of the field; and Saul said, What aileth the people that they weep? And they told him the tidings of the men of Jabesh. 6. And the spirit of God came upon Saul when he heard those tidings, and his anger was kindled greatly. 7. And he took a yoke of oxen, and hewed them in pieces, and sent them throughout all the coasts of Israel by the hands of. messengers, saying, Whosoever cometh not forth after Saul and after Samuel, so shall it be done unto his oxen. And the fear of the LORD fell on the people, and they came out with one consent.

Utter defeat of the barbarous enemy—8. And when he numbered them in Bezek, the children of Israel were three hundred thousand, and the men of Judah thirty

its previous history, when its maidens were carried off to supply Benjamin with wives, see Judg. 21: vol. 2, p. 191; and for the sequel to the present narrative, 31:11; *2* Sam. 2, below, pp. 99, 108. The Ammonites had figured in Hebrew history once before, **in** conflict with Jephthah (Judg. 11). They were considered to be distantly akin to the Hebrews: their habitat was around the sources of the Jabbok, east of Gad. This King Nahash ("the Serpent") subsequently befriended the outlaw David, out of animosity to his present conqueror, Saul (2 Sam. 10 : 2).

7. *Cf.* the medieval despatch of the war-arrow, or the Fiery Cross of the Highlands.

8. Numbers exaggerated, as usual in ancient documents, sacred and profane alike. Deborah (Judg. v. 8) put the whole national army at 40,000 men; and, especially in the face of continuous hostility, it could hardly have grown to 330,000 in the century or less since her day.

Bezek. Ten miles west of Jordan, nearly opposite Jabesh.

thousand. 9. And they said unto the messengers that came, Thus shall ye say unto the men of Jabesh-gilead, Tomorrow, by that time the sun be hot, ye shall have help. And the messengers came and shewed it to the men of Jabesh: and they were glad. 10. Therefore the men of Jabesh said, Tomorrow we will come out unto you, and ye shall do with us all that seemeth good unto you. 11. And it was so on the morrow, that Saul put the people in three companies; and they came into the midst of the host in the morning watch, and slew the Ammonites until the heat of the day: and it came to pass, that they which remained were scattered, so that two of them were not left together.

The kingship is ratified at Gilgal—12. And the people said unto Samuel, Who is he that said, Shall Saul reign over us? bring the men, that we may put them to death. 13. And Saul said, There shall not a man be put to death this day: for to day the LORD hath wrought salvation in Israel. 14. Then said Samuel to the people, Come, and let us go to Gilgal, and renew the kingdom there. And all the people went to Gilgal; and there they made Saul king before the LORD in Gilgal; and there they sacrificed sacrifices of peace offerings before the LORD; and there Saul and all the men of Israel rejoiced greatly.

SAMUEL'S FAREWELL ADDRESS ON ABDICATION OF HIS OFFICE AS JUDGE OF THE THEOCRACY

1 Samuel 12

He protests his integrity—1. And Samuel said unto all Israel, Behold, I have hearkened unto your voice in all that ye said unto me, and have made a king over you. And now, behold, the king walketh before you: and I am old and gray-headed: and behold, my sons are with you: and I have walked before you from my childhood unto this day. 3. Behold, here I am: witness

12-14 are an editorial addition designed to harmonize the two accounts of Saul's accession which we have already considered.

12:1. This fine rhetorical address closely resembles the farewell of Joshua (Josh. 13).

against me before the LORD, and before his anointed: whose ox have I taken? or whose ass have I taken? or whom have I defrauded? whom have I oppressed? or of whose hand, have I received any bribe to blind mine eyes therewith? and I will restore it you. 4. And they said, Thou hast not defrauded us, nor oppressed us, neither hast thou taken ought of any man's hand. 5. And he said unto them, The LORD is witness against you, and his anointed is witness this day, that ye have not found ought in my hand. And they answered, He is witness.

Their own history is a witness to God's goodness—6. And Samuel said unto the people, It is the LORD that advanced Moses and Aaron, and that brought your fathers up out of the land of Egypt. 7. Now therefore stand still, that I may reason with you before the LORD of all the righteous acts of the LORD, which he did to you and to your fathers. 8. when Jacob was come into Egypt, and your fathers cried unto the LORD, then the LORD sent Moses and Aaron, which brought forth your fathers out of Egypt, and made them dwell in this place. 9. And when they forgat the LORD their God, he sold them into the hand of Sisera, captain of the host of Hazor, and into the hand of the Philistines, and into the hand of the king of Moab, and they fought against them. 10. And they cried unto the LORD, and said, Ye have sinned, because we have forsaken the LORD, and have served Baalim and Ashtaroth: but now deliver us out of the hand of our enemies, and we will serve thee. 11. And the LORD sent Jerubbaal, and Bedan, and Jephthah, and Samuel, and delivered you out of the hand of your enemies on every side, and ye dwelled safe. 12. And when ye saw that Nahash the king of the children of Ammon came against you, ye said unto me, Nay; but a king shall reign over us: when the LORD your God was your king.

So now under the king, obedience to God will win His favor—13. Now therefore behold the king whom ye

11. **Bedan** is a corruption of Barak, the letters of which, in the Hebrew, are much like those of Bedan.

Samuel. The Deuteronomic editor of Samuel's words has no scruples in making Samuel catalogue himself among the greatest of the Judges—and rightly.

have chosen, and whom ye have desired! and, behold, the LORD hath set a king over you. 14. If ye will fear the LORD, and serve him, and obey his voice, and not rebel against the commandment of the LORD, and both ye and also the king that reigneth over you continue following the LORD your God: well: 15. but if ye will not obey the voice of the LORD, but rebel against the commandment of the LORD, then shall the hand of the LORD be against you, as it was against your fathers.

A sign convinces them of their error in desiring a king—Now therefore stand and see this great thing, which the LORD will do before your eyes. 17. Is it not wheat harvest today? I will call unto the LORD, and he shall send thunder and rain; that ye may perceive and see that your wickedness is great, which ye have done in the sight of the LORD, in asking you a king. 18. So Samuel called unto the LORD; and the LORD sent thunder and rain that day: and all the people greatly feared the LORD and Samuel. 19. And all the people said unto Samuel, Pray for thy servants unto the LORD thy God, that we die not: for we have added unto all our sins this evil, to ask us a king.

His final exhortation—20. And Samuel said unto the people, Fear not: ye have done all this wickedness: yet turn not aside from following the LORD, but serve the LORD with all your heart; 21. and turn ye not aside after vain things, which cannot profit nor deliver; for they are vain. 22. For the LORD will not forsake his people for his great name's sake: because it hath pleased the LORD to make you his people.

He resigns his office as Jehovah's representative, but retains the privilege of interceding for Israel—23. Moreover, as for me, God forbid that I should sin against the LORD in ceasing to pray for you: but I will teach you the good and the right way: 24. only fear the LORD, and serve him in truth with all your heart: for consider how great things he hath done for you. 25. But if ye shall still do wickedly, ye shall be consumed, both ye and your king.

PART II

SAUL THE KING

INTRODUCTORY

ONE preliminary word only need be said. In estimating the character of Saul, the reader should remember that, as before, the authors of our two main narratives write from wholly different points of view. The older writer presents Saul as a brave, impulsive, generous, and devout rnan; touched, however, with a melancholia which eventually developed into temporary madness. The younger writer has nothing good to say of him, but regards him, from the outset, as an intruder of whom the theocracy were better quit.

THE FAMILY OF SAUL

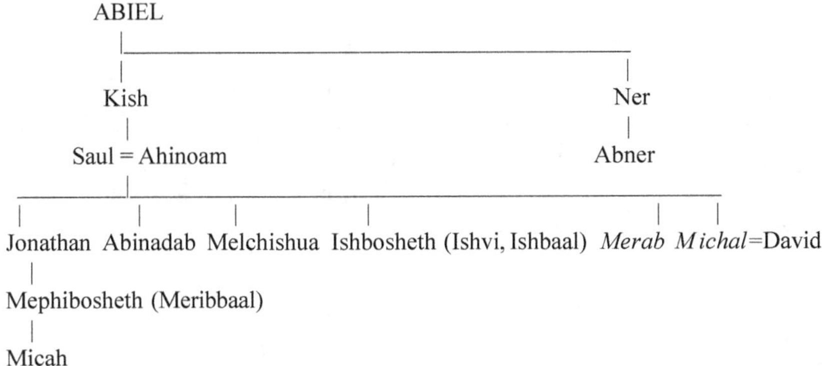

The names of women are printed in italics.

THE WAR OF INDEPENDENCE:
THE BATTLE OF MICHMASH
1 Samuel 13:2—14:46 and 52

Opening of Saul's first campaign against the Philistines—9:2. And Saul chose him three thousand men of Israel;

whereof two thousand were with Saul in Michmash and in mount Beth-el, and a thousand were with Jonathan in *Geba* of Benjamin: and the rest of the people he sent every man to his tent. 3. And Jonathan smote the garrison of the Philistines that was in *Gibeah,* and the Philistines heard of it. And Saul blew the trumpet throughout all the land, saying, Let the Hebrews hear. 4. And all Israel heard say that Saul had smitten a garrison of the Philistines, and that Israel also was had in abomination with the Philistines. And the people were called together after Saul to Gilgal.

Gathering of the Philistine forces—5. And the Philistines gathered themselves together to fight with Israel, thirty thousand chariots, and six thousand horsemen, and people as the sand which is on the seashore in multitude: and they came up, and pitched in Michmash, eastward from Beth-aven. 6. When the men of Israel saw that they were in a strait (for the people were distressed), then the people did hide themselves in caves, and in thickets, and in rocks, and in high places, and in pits. 7. And some of the Hebrews went over Jordan to the land of Gad and Gilead. As for Saul, he was yet in Gilgal, and all the people followed him trembling.

[Now Samuel had commanded Saul, saying,] 10:8. Thou shalt go down before me to Gilgal; and behold, I will come down unto thee, to offer burnt offerings and to sacrifice sacrifices of peace offerings: seven days shalt

2. See a map. Saul is at Michmash, on the north side of a narrow ravine; Jonathan just opposite, at Geba on the south side. Thus, they held the pass between them. Michmash was "the very citadel of Israel's hill country." He who held it (a) commanded one of the best trade routes from the Shephelah to Jordan: (b) cut off communication between the northern and the southern tribes. Hence the Philistines were anxious to secure it and did so (verse 4).

3. From Geba Jonathan made a raid on the Philistine "Resident" at Gibeah, his home, about three miles away, and cut him and his garrison down.

4. Saul clearly soon suffered a defeat and had to evacuate Michmash. But Jonathan, still held out at Geba, which now became the solitary rallying-post of the demoralized Hebrews. The enemy overran the entire country, plundering (verse 17 *seq.*). The true original account of the strategic movement is, however, interrupted by the rather tiresome intrusion into the narrative, from another source, of the story of Saul's rejection (verses 4 *b,* 7 *b,* 8-14).

thou tarry, till I come to thee and shew thee what thou shalt do.

*Saul's sin and consequeni rejection (1st account)—13:*8. And he, tarried seven days, according to the set time that Samuel had appointed: but Samuel came not to Gilgal; and the people were scattered from him. 9. And Saul said, Bring hither a burnt offering to me, and peace offerings. And he offered the burnt offering. 10. And it came to pass, that as soon as he had made an end of offering the burnt offering, behold, Samuel came; and Saul went on to meet him, that he might salute him. 11. And Samuel said, What hast thou done? And Saul said, Because I saw that the people were scattered from me, and that thou earnest not within the days appointed, and that the Philistines gathered themselves together at Michmash; 12. therefore said I, The Philistines will come down now upon me to Gilgal, and I have not made supplication unto the LORD: I forced myself therefore and offered a burnt offering. 13. And Samuel said to Saul, Thou hast done foolishly: thou hast not kept the commandment of the LORD thy God, which he commanded thee: for now would the LORD have established thy kingdom upon Israel fore ver. 14. But now thy kingdom shall not continue: the LORD hath sought him a man after his own heart, and the LORD hath commanded him to be captain over his

8. **had appointed,** viz. in 1 0 : 8, at the secret anointing—a verse which we have transferred from that passage to this, which is clearly its proper context.

13. What was Saul's sin? That he had disobeyed Samuel's order to wait? But he had not. That he had usurped priestly privileges in sacrificing? But he had not. Sacrifice was not then the exclusive prerogative of the priest: Gideon, David, Elijah, etc., offer it without question; nor is there any suggestion in our text that his fault lay there. That he had been impatient? The narrative hardly bears out this charge. We must conclude either (1) that the editor's irremediable dislocation of the original text has caused the omission of some crucial verse explaining the mystery; or (2) that the philosophic writer of this passage— it is a late, and reflective one—wishing to show, that Saul's character must have been unacceptable to God and uns itable for the duties of monarchy, since in fact he founded no dynasty—punishment must have been preceded by sin—unwisely selected this as a convenient occasion for ventilating his theory. The doublet of the story (chap. 15 below) is far more intelligible and just.

people, because thou hast not kept that which the LORD commanded thee.

Saul at Geba with a small force—15. And Samuel arose, and gat him up from Gilgal unto *Geba* of Benjamin.   And Saul numbered the people that were present with him, about six   hundred   men. 16. And Saul,   and   Jonathan his son, and the people that were present with them, abode in *Geba* of Benjamin: but the Philistines encamped in Michmash.

Devastations by the Philistines—17. And the spoilers came out of the camp of the Philistines in three companies: one company turned unto the way that leadeth to Ophrah, unto the land of Shual: 18. and another company turned the way   to Beth-horon: and   another company turned to the way of the border that looketh to the valley of Zeboim toward the wilderness.   19. Now there was no smith found throughout all the land of Israel: for the Philistines said, Lest the Hebrews make them swords or pears: 20.   but all the Israelites went down to the Philistines, to sharpen every man his share, and his coulter, and his axe, and his mattock. 22.   So it came to pass in the day of battle, that there was neither sword nor spear found in the hand of any of the people that were with Saul and Jonathan: but with Saul and with Jonathan his son was there found. 23. And the garrison of the Philistines went out to the passage of Michmash.

Jonathan's rash exploit—14:1. Now it came to pass upon a day, that Jonathan the son of Saul said unto the young man that bare his armor, Come, and let us go over to the Philistines' garrison, that is on the other side. But he told not his father. 2. And Saul tarried in the uttermost part of *Geba* under a pomegranate tree which is *by the threshing floor:* and the people that were with him were about six hundred men; 3. and Ahiah, the son of Ahitub, Ichabod's brother, the son of Phinehas, the son of Eli, the Lord's priest in Shiloh, *carrying the* ephod. And the people

17. North to **Ophrah** in Ephraim, west to Beth-horon, south-east towards the Jordan Valley (see *H.G.H.L.,* p. 291).

19 *seq.* A quaint exaggeration by a late interpolator desirous of heightening the effect. Coulter is the "cutter," or blade of the plough.

3. **Ahlah,** or Ahijah, also called Ahimelech (chap. 2 1 ; 2), the names heing synonymous. See genealogical tree, p. 12.

knew not that Jonathan was gone.

Description of the ravine—4. And between the passages, by which Jonathan sought to go over unto the Philistines' garrison, there was a sharp rock on the one side, and a sharp rock on the other side: and the name of the one was Bozez, and the name of the other Seneh. 5. The forefront of the one was situated nortlward over against Michmash, and the other southward over against *Geba.*

The plan of attack—6. And Jonathan said to the young man that bare his armor, Come, and let us go over unto the garrison of these uncircumcised: it may be that the LORD will work for us: for there is no restraint to the LORD to save by many or by few. 7. And his armorbearer said unto him, Do all that is in thine heart: turn thee; behold, I am with thee according to thy heart. 8. Then said Jonathan, Behold, we will pass over unto these men, and we will discover ourselves unto them. 9. If they say thus unto us, Tarry until we come to you; then we will stand still in our place and will not go up unto them. 10. But if they say thus, Come up unto us; then we will go up: for the LORD hath delivered them into our hand: and this shall be a sign unto us.

Success of Jonathan—11. And both of them discoveredthemselves unto the garrison of the Philistines: and the Philistines said, Behold, the Hebrews come forth out of the holes where they had hid themselves. 12. And the men of the garrison answered Jonathan and his armorbearer, and said, Come up to us, and we will shew you a thing. And Jonathan said unto his armor-bearer, Come up after me: for the LORD hath delivered them into the hand of Israel. 13. And Jonathan climbed up upon his hands and upon his feet, and his armor-bearer after him: and they fell before Jonathan; and his armor-bearer

5. **Bozez,** " the shining," on the north side; **Seneh,** "the thorny," on the south *(H.G.H.L.,* p. 250).

9. For the omen as an indication of God's will see above, 6:7 *n.* We are doubtless meant to understand that the language of the Philistines would give a hint to Jonathan as to their probable strength; how precisely we cannot say.

12. **a thing.** This is contemptuous badinage, almost a slang phrase, " we'll show you a thing or two."

slew after him. 14. And that first slaughter, which Jonathan and his armor-bearer made, was about twenty men, within as it were a half- acre of land, which a yoke of oxen might plow.

Which has unhoped-for consequences—15. And there was trembling in the host, in the field, and among all the people: the garrison, and the spoilers, they also trembled: and the earth quaked: so it was a very great trembling. 16. And the watchmen of Saul in *Geba* of Benjamin looked; and behold, the multitude melted away; and they went on beating down one another. 17. Then said Saul unto the people that were with him, Number now, and see who is gone from us. And when they had numbered, behold, Jonathan and his armor-bearer were not there. 18. And Saul said unto Ahiah, Bring hither the ephod. For he carried the ephod at that time before Israel.

A general rout of the enemy—19. And it came to pass, while Saul talked unto the priest, that the noise that was in the host of the Philistines went on and increased: and Saul said unto the priest, Withdraw thine hand. 20. And Saul and all the people that were with him assembled themselves, and they came to the battle: and behold, every man's sword was against his fellow, and there was a very great discomfiture. 21. Moreover the Hebrews that were with the Philistines *heretofore,* which went up with them into the camp from the country round about, even they also turned to be with the Israelites that were with Saul and Jonathan. 22. Likewise all the men of Israel which had hid themselves in mount Ephraim, when they heard that the Philistines fled, even they also followed hard after them in the battle. 23. So the LORD saved

18. The text printed in italics gives the Greek (LXX) version and is obviously right (Smith, p. 112). A.V. renders the Hebrew text which, by a scribe's error here, make *the Ark* to be brought up by Ahijah. The Ark was, we know, at Kirjath-jearim. For the consultation of God's will by the Ephod see above, 2 : 18 *n.,* and any Bible Dictionary.

19. **Withdraw.** Saul quickly changed his mind, and now would not wait for the oracle's answer to be obtained. He now suddenly felt, with Pericles, that the opportunity for a crushing blow must not be lost: *Kairoi polemon ou menetoi* (Thuc. 1:142). Saul was obviously a mass of "nerves." His nervousness and indecision were exhibited on many occasions, *e.g.,* when he "hid behind the stuff."

Israel that day: and the battle passed over unto Beth-aven.

Saul's taboo on food, 24. And the men of Israel were distressed that day: for Saul had adjured the people, saying, Cursed be the man that eateth any food until evening, that I may be avenged on mine enemies. So, none of the people tasted any food. *25.* And all they of the land came to a wood; and there was honey upon the ground. 26. And when the people were come unto the food, behold, the honey dropped; but no man put his hand *to* his mouth: for the people feared the oath.

Unwittingly violated by his son—27. But Jonathan heard not when his father charged the people with the oath; wherefore he put forth the end of the rod that was in his hand, and dipped it in an honeycomb, and put his hand *to* his mouth; and his eyes were enlightened. 28. Then answered one of the people, and said, Thy father straitly charged the people with an oath, saying, Cursed be the man that eateth any food this day. And the people were faint. 29. Then said Jonathan, My father hath troubled the land: see, I pray you, how mine eyes have been enlightened, because I tasted a little of this honey. 30. How much more, if haply the people had eaten freely today of the spoil of their enemies which they found? for had there not been now a much greater slaughter among the Philistines? 31. And they smote the Philistine? that day from Michmash to Aijalon: and the people were very faint. 32. And the people flew upon the spoil, and, took sheep, and oxen, and calves, and slew them on the ground: and the people did eat them with the blood.

23. **Beth-aven.** The mountainous "wilderness" north-west of Michmash.

24. Saul, according to the religious idea of primitive times, was doing a right action in depriving the army of food. This was a recognized method of retaining the favor and help of the Deity. It was the logical expression of his zeal for God's honor. In this older document *(St)* he is painted as a religious, devout man. As a piece of practical military policy, it was foolish to employ an army on an empty stomach, and Jonathan's criticism on his father's orders wins our sympathy. The contrary view is, however, held by some military critics.

32. The blood was regarded as the seat of the "soul," *i.e.,* as the principle of life. It was therefore always treated with religious

Ceremonial reparation made for eating meat "with the blood."—33. Then they told Saul, saying, Behold, the people's in against the LORD, in that they eat with the blood. And he said, Ye have transgressed: roll a great stone unto me this day. 34. And Saul said, Disperse yourselves among the people, and say unto them, Bring me hither every man his ox, and every man his sheep, and slay them here, and eat; and sin not against the LORD in eating with the blood. And all the people brought every man his ox with him that night, and slew them there. 35. And Saul built an altar unto the LORD: the same was the first altar that he built unto the LORD.

" The oracle is dumb"—36. And Saul said, Let us go down after the Philistines by night, and spoil them until the morning light, and let us not leave a man of them. And they said, Do whatsoever seemeth good unto thee. Then said the priest, Let us draw near hither unto God. 37. And Saul asked counsel of God, Shall I go down after the Philistines? wilt thou deliver them into the hand of Israel? But he answered him not that day.   38. And Saul said, Draw ye near hither, all the chief of the people: and know and see wherein this sin hath been this day. 39. For, as the LORD liveth, which saveth Israel, though it be in Jonathan my son, he shall surely die.   But there was not a man among all the people that answered him. 40. Then said he unto all Israel, Be ye on one side, and I and Jonathan my son will be on the other side.   And the people said unto Saul, Do what seemeth good unto thee. 41. Therefore Saul said unto the L ORD God of Israe1, Give a perfect lot. And Saul and Jonathan were taken: but the people escaped.

Saul condemns his son to death—42. And Saul said, Cast lots between me and Jonathan my son.   And Jonathan was taken. 43. Then Saul said to Jonathan, Tell me what thou hast done.

awe in ancient time. In Hebrew legislation strict rules were made and repeated forbidding the eating of flesh until the hlood had been drained from it. The idea that the blood is the life is the fundamental principle of all sacrifice (vol. 1 , p. 32; vol. 2, p. 51; Deut. 1 2 : 23, etc.;   *Rel. Sem.,* pp. 40, 234).
     41. The   guilty person is discovered by the sacred lot—as Achan was (Josh. 7).   Our text is imperfect: the LXX here preserves a fuller text describing clearly the application of the sacred lots, the Urim and Thummim.

And Jonathan told him, and said, I did but taste a little honey with the end of the rod that was in mine hand, and, lo, I am ready to die. 44. And Saul answered, God do so and more also: for thou shalt surely die, Jonathan. 45. And the people said unto Saul, Shall Jonathan die, who hath wrought this great salvation in Israel? God forbid: as the LORD liveth, there shall not one hair of his head fall to the ground; for he hath wrought with God this day. So, the people rescued Jonathan, that he died not. 46. Then Saul went up from following the Philistines: and the Philistines went to their own place.

Small results of the victory—52. And there was sore war against the Philistines all the days of Saul: and when Saul saw any strong man, or any valiant man, he took him unto him.

SAUL'S SIN AND REJECTION (SECOND ACCOUNT)

1 Samuel 15

A military mission against Amalek—1. Samuel also said unto Saul, The LORD sent me to anoint thee to be king over

44. God do . . . also. See 3:17 *n.*

45. This incident opens up interesting questions on (1) Antiquities, *e.g.* Taboo, Sacrifice, Lots; (2) the characters of Saul and Jonathan. There is no space to pursue these here, but the student is advised to do so (see *Bib. Diets.; Rel. Sem.;* Smith; Kenn. *ad loc.* etc.).

52. The victory of Michmash had no permanent effect: it merely meant the capture of the enemy's camp and a subsequent guerilla warfare all through Saul's reign. Saul adopted, however, a wise policy in attracting stout warriors to his military capital at Gibeah: this presently brought David to his court.

15:1 This expedition was undertaken solely in the interests of Judah, a tribe which, with Benjamin, Saul attached closely to him self. The Amalekites were a "powerful, widely dispersed tribe of nomads whose original home was" in the Semitic peninsula. They predominated, however, rather in the district between Kadesh. and Judah. During the Exodus Israel defeated them at Rephidim (Exod. 17) and was defeated by them at Hormah (Num. 14).

Observe that Samuel, though he had retired, is still in the writer's eyes the virtual theocratic Judge of Israel and representative of Jehovah. His power is greater, and his plainness of speech in dealing frankly with a king no less, than that of the prophets Nathan and Gad, etc., in the next era.

his people, over Israel: now therefore hearken thou unto the voice of the words of the LORD. 2. Thus saith the LORD of hosts, I remember that which Amalek did to Israel, how he laid wait for him in the way, when he came up from Egypt.   3. Now go and smite Amalek, and utterly destroy all that they have, and spare them not; but slay both man and woman, infant and suckling, ox and sheep, camel and ass. 4. And Saul gathered the people together, and numbered them in Telaim, two hundred thousand footmen, and ten thousand men of Judah.   5. And Saul came to a city of Amalek, and laid wait in the valley.

Saul's victory and disobedience—6. And Saul said unto the. Kenites, Go, depart, get you down from among the Amalekites, lest I destroy you with them: for ye shewed kindness to all the children of Israel, when they came up out of Egypt. So the Kenites departed from among the Amalekites. 7. And Saul smote the Amalekites from Havilah until thou comest to Shur, that is over against Egypt.   8. And he took Agag the king of the Amalekites alive, and utterly destroyed all the people with the edge of the sword. 9. But Saul and the people spared Agag, and the best of the sheep, and of the oxen, and of the fatlings, and the lambs, and all that was good, and would not utterly destroy them: but everything that was vile and refuse, that they destroyed utterly.

Samuel confronts him—10. Then came the word of the **LORD** unto Samuel, saying, 11. It repenteth me that I have set up Saul to be king: for he is turned back from following me, and hath not performed my commandments. And it grieved Samuel; and he cried unto the

4. **Telaim.**   On the southern border of Judah, on the route to the Amalekite country.

6. Some of the Kenites whose home was in the south country among the Midianites, had joined the Hebrews in their invasion of Palestine, and settled in the south of Judah. Subsequently, "true to their nomadic origin," they filtered south through the Negeb and coalesced with Amalek.   Jethro is stated to have been a Kenite (Judg; 1:16, 4:11, etc.; *H.G.H.L.* p. 277).

7. **Havilah.**   Unknown.   Shur is the "wilderness" on the eastern frontier of Egypt, which takes its name from the line of frontier walls (Shur) and fortresses which in old days ran along the Isthmus of Suez.

LORD all night. 12. And when Samuel rose early to meet Saul in The morning, it was told Samuel, saying Saul came to Carmel, and behold, he set him up a place: and is gone about, and passed on, and gone down to Gilgal. 13. And Samuel came to Saul: and Saul said unto him, Blessed be thou of the LORD: I have performed the commandment of the LORD. 14. And Samuel said, What meaneth then this bleating of the sheep in mine ears and the lowing of the oxen which I hear? 15. And Saul said, They have brought them from the Amalekites: for the people spared the best of the sheep and of the oxen, to sacrifice unto the LORD thy God; and the rest we have utterly destroyed.

Samuel's rebuke—16. Then Samuel said unto Saul, Stay, and I will tell thee what the LORD hath said to me this night. And he said unto him, Say on. 17. And Samuel said, When thou wast little in thine own sight, wast thou not made the head of the tribes of Israel, and the LORD anointed thee king over Israel? 18. And the LORD sent thee on a journey, and said, Go and utterly destroy the sinners the Amalekites, and fight against them until they be consumed. 19. Wherefore then didst thou not obey the voice of the LORD, but didst fly upon the spoil, and didst evil in the sight of the LORD?

Saul's shift to excuse himself—20. And Saul said unto Samuel, Yea, I have obeyed the voice of the LORD, and have gone the way which the LORD sent me, and have brought Agag the king of Amalek, and have utterly destroyed the Amalekites. 21. But the people took of the spoil, sheep and oxen, the chief of the things which should have been utterly destroyed, to sacrifice unto the LORD thy God in Gilgal. 22. And Samuel said, Hath the LORD as great delight in burnt offerings and sacrifices, as in obeying the voice of the LORD? Behold, to obey is better than sacrifice, and to hearken than the fat of rams. 23. For REBELLION is as the sin of witchcraft, and stubbornness is as iniquity and

12. Carmel (25:2)—seven rniles south of Hebron, the farm of the churl Nabal. **place**, i.e., a trophy of his victory.

20. Saul shifts the blame on to **the people**. Besides, he says, Jehovah will get His proper share from the sacrifice: that is my justification. "Falsehood," "hypocrisy," "impudence," say his critics, harshly but perhaps rightly.

23. **stubbornness . . . idolatry**. The Heb. says, "Arrogance is as the iniquity of teraphim." Teraphim were the familiar images

idolatry. Because thou hast rejected the word of the LORD, he hath also rejected thee from being king.

He confesses—24. And Saul said unto Samuel, I have sinned: for I have transgressed the commandment of the LORD, and thy words: because I feared the people, and obeyed their voice. 25. Now therefore, I pray thee, pardon my sin, and turn again with me, that I may worship the LORD. 26. And Samuel said unto Saul, I will not return with thee: for thou hast rejected the word of the LORD, and the LORD hath rejected thee from being king over Israel. 27. And as Samuel turned about to go away, he laid hold upon the skirt of his mantle, and it rent. And Samuel said unto him, The LORD hath rent the kingdom of Israel from thee this day, and h ath given it to a neighbor of thine, that is better than thou. 29. And also the Strength of Israel will not lie nor repent: for he is not a man, that he should repent. 30. Then he said, I have sinned: yet honor me now, I pray thee, before the elders of my people, and before Israel, and turn again with me, that I may worship the LORD thy God. 31. So Samuel turned again after Saul; and Saul worshipped the LORD.

Slaughter of Agag—32. Then said Samuel, Bring ye   hither

which play a large part as a means of divination in the religious customs of ancient Israel. By the time this passage was written they were utterly condemned as idolatrous—a result of the spiritual teaching of the prophets. For the whole verse *cf.* Hos. 6 : 6: " I desire mercy [*hesed* = "lovingkindness"] and not sacrifice, and the knowledge of God more than burnt offerings": Micah 6 : 6-8, etc. In these words "the author of this chapter brings to a luminous point the whole ethical teaching of the Hebrew prophets from Amos downwards . . . The O.T. has no word for ' duty': its moral ideal is embodied in the words ' as the Lord commanded'" (Kenn.). Saul had singularly failed in his "duty."

28. For the significance of the rent garment compare the interview of Ahijah, the prophet, with Jeroboam (1 Kings 11:29).

29. **"the Strength of Israel"** Samuel pointedly uses this title in speaking of Jehovah in order to make Saul feel the contrast between God's immovable strength and his own weakness. Saul was outwardly the strong man, inwardly weak, and vacillating.

32. **delicately** perhaps = mincingly, as if to ingratiate himself and avoid his fate: a demeanor further exhibited in his words: "You cannot really mean to kill me?" LXX has *tremon* ("trembling"),

to me Agag the king of the Amalekites. And Agag came unto him delicately. And Agag said, Surely the bitterness of death is past. 33. And Samuel said, As thy sword hath made women childless, so shall thy mother be childless among women. And Samuel hewed Agag in pieces before the LORD in Gilgal.

Saul shall see Samuel's face no more—34. Then Samuel went to Ramah; and Saul went up to his house to Gibeah of Saul. 35. And Samuel came no more to see Saul until the day of his death: nevertheless Samuel mourned for Saul.

DAVID'S EARLY LIFE AND INTRODUCTION TO
SAUL'S COURT

From this point the dramatic interest of the story centers in David. The vicissitudes of fortune which at length set him on the throne of Judah, and subsequently of all Israel, are portrayed with a vividness which puts the historical fortunes of Saul in the background. Unfortunately the Hebrew text presents literary and historical difficulties—repetitions, inaccuracies, contradictions which in places are frankly insuperable. We can only attempt *to* present the stories in some sort of intelligible shape. David is introduced to the reader as a new character three times: these three independent accounts, with their circumstances, are here given, marked respectively A, B, and C; in the Bible text the compiler has made an eminently unsuccessful endeavor to weld them into one.

instead of "delicately," and simply *pikros ha thanatos* ("death is bitter") —which robs the passage of its color. The original texts, however, do not make it clear whether Agag is meant to be specious, or defiant, or craven.

33. A massacre in cold blood, though abhorrent to us, appeared as duty to the most conscientious men of that time. The enemy were regarded as being under a religions ban, devoted to God, and therefore it was wicked to spare them.

35 *a.* This statement is contradicted by 19:23——a passage which, however, is of very late origin and little historical value.

DAVID'S YOUTH

A. (FIRST STORY) DAVID, THE YOUNG SHEPHERD, ANOINTED BY SAMUEL

1 Samuel 15:35b—16:13

God chooses a successor to Saul—15: 35 b. And the LORD repented that he had made Saul king over Israel. 15:1. And the LORD said unto Samuel, How long wilt thou mourn for Saul, seeing I have rejected him from reigning over Israel? fill thine horn with oil, and go, I will send thee to Jesse the Bethlehemite: for I have provided me a king among his sons 2. And Samuel said, How can I go? if Saul hear it, he will kill me. And the LORD said, Take an heifer with thee, and say, I am come to sacrifice to the LORD. 3. And call Jesse to the sacrifice, and I will shew thee what thou shalt do: and thou shalt anoint unto me him whom I name unto thee. 4. And Samuel did that which the LORD spake, and came to Bethlehem. And the elders of the town trembled at his coming, and said, Comest thou peaceably? 5. And he said, Peaceably. I am come to sacrifice unto the LORD: sanctify yourselves and come with me to the sacrifice. And he sanctified Jesse and his sons and called them to the sacrifice.

Jesse's sons pass in review before Samuel—6. And it came to pass, when they were come, that he looked on Eliab, and said, Surely the LORD'S anointed is before him. 7. But the LORD said unto Samuel, Look not on his countenance, or on the height of his stature; because I have refused him: for the LORD seeth not as man seeth; for man looketh on the outward appearance, but the LORD looketh on the heart. 8. Then Jesse called Abinadab and made him pass before Samuel. And he said, Neither hath the LORD chosen his. 9. Then Jesse made Shammah to pass by. And he said, Neither hath the LORD chosen this. 10. Again, Jesse made seven of his sons to pass before Samuel. And Samuel said unto Jesse, The LORD hath not chosen these.

David is Jehovah's choice—11. And Samuel said unto Jesse, Are here all thy children? And he said, There remaineth yet

---

4. The unexpected arrival of so great a man, Jehovah's representative, caused consternation in the little Judean village.

the youngest, and behold, he keepeth the sheep. And Samuel said unto Jesse, Send and fetch him: for we will not sit down till he come hither. 12. And he sent, and brought him in. Now he was ruddy, and withal of a beautiful countenance, and goodly to look to. And the LORD said, Arise, anoint him: for this is he. 13. Then Samuel took the horn of oil and anointed him in the midst of his brethren: and the spirit of the LORD came upon David from that day forward. So, Samuel rose up, and went to Ramah.

B. (SECOND STORY). DAVID, THE SKILLED MUSICIAN, AND GOLIATH

1 Samuel 16:14—17:11, 32-53

Saul's mental disease—16:14. But the spirit of the LORD departed from Saul, and an evil spirit from the LORD troubled him. 15. And Saul's servants said unto him, Behold now, an evil spirit from God troubleth thee. Let our Lord now command thy servants, which are before thee, to seek out a man, who is a cunning player on an harp: and if it shall come to pass, when the evil spirit from God is upon thee, that he shall play with his hand, and thou shalt be well. 17. And Saul said unto his servants, Provide me now a man that can play well, and bring him to me. 18. Then answered one of the servants, and said, Behold, I have seen a son of Jesse the Bethlehemite, that is cunning in playing, and a mighty valiant man, and a man of war, and prudent in matters, and a comely person, and the LORD is with him.

12. Kennedy aptly quotes Browning's *Saul:*
"God's child with His dew
On thy gracious gold hair."

16:14. Saul suffered from a kind of melancholia, developing occasionally into dangerous mania. That disease was held by the Hebrews to be a visitation of evil spirits, implying the withdrawal of God's favor, is a familiar idea both in the Old and New Testaments. An evil spirit, as much as anything else in nature, is created by and subject to God; there is, therefore, no difficulty in the phrase, "an evil spirit from Jehovah."

18. **mighty. . .war.** The epithets are, perhaps, hardly consistent

Alleviated by David's musical art—19. Wherefore Saul sent messengers unto Jesse, and said, Send me David thy son, which is with the sheep. 20. And Jesse took an ass laden with bread, and a bottle of wine, and a kid, and sent them by David his son unto Saul. 21. And David came to Saul and stood before him: and he loved him greatly; and he became his armor-bearer. 22. And Saul sent to Jesse, saying, Let David, I pray thee, stand before me; for he hath found favor in my sight. 23. And it came to pass, when the evil spirit from God was upon Saul, that David took an harp, and played with his hand: so Saul was refreshed, and was well, and the evil spirit departed from him.

Another campaign in the war of independence—17:1. Now the Philistines gathered together their armies to battle, and were gathered together at Shochoh, which belongeth to Judah, and pitched between Shochoh and Azekah, in Ephes-dammim. 2. And Saul and the men of Israel were gathered together, and pitched by the valley of Elah, and set the battle in array against the Philistines. 3. And the Philistines stood on a mountain on the one side and Israel stood on a mountain on the other side: and there was a valley between them.

Goliath's challenge—4. And there went out a champion out of the camp of the Philistines, named Goliath, of Gath, whose height was six cubits and a span. 5. And he had an helmet of brass upon his head, and he was armed with a coat of mail; and the weight of the coat was five thousand shekels of brass. 6. And he had greaves

with David's present youth and inexperience, which all three of our documents agree in asserting and the historical situation makes certain. He could not have been more than about twenly years old (see p. xxiii).

17:1. The battlefield, twelve miles west of Bethlehem, on the edge of the Shephelah, is described in *H.G.H.L.,* pp. 227-8.

4. **Goliath** was 9 ft. 9 in. high (a span = half a cubit); his cuirass weighed 200 lbs., his spearhead 24 lbs. There are many convergent indications that David's opponent in this battle in the original records was anonymous: later admirers sought to enlarge the renown of his victory by identifying his nameless victim with the giant Goliath, who below (2 Sam. 21:19) is reported to have been killed by one Elhanan. (Sec Kenn. *ad loc.* for an original examination of the question.)

of brass upon his legs, and a *javelin* of brass between his shoulders. 7. And the staff of his spear was like a weaver's beam; and his spear's head weighed six hundred shekels of iron: and on bearing a shield went before him. 8. And he stood and cried unto the armies of Israel, and said unto them, Why are ye come out to set your battle in array? am not I a Philistine, and ye servants to Saul? choose you a man for you, and let him come down to me. 9. If he be able to fight with me, and to kill me, then will we be your servants: but if I prevail against him, and kill him, then shall ye be our servants, and serve us. 10. And the Philistine said, I defy the armies of Israel this day; give me a man, that we may fight together. 11. When Saul and all Israel heard those words of the Philistine, they were dismayed, and greatly afraid.

David accepts the challenge—32. And David said to Saul, Let no man's heart fail because of him; thy servant will go and fight with this Philistine. 33. And Saul said to David, Thou art not able to go against this Philistine to fight with him: for thou art but a youth, and he a man of war from his youth. 34. And David said unto Saul, Thy servant kept his father's sheep, and *when* there came a lion, *or* a bear, and took a lamb out of the flock, 35. I went out after him, and smote him, and delivered it out of his mouth: and when he arose against me, I caught him by his beard, and smote him, and slew him. 36. Thy servant slew both the lion and the bear: and this uncircumcised Philistine shall be as one of them, seeing he hath defied the armies of the living God. 37. David said moreover, The LORD that delivered me out of the paw of the lion, and out of the paw of the bear, he will deliver rne out of the hand of this Philistine. And Saul said unto David, Go, and the LORD be with thee.

He refuses the loan of Saul's armor—38. And Saul armed David with his armor, and he put an helmet of brass upon his head; also he armed him with a coat of mail. 39. And David girded his sword upon his armor, and he assayed to go; for he had not proved it. And David said unto Saul, I cannot go with these; for I have

---

39. David tried in vain to walk in this unaccustomed armor, in the use of which he had no experience.

not proved them.　And David put them off him.　40. And he took his staff in his hand and chose him five smooth stones out of the brook and put them in a shepherd's bag which he had, even in a scrip; and his sling was in his hand:　and he drew near to the Philistine.

And advances to the duel—42. And when the Philistine looked about, and saw David, he disdained him: for he was but a youth, and ruddy, and of a fair countenance. 43. And the Philistine said unto David, Am I a dog, that thou comest to me with staves? And the Philistine cursed David by his gods.　44. And the Philistine said to David, Come to me, and I will give thy flesh unto the fowls of the air, and to the beasts of the field.　45. Then said David to the Philistine, Thou comest to me with a sword, and with a spear, and with a *javelin:*　but I come to thee in the name of the LORD of hosts, the God of the armies. of Israel, whom thou hast defied. 46. This day will the LORD deliver thee into mine hand; and I will smite thee, and take thine head from thee;　and I will give the carcasses of the host of the Philistines this day unto the fowls of the air, and to the wild beasts of the earth; that all the earth may know that there is a God in Israel. 47. And all this assembly shall know that the LORD saveth not with sword and spear: for the battle is the Lord's, and he will give you into our hands.

Fall of the giant, followed by a rout of the Philistines—48. And it came to pass, when the Philistine arose, and came and drew nigh to meet David, that David hasted, and ran toward the army to meet the Philistine.　49. And David put his hand in his bag, and took thence a stone, and slang it, and smote the Philistine in his forehead, that the stone sunk into his forehead; and he fell upon his face to the earth.　51. Therefore David ran, and stood upon the Philistine, and took his sword, and drew it out of the sheath thereof, and slew him, and cut off his head therewith. And when the Philistines saw their champion was dead, they fled. 52. And the men of Israel and of Judah arose, and shouted, and pursued the Philistines, until thou come to *Gath,* and to the gates of Ekron. And the wounded of the Philistines fell down by the way to Shaaraim, even unto Gath, and unto Ekron. 53. And the children of Israel returned from chasing after the Philistines, and they spoiled their tents.

C. (THIRD STORY). THE YOUNG DAVID AND HIS BROTHERS

1 Samuel 17:12-30; 55-58

David is sent on an errand to the camp—17:12. Now David was the son of that Ephrathite of Bethlehem-judah whose name was Jesse; and he had eight sons: and the man went among men for an old man in the days of Saul. And the three eldest sons of Jesse went and followed Saul to the battle: and the names of his three sons that went to the battle were Eliab the firstborn, and next unto him Abinadab, and the third Shammah. 14. And David was the youngest: and the three eldest followed Saul. [16. And the Philistine drew near morning and evening and presented himself forty days.] 17. And Jesse said unto David his son, Take now for thy brethren an ephah of this parched corn, and these ten loaves, and run to the camp to thy brethren; 18. and carry these ten cheeses unto the captain of their thousand, and look how thy brethren fare, and take their pledge.

There he hears Goliath's challenge—19. Now Saul, and they, and all the men of Israel, were in the valley of Elah, fighting with the Philistines. 20. And David rose up early in the morning, and left the sheep with a keeper, and took, and went, as Jesse had commanded him; and he came to the trench, as the host was going forth to the fight and shouted for the battle. 21. For Israel and the Philistines had put the battle in array, army against army. *22.* And David left his carriage in the hand of the keeper of the carriage, and ran into the army, and came and saluted his brethren. 23. And as he talked with them, behold, there came up the champion, the

12. **Ephrathlte** here, as in *Ruth*= a Bethlehemite.

17. **ephah** = 6¼ gallons; or, by another system of measurement, 8½ gallons, *i.e.,* about a bushel.

18. **thousand.** For a sketch of the military organization, see below, p. 138.
pledge. "Bring me some assurance that they are alive and well."

22. carriage. Old word for baggage; burden.

Philistine of Gath, Goliath by name, out of the armies of the Philistines, and spake according to the same words: and David heard them. 24. And all the men of Israel, when they saw the man, fled from him, and were sore afraid.

The soldiers kindle David's ambition to fight the giant—25. And the men of Israel said, Have ye seen this man that is come up? surely to defy Israel is he come up: and it shall be, that the man who killeth him, the king will enrich him with great riches, and will give him his daughter, and make his father's house free in Israel. 26. And David spake to the men that stood by him, saying, What shall be done to the man that killeth this Philistine, and taketh away the reproach from Israel? for who is this uncircumcised Philistine, that he should defy the armies of the living God? 27. And the people answered him after this manner, saying, So shall it be done to the man that killeth him.

An elder brother's ill-natured rebuke—28. And Eliab his eldest brother heard when he spake unto the men; and Eliab's anger was kindled against David, and he said, why earnest thou down hither? and with whom hast thou left those few sheep in the wilderness? I know thy pride, and the naughtiness of thine heart; for thou art come down that thou mightest see the battle. 29. And David said, What have I now done? Is there not a cause? 30. And he turned from him toward another, and spake after the same manner: and the people answered him again after the former manner. *[Here must have fallowed in the original an account of David's fight with the giant.]*

David is presented to Saul—55. And when Saul saw David go forth against the Philistine, he said unto Abner, the captain of the host, Abner, whose son is this youth? And Abner said, As thy soul liveth, O King, I cannot tell. 56. And the king said, Enquire thou whose son the stripling is. 57. And as David returned from the slaughter of the Philistine, Abner took him, and brought him before Saul

23. **same words.** The compiler, having pieced this narrative into the second story, B., in the Heb. text, means to refer to Goliath's challenge (17:8 *seq.*).
25. **free,** *i.e.,* from taxes and forced labor.
29. "Have I not a sufficient cause for coming, namely, my father's command?"

with the h e a d of the Philistine in his hand. 58. And Saul said to him, Whose son art thou, thou young man? And David answered, I am the son of thy servant Jesse the Bethlehemite.

DAVID AT COURT: HIS SUCCESS AND POPULARITY ROUSE SAUL'S JEALOUSY

1 Samuel 18:1—19:17

Jonathan's covenant of blood-brotherhood with David—18:1. And it came to pass, when he had made an end of speaking unto Saul, that the soul of Jonathan was knit with the soul of David, and Jonathan loved him as his own soul. 2. And Saul took him that day and would let him go no more home to his father's house. 3. Then Jonathan and David made a covenant, because he loved him as his Own soul. 4. And Jonathan stripped himself of the robe that was upon him, and gave it to David, and his garments, even to his sword, and to his bow, and to his girdle.

David's promotion—5. And David went out whithersoever Saul sent him and behaved himself wisely: and Saul set him over the men of war, and he was accepted in the sight of all the people, and also in the sight of Saul's servants.

Saul grows envious of him—6. And it came to pass as they came, when David was returned from the slaughter of the Philistine, that the women came out of all cities of Israel, singing and dancing, to meet king Saul, with tabrets, with joy, and with instruments of musick. 7. And the women answered one another as they played, and said,

> Saul hath slain his thousands,
> And David his ten thousands.

18:3. For the ritual and significance of this covenant see *Rel. Sem.*, 1st ed., pp. 296-9, 317; revised. ed. p. 335. By it the two parties are regarded as being made, physically, brothers of each other. The blood is the life; and in the ritual, drops either of their own blood, or later that of a victim in its stead, were shed and tasted jointly. Hereby the two lives were made one.

4. **garments,** *i.e.,* armor. *Cf.* Glaucus and Diomede, *Iliad* 6:230 *seq.*

6. The correct sequence of events is by no means preserved in the texts and is impossible to restore. In the women's chorus the reference to ten thousands would be more appropriate to some other and later achievement in David's career.

8. And Saul was very wroth, and the saying displeased him; and he said, They have ascribed unto David ten thousands, and to me they have ascribed but thousands: and what can he have more but the kingdom?   9. And Saul eyed David from that day and forward.

Saul removes David from personal attendance on him—12. And Saul was afraid of David, because the LORD was with him, and was departed from Saul. 13. Therefore Saul removed him from him and made him his captain over a thousand; and he went out and came in before the people. 14 And David behaved himself wisely in all his ways; and the LORD was with him. 15. Wherefore when Saul saw that he behaved himself very wisely, he was afraid of him. 16. But all Israel and Judah loved David, because he went out and came in before them.

An insincere offer of marriage—17. And Saul said to David, Behold my elder daughter Merab, her will I give thee *to w*ife: only be thou valiant for me, and fight the LORD'S battles. For Saul said, Let not mine hand be upon him, but let the hand of the Philistines be upon him. 18. And David said unto Saul, who am I? and what is my life, or my father's family in Israel, that I should be son in law to the king? 19. But it came to pass at the time when Merab Saul's daughter should have been given to David, that she was given unto Adriel the Meholathite to wife.

David's marriage with Saul's younger daughter—20. And Michal Saul's daughter loved David: and they told Saul, and the thing pleased him. 21. And Saul said, I will give him her, that she may be a snare to him, and that the hand of the Philistines may be against him. 22. And Saul commanded his servants saying, Commune with David secretly, and say, Behold, the king hath delight in thee and all his servants love thee: now therefore be the king's son in law. *23.* And Saul's servants spake those words in the ears of David. And David said, Seemeth it to you a light thing to be a king's son in law, seeing that I am a poor

13. **went . . . in,** *i.e.,* in fulfilling his military duties he was much in the public eye.

17. The king secretly hoped that David would fall in battle. David himself imitated this policy in dealing subsequently with Uriah (2 Sam. 11:15).

man, and lightly esteemed?   24. And the servants of Saul told him, saying, On this manner spake David.   25. And Saul said, Thus shall ye say to David, the king desireth not any dowry, but an hundred trophies of the Philistines to be avenged of the king's enemies. But Saul thought to make David fall by the band of the Philistines. 26. And when his servants told David these words, it pleased David well to be the king's son in law. And the days were not expired, 27. when David arose and went, he and his men, and slew of the Philistines two hundred men; and David brought the trophies, and gave them in full tale to the king, that he might be the king's son in law. And Saul gave him Michal his daughter to wife.   28. And Saul saw and knew that the LORD was with David, and that all Israel loved him. 29. And Saul was yet the more afraid of David.

In his mania he attempts David's life—10. And it came to pass on the morrow, that the evil spirit from God came upon Saul, and he prophesied in the midst of the house: and David played with his hand, as at other times: and there was a javelin in Saul's hand. 11. And Saul cast the javelin; for he said, I will smite David even to the wall with it. And David avoided out of his presence twice.

Jonathan befriends his "brother"—19:1. And Saul spake to Jonathan his son, and to all his servants that they should kill David. 2. But Jonathan Saul's son delighted much in David: and Jonathan told David, saying, Saul my father seeketh to kill thee: now therefore, I pray thee, take heed to thyself until the morning, and abide in a secret place, and hide thyself: 3. And I will go out and stand beside my father in the field where thou art, and I will commune with my father of thee; and what I see, that I will tell thee.

His intercession causes a temporary reconciliation—4. And Jonathan spake good of David unto Saul his father, and said unto him, Let not the king sin against his servant,

25. **dowry,** *i.e.,* according to the universal custom of antiquity the price paid by the bridegroom or his people to the bride's parents; Gk. *eeova,* not *pherne* which = dowry in our sense of the word.

26 *b.* Saul apparently had set a limit within which the exploit was to be performed.

10. **prophesied**. Rather, "raved" in melancholic passion.

III-5

against David; because he hath not sinned against thee, and because his works have been to thee-ward very good: 5. for he did put his life in his hand, and slew the Philistine, and the LORD wrought a great salvation for all Israel: thou sawest it, and didst rejoice: wherefore then wilt thou sin against innocent blood, to slay David without a cause? 6. And Saul hearkened unto the voice of Jonathan: and Saul swore, As the LORD liveth, he shall not be slain. 7. And Jonathan called David, and Jonathan showed him all those things. And Jonathan brought David to Saul, and he was in his presence, as in times past.

A recurrence of Saul's mania—8. And there was war again: and David went out, and fought with the Philistines, and slew them with a great slaughter; and they fled from him. 9. And the evil spirit from the LORD was upon Saul, as he sat in the house with his javelin in his hand: and David played with his hand. 10. And Saul sought to smite David even to the wall with the javelin; but he slipped away out of Saul's presence, and he smote the javelin into the wall: and David fled and escaped that night.

Michal saves David by a stratagem—11. Saul also sent messengers unto David's house, to watch him, and to slay him in the morning: and Michal David's wife told him, saying, If thou save not thy life to night, tom orrow thou shalt be slain. 12. So Michal let David down through a window: and he went, and fled, and escaped. 13. And Michal took an image, and laid it in the bed, and put a pillow of goats' hair for his bolster and covered it with a cloth. 14. And when Saul sent messengers to take David, she said, He is sick. 15. And Saul sent the messengers again *to* see David, saying, Bring him up to me in the bed, that I may slay him. 16. And when the messengers were come in, behold, there was an image in the bed, with a pillow of goats' hair for his bolster. 17. And Saul said unto Michal, Why hast thou deceived me so, and sent away mine enemy, that he is escaped? And Michal answered Saul, He said unto me, Let me go: why should I kill thee?

13. **image.** Heb. *teraphim,* the primitive sacred image with a head obviously of human shape.
17. **why should I? . . .** is a threat: " I'll kill you if you do not." Michal pretends that her husband had thus threatened her.

JONATHAN MAKES A LAST ATTEMPT TO RECONCILE HIS HALF-INSANE FATHER TO DAVID

1 Samuel 20

David appeals to Jonathan—1. And David came and said before Jonathan, What have I done? what is mine iniquity? and what is my sin before thy father, that he seeketh my life? 2. And he said unto him, God forbid; thou shalt not die: behold, n1y father will do nothing either great or small, but that he will show it me: and why should my father hide this thing from me? it is not so. 3. And David sware moreover, and said, Thy father certainly knoweth that I have found grace in thine eyes: and he saith, Let not Jonathan know this, lest he be grieved; but truly as the LORD liveth, and as thy soul liveth, there is but a step between me and death. 4. Then said Jonathan unto David, Whatsoever thy soul desireth, I will even do it for thee.

And suggests a plan for discovering Saul's feelings towards him—5. And David said unto Jonathan, Behold, tomorrow is the new moon, and I should not fail to sit with the king at meat: but let me go, that I may hide myself in the field unto the third day at even. 6. If thy father at all miss me, then say, David earnestly asked leave of me that he might run to Bethlehem his city: for there is a yearly sacrifice there for all the family. 7. If he says thus, It is well; thy servant shall have peace: but if he be very wroth, then be sure that evil is determined by him. 8. Therefore thou shalt deal kindly with thy servant; for thou hast brought thy servant into a covenant of the LORD with thee: notwithstanding, if there be in me iniquity, slay me thyself: for why shouldest thou bring me *to* thy

1. Before finally fleeing from the court, after this last attempt on his life, David determines to ascertain through his friend whether reconciliation is still possible.

2. Jonathan's apparent ignorance of his father's designs is not quite in harmony with the scene recorded in chap. xix. 1-7 above.

5. **the new moon,** like the Sabbath, was observed as a day of rest and family reunion.

8. **covenant of Jehovah.** The blood-brotherhood, witnessed and sanctified by Jehovah (18:3).

father? 9. And Jonathan said, Far be it from thee: for if I knew certainly that evil were determined by my father to come upon thee, then would not I tell it thee? 10. Then said David to Jonathan, Who shall tell me if thy father answer thee roughly?

Jonathan's promise—11. And Jonathan said unto David, Come, and let us go out into the field. And they went out both of them into the field. 12. And Jonathan said unto David, O LORD God of Israel, when I have sounded my father about tomorrow any time, or the third day, and, behold, if there be good toward David, and I then send not unto thee, and shew it thee; 13. the LORD do so and much more to Jonathan: but if it please my father to do thee evil, then I will shew it thee, and send thee away that thou mayest go in peace: and the LORD be with thee, as he hath been with my father.

He implores David's compassion in the future—14. And thou shalt not only while yet I live shew m the kindness of the LORD: 15. but if I should die thou shalt not cut off thy kindness from my house for ever: no, not when the LORD hath cut off the enemies of David everyone from the face of the earth. 16. So Jonathan made a covenant with the house of David, saying, Let the LORD even require it at the hand of David. 17. And Jonathan swore yet again to David because he loved him: for he loved him as he loved his own soul.

Their scheme for communication—18. Then Jonathan said to David, Tomorrow is the new moon: and thou shalt be missed, because thy seat will be empty. 19. And when thou hast stayed three days, then thou shalt go down quickly, and come to the place where thou didst hide thyself when the business was in hand, and shalt remain by

10. The question implies that if Saul was still incensed with David it would not be safe for him and Jonathan to converse openly; so in verse 18 Jonathan invents a method of communication. The intervening verses temporarily break the sequence of the narrative.

14. Jonathan foresees the downfall of his own house and the future ascendancy of David's house.

17. Jonathan repeats to David the assurance he gave in verse 13.

19. What business is meant is unknown; text corrupt. Possibly the allusion is to 19:2, David's previous recourse to a hiding place.

the stone Ezel. 20. And I will shoot three arrows on the side thereof, as though I shot at a mark. 21. And, behold, I will send a lad, saying, Go, find out the arrows. If I expressly say unto the lad, Behold, the arrows are on this side of thee, take them: then come thou: for there is peace to thee, and no hurt; as the LORD liveth. 22. But if I say thus unto the young man, Behold, the arrows are beyond thee; go thy way: for the LORD hath sent thee away. 23. And as touching the matter which thou and I have spoken of, behold, the LORD be between thee and me forever.

Saul, observing David's absence—24. So David hid himself in the field, and when the new moon was come, the king sat him down to eat meat. 25. And the king sat upon his seat, as at other times, even upon a seat by the wall: and Jonathan *was in front,* and Abner sat by Saul's side, and David's place was empty. 26. Nevertheless Saul spake not anything that day: for he thought, Something hath befallen him, he is not clean: surely he is not clean. 27. And it came to pass on the morrow, which was the second day of the month, that David's place was empty: and Saul said unto Jonathan his son, Wherefore cometh not the son of Jesse to meat, neither yesterday, nor to day? 28. And Jonathan answered Saul, David earnestly asked leave of me to go to Bethlehem: 29. and he said, Let me go, I pray thee; for our family hath a sacrifice in the city; and my brother, he hath commanded me to be there: and now, if I have found favor in thine eyes, let me get away, I pray thee, and see my brethren. Therefore, he cometh not unto the king's table.

Is beside himself with passion—30. Then Saul's anger was kindled against Jonathan, and he said unto him, Thou son of the perverse rebellious woman, do not I know that thou hast chosen the son of Jesse to thine

19. **by the stone Ezel.** Read as LXX: "by yonder mound" (see verse 41).

25. **Abner,** Saul's cousin, was commander of the army.

26. **not clean,** *i.e.,* he is prevented from coming to the fast by some ceremonial defilement. See Leviticus and Deut. *passim.*

30. **son of, etc**——"Son of a rebellious slave-girl!" To insult a man by reviling his parents or ancestors is a familiar Eastern habit——in modern days, too.

own confusion? 31. For as long as the son of Jesse liveth upon the ground, thou shalt not be established, nor thy kingdom. Wherefore now send and fetch him unto me, for he shall surely die. 32. And Jonathan answered Saul his father, and said unto him, Wherefore shall he be slain? what hath he done? 33. And Saul cast a javelin at him to smite him: whereby Jonathan knew that" it was determined of his father to slay David. 34. So Jonathan arose from the table in fierce anger, and did eat no meat the second day of the month: for he was grieved for David, because his father had done him shame.

The news communicated to David—35. And it came to pass in the morning, that Jonathan went out into the field at the time appointed with David, and a little lad with him. 36. And he said unto his lad, Run, find out now the arrows which I shoot. And as the lad ran, he shot an arrow beyond him. 37. And when the lad was come to the place of the arrow which Jonathan had shot, Jonathan cried after the lad, and said, Is not the arrow beyond thee? 38. And Jonathan cried after the lad, Make speed, haste, stay not. And Jonathan's lad gathered up the arrows and came to his master. 39. But the lad knew not anything: only Jonathan and David knew the matter. 41. And David arose *from beside the mound* and departed; and Jonathan went into the city.

DAVID AS AN OUTLAW: HIS WANDERINGS

1. To RAMAH

1 Samuel 19:18-24

18. So David fled, and escaped and came to Samuel to Ramah, and told him all that Saul had done to him.

41. The original here gives three verses which "stultify the whole preceding account": they make the friends take an affecting farewell. This, as we have seen, was impossible. The sole reason for the elaborate scheme with the arrows was that in the present state of Saul's temper it was dangerous for Jonathan to be seen, or risk being seen, with David. (See Smith, *ad loc.*).

18. On his virtual exile from court David led the life of a rover. It is not possible to follow the successive incidents of his career with exactness. Most probably he fled first southwards to his

And he and Samuel went and dwelt in *the cloister in Ramah*. 19. And it was told Saul; saying, Behold, David is at *the cloister* in Ramah. 20. And Saul sent messengers to take David: and when they saw the company of the prophets prophesying, and Samuel standing as appointed over them, the Spirit of God was upon the messengers of Saul, and they also prophesied. 21. And when it was told Saul, he sent other messengers, and they prophesied likewise. And Saul sent messengers again the third time, and they prophesied also. 22. Then went he also to Ramah, and came to the well of the threshing-fioor which is on the height: and he asked and said, Where are Samuel and David? And one said, Behold, they be at the cloister in Ramah. 23. And he went *thence* to *the cloister* in Ramah: and the Spirit of God was upon him also, and he went on, and prophesied, until he came to *the cloister* in Ramah. 24. And he stripped off his clothes also, and prophesied before Samuel in like manner, and lay down naked all that day and all that night. Wherefore they say, Is Saul also among the prophets?

2. TO NOB: TRAGIC SEQUEL TO HIS VISIT

1 Samuel 21:1-9, 2 2 : 6-23

David demands the shewbread from the priest—21:1. Then came David to Nob to Ahimelech the priest, and Ahimelech was afraid at the meeting of David, and said unto him, Why art thou alone, and no man with thee? 2. And David said unto Ahimelech the priest, The king

own people, where, in fact, we shall find him shortly. Meanwhile a late and untrustworthy section of the text brings him at the outset of his wanderings to Ramah.

cloister.   The rendering accepted by many scholars of the Heb. *Naioth.* It is presumed to be the common dwelling-place of the prophetic company here introduced.

24.   In 10:12 we have already read the more authentic account of the origin of this proverb.

21:1. **Ahimelech,** or Ahijah, Eli's great-grandson.

Nob, 2½ miles north of Jerusalem, had been the religious "capital" of the country since the battle of Aphek (p. 18). It lay on David's route from Ramah and Gibeah down south to his own clan. The priest was startled at the arrival of the king's son-in-law thus unattended, unarmed, and unprovided with food.

hath commanded me a business, and hath said unto me, Let no man know anything of the business whereabout I send thee, and what I have commanded thee: and I have appointed my servants to such and such a place. 3. Now therefore what is under thine hand? give me five loaves of bread in mine hand, or what there is present. 4. And the priest answered David, and said, There is no common bread under mine hand, but there is hallowed bread; 6. so the priest gave him hallowed bread: for there was no bread there but the shewbread, that was taken from before the LORD, to put hot bread in the day when it was taken away. 7. Now a certain man of the servants of Saul was there that day, detained before the LORD; and his name was Doeg, an Edomite, the chiefest of the herdmen that belonged to Saul.

And obtains a famous sword—8. And David said unto Ahimelech, And is there not here under thine hand spear or sword? for I have neither brought my sword nor my weapons with me, because the king's business required haste. 9. And the priest said, The sword of Goliath the Philistine, whom thou slewest in the valley of Elah, behold, it is here wrapped in a cloth behind the ephod: if thou wilt take that, take it: for there is no other save that here. And David said, There is none like that; give it me.

To Saul, venting his spleen on his courtiers—22: 6. Now Saul abode in Gibeah under a tree on the height, having his spear in his hand, and all his servants were standing about him. 7. And Saul said unto his servants that stood about him, Hear now, ye Benjamites; will the son of Jesse give every one of you fields and vineyards, and make you all captains of thousands, and captains of hundreds; 8. that all of you have conspired against me,

4. The presence-bread, or shewbread, in later days could only lawfully be eaten by the priests themselves *(cf.* Matt. 12: 4); but in David's day, perhaps, anyone who was ceremonially "clean" might eat it: so the priest had no scruple in giving it *to* David.

6. There was no bread there except the stale shewbread which had been removed, on its proper day, from the presence-table to make room for the hot fresh shewbread.

7. **detained,** *i.e.,* kept in the precincts until he was ceremonially "clean" for the performance of some religious duty or other.

9. **ephod.** It is not clear here whether the sacred image or the priestly garment is meant; probably the former. See p. 11.

and there is none that sheweth me that my son hath made a league with the son of Jesse, and there is none of you that is sorry for me, or sheweth unto me that my son hath stirred up my servant against me, to lie in wait, as at this day?

Doeg tells a tale—9. Then answered Doeg the Edomite, which was *standing by* the servants of Saul, and said, I saw the son of Jesse coming to Nob, to Ahimelech the son of Ahitub. 10. And he inquired of the LORD for him, and gave him victuals, and gave him the sword of Goliath the Philistine.

Ahimelech is haled to Gibeah—11. Then the king sent to call Ahimelech the priest, the son of Ahitub, and all his father's house, the priests that were in Nob; and they came all of them to the king. 12. And Saul said, Hear now, thou son of Ahitub. And he answered, Here I am, my Lord. 13. And Saul said unto him, Why have ye conspired against me, thou and the son of Jesse, in that thou hast given him bread, and a sword, and hast enquired of God for him, that he should rise against me, to lie in wait, as at this day? 14. Then Ahimelech answered the king, and said, And who is so faithful among all thy servants as David, which is, the king's son in law, and goeth at thy bidding, and is honorable in thine house? 15. Did I then begin to enquire of God for him? be it far from me: let not the king impute anything unto his servant, nor to all the house of my father: for thy servant knew nothing of all this, less or more. 16. And the king said, Thou shalt surely die, Ahimelech, thou, and all thy father's house.

And butchered, with all the priests—17. And the king said unto the footmen that stood about him, Turn, and slay the priests of the LORD; because their hand also is with David, and because they knew when he fled, and did not shew it to me. But the servants of the king would not put forth their hand to fall upon the priests of the LORD. 18. And the king said to Doeg, Turn thou, and fall upon the priests. And Doeg the Edomite turned, and he fell

15. "Is this the *first* time I have enquired of God on his behalf? No, I have often done so unreproved: so this is no proof of disloyalty to you."

upon the priests, and slew on that day fourscore and five persons that did wear a linen ephod. 1 9 . And Nob, the city of the priests, smote he with the edge of the sword, both men and women, children and sucklings, and oxen, and asses, and sheep, with the edge of the sword.

Except Abiathar—20. And one of the sons of Ahimelech the son of Ahitub, named Abiathar, escaped, and fled after David. 21. And Abiathar shewed David that Saul, had slain the LORD'S priests. 22. And David said unto Abiathar, I knew it that day, when Doeg the Edomite was there, that he would surely tell Saul: I have occasioned the death of all the persons of thy father's house. 23. Abide thou with me, fear not: for he that seeketh my life seeketh thy life: for with me thou shalt be in safeguard.

3. TO THE CAVE OF ADULLAM, WHERE HE BECOMES CAPTAIN OF AN OUTLAW BAND

1 Samuel 22:1-5

1. David therefore departed thence and escaped to the cave Adullam: and when his brethren and all his father's house heard it, they went down thither to him. 2. And every one that was in distress, and every one that was in debt, and every one that was discontented, gathered themselves unto him; and he became a captain over them: and there were with him about four hundred men.
He sends his parents, for safety, to Moab—3. And David went thence *to* Mizpeh of Moab: and he said unto the king of Moab, Let my father and my mother, I pray thee, come forth, and be with you, till I know what God will

20. David meanwhile had fled further south to Adullam.
23. Rather: "he that seeketh *thy* life seeketh *my* life also."
22:1. **thence**, *i.e.,* from Nob (21:9).
cave. Rather, "stronghold" – "the hold." From this incident "Adullamites," as a term for a small body of malcontents, has become proverbial. The position, twelve miles south-west of Bethlehem, is admirably described in *H.G.H.L.,* p. 229.
3. David's great-grandmother, Ruth, was a Moabitess: hence the present appeal.

do for me. 4. And he brought them before the king of Moab: and they dwelt with him all the while that David was in the hold. 5. And the prophet Gad said unto David, Abide not in *Mizpeh*; depart, and get thee into the land of Judah. Then David departed, and came into the forest of Hareth.

4. To KEILAH

1 Samuel 23:1-13

1. Then they told David, saying, Behold, the Philistines fight against Keilah, and they rob the threshing-floors. 2. Therefore David enquired of the LORD, saying, Shall I go and smite these Philistines? And the LORD said unto David, Go, and smite the Philistines, and save Keilah. (6. For it came to pass, when Abiathar the son of Ahimelech fled to David to Adullam, that he came down with an ephod in his hand.) 3. And David's men said unto him, Behold, we be afraid here in Judah: how much more then if we come to Keilah against the armies of the Philistines? 4. Then David enquired of the LORD yet again. And the LORD answered him and said, Arise, go down to Keilah; for I will deliver the Philistines into thine hand. 5. So David and his men went to Keilah, and fought with the Philistines, and brought away their cattle, and smote them with a great slaughter. So David saved the inhabitants of Keilah.

Saul proposes to entrap him there—7. And it was told, Saul that David was come to Keilah. And Saul said, God hath delivered him into mine hand; for he is shut in, by entering into a town that hath gates and bars. 8. And

5. Gad (see p. xx, and 2 Sam. 24:11, below).

David returns from his short visit to Moab to his headquarters at Adullam, the district surrounding which was (apparently) known as the Forest of Hareth.

23:1. From Adullam David with his four hundred free-lances, who soon grew to six hundred, marched to rescue a frontier town from the Philistines. Keilah is three miles south of Adullam.

2. **enquired**. How? obviously by the employment of the oracular ephod, the traditional method. Verse 6 (originally a marginal note by a scribe) has been misplaced, and the words "to Keilah" wrongly added to it instead of "to Adullam."

Saul called all the people together to war, to go down to Keilah, to besiege David and his men. 9. And David knew that Saul secretly practiced mischief against him; and he said to Abiathar the priest, Bring hither the ephod. 10. Then said David, O LORD God of Israel, thy servant hath certainly heard that Saul seeketh to come to Keilah, to destroy the city for my sake. 11. Will the men of Keilah deliver me up into his hand? will Saul come down, as thy servant hath heard? O LORD God of Israel, I beseech thee, tell thy servant. And the LORD said, He will come down. 12. Then said David, Will the men of Keilah deliver me and my men into the hand of Saul? And the LORD said, They will deliver thee up.

But the sacred oracle had warned David in time—13. Then David and his men, which were about six hundred, arose and departed out of Keilah, and went whithersoever they could go. And it was told Saul that David was escaped from Keilah; and he forbare to go forth.

TO THE WILDERNESS OF JUDAH

(a) Ziph

1 Samuel 2 3 : 1 4-28

14. And David abode in the wilderness in strongholds and remained in a mountain in the wilderness of Ziph. And Saul sought him every day, but God delivered him not into his hand. 15. And David saw that Saul was come out to seek his life: and David was in the wilderness of Ziph in a wood.

Renewal of the blood-brotherhood between Jonathan and David—16. And Jonathan Saul's son arose, and went to David into the wood, and strengthened his hand in God. 17. And he said unto him, Fear not: for the hand of Saul

14. **Wilderness of Ziph.** Four miles south-east of Hebron, stretching towards the Dead Sea. A vivid picture of the district is given in *H.G.H.L.,* p. 306. It is too long to quote, but the reader is earnestly advised to consult this invaluable work. History cannot be understood without visualizing the stage on which it is enacted.

15. **a wood.** Probably we should read a proper name here— "in Horesha."

my father shall not find thee; and thou shalt be king over Israel, and I shall be next unto thee; and that also Saul my father knoweth. 18. And they two made a covenant before the LORD: and David abode in the wood and Jonathan went to his house.

David's narrow escape—19. Then came up the Ziphites to Saul to Gibeah, saying, Doth not David hide himself with us in strong holds in the wood, in the hill of Hachilah, which is on the south of Jeshimon? 20. Now therefore, O king, come down according to all the desire of thy soul to come down; and our part shall be to deliver him into the king's hand. 22. And Saul said, Blessed be ye of the LORD; for ye have compassion on me. 22. Go, I pray you, prepare yet, and know and see his place where his haunt is, and who hath seen him there: for it is told me that he dealeth very subtly. 23. See therefore and take knowledge of all the lurking places where he hideth himself, and come ye again to me with the certainty, and I will go with you: and it shall come to pass, if he be in the land, that I will search him out throughout all the thousands of Judah. 24. And they arose and went to Ziph before Saul: but David and his men were in the wilderness of Maon, in the plain on the south of Jeshimon. 25. Saul also and his men went to seek him. And they told David: wherefore he came down into a rock *which is* in the wilderness of Maon. And when Saul heard that, he pursued after David in the wilderness of Maon. 26. And Saul went on this side of the mountain, and David and his men on that side of the mountain: and David made haste to get away for fear of Saul; for Saul and his men compassed David and his men round about to take them.

A   providential   Philistine   demonstration   recalls   Saul—

19. **Hachilah**. Between Ziph village and the Dead Sea. **Jeshimon** (= "the waste") is the high desert running north and south between the shore of the Dead Sea and the highlands of Judah, a howling waste thirty-five miles by fifteen, of "a haggard and crumbling appearance" (H.G.H.L., p. 312 seq.).

24. David had fled some five miles south on the approach of Saul's scouts (see: Murray's Map).

plain. Heb. the Arabah—the great rift running north and south right from the source of Jordan to the desert near the Gulf of Akaba.

But there came a messenger unto Saul, saying, haste thee, and come; for the Philistines have invaded the land. 28. Wherefore Saul returned from pursuing after David, and went against the Philistines: therefore they called that place Sela-hammahlekoth.

(b) En-gedi

1 Samuel 23:29—24

Saul returns relentless to the hunt—23:29. And David went up from thence and dwelt in strong holds at En-gedi. 24:1. And it came to pass, when Saul was returned from following the Philistines, that it was told him, saying, Behold, David is in the wilderness of En-gedi. 2. Then Saul took three thousand chosen men out of Israel and went to seek David and his men upon the rocks of the wild goats.

David's magnanimity: first occasion—3. And he came to the sheepcotes by the way, where was a cave; and Saul went in and David and his men remained in the sides of the cave. 4 *a.* And the men of David said unto him, Behold the day of which the LORD said unto thee, Behold, I will deliver thine enemy into thine hand, that thou mayest do to him as it shall seem good unto thee. 6. And he said unto his men, The LORD forbid that I should do this thing unto my master, the LORD's anointed, to stretch forth mine hand against him, seeing he is the anointed of the LORD. *7 a.* So David stayed his servants with these: words, and suffered them not to rise against Saul. 4 *b.* Then David arose and cut off the skirt of Saul's robe privily. *7 b.* But Saul rose up out of the cave and went on his way. 5. And it came to pass afterward, that David's heart smote him, because he had cut off Saul's skirt 8 . David also arose afterward, and went out of

28. Sela-hammahlekoth = "Rock of Divisions."

29. En-gedi = "the well of the wild goat." A lovely, green, well watered oasis near the shore of the Dead Sea, due east from **Ziph** *(H.G.H.L.,* p. 269 *seq.).* Saul's cave was "by the way," some three miles north of En-gedi.

24:4 *a.* The occasion when this divine oracle was given is not recorded.

5. David had Saul's life at his mercy; but his conscience was stricken even by this mild indignity he had put upon Jehovah's anointed.

the cave, and cried after Saul, saying, My Lord the king. And when Saul looked behind him, David stooped with his face to the earth, and bowed himself.

He pleads with the king—9. And David said to Saul, Wherefore hearest thou men's words, saying, Behold, David seeketh thy hurt? 10. Behold, this day thine eyes have seen how that the LORD had delivered thee to day into mine hand in the cave: and some bade me kill thee: but mine eye spared thee; and I said, I will not put forth mine hand against my Lord; for he is the LORD'S anointed. 11. Moreover, my father, see, yea, see the skirt of thy robe in my hand: for in that I cut off the skirt of thy robe, and killed thee not, know thou and see that there is neither evil nor transgression in mine hand, and I have not sinned against thee; yet thou huntest my soul to take it. 12. The LORD judge between me and thee, and the LORD avenge me of thee. But mine hand shall not be upon thee. 13. As saith the proverb of the ancients, Wickedness proceedeth from the wicked: but mine hand shall not be upon thee. 14. After whom is the king of Israel come out? after whom dost thou pursue? after a dead dog, after a flea. 15. The LORD therefore be judge, and judge between me and thee, and see, and plead my cause, and deliver me out of thine hand.

The king's heart is touched—16. And it came to pass when David had made an end of speaking these words unto Saul, that Saul said, Is this thy voice, my son David? And Saul lifted up his voice, and wept. 17. And he said to David, Thou art more righteous than I: for thou hast rewarded me good, whereas I have rewarded thee evil. 18. And thou hast shewed this day how that thou hast dealt well with me: forasmuch as when the LORD had delivered me into thine hand, thou killedst me not. 19. For if a man find his enemy, will he let him go well away? wherefore the LORD reward thee good for that thou hast done unto me this day.

David's oath to Saul—20. And now, behold, I know

12.   "I leave my cause in the hands of God; I will not touch thee."

13. "I am not a wicked man, and therefore I shall do no evil to you." But some think that the proverb means, " Your own wickedness will recoil on your own head."

well that thou shalt surely be king, and that the kingdom of Israel shall be established in thine hand. 2 1 . Swear now therefore unto me by the LORD, that thou wilt not cut off my seed after me, and that thou wilt not destroy my name out of my father's house. *22.* And David sware unto Saul. And Saul went home: but David and his men gat them up unto the hold.

(c) *Ziph again. David's Magnanimity: second occasion*

1 Samuel 26

1. And the Ziphites came unto Saul to Gibeah, saying, Doth not David hide himself in the hill of Hachilah, which is before Jeshimon? 2. Then Saul arose, and went down to the wilderness of Ziph, having three thousand chosen men of Israel with him, to seek David in the wilderness of Ziph. 3. And Saul pitched in the hill of Hachilah, which is before Jeshimon, by the way. But David abode in the wilderness, and he saw that Saul came after him into the wilderness. 4. David therefore sent out spies and understood that Saul was come in very deed.

David's bold adventure by night—5. And David arose and came to the place where Saul had pitched: and David beheld the place where Saul lay, and Abner the son of *Ner,* the captain of his host: and Saul lay in the trench, and the people pitched round about him, 6. Then answered David and said to Ahimelech the Hittite, and to Abishai the son

22. **hold,** *i.e.,* his fort at En-gedi.

26:1. This chapter is probably a duplicate from an earlier and more authentic source *(Sl)* of the events recorded in the two preceding paragraphs.

5. **trench,** as in 27:20 = either entrenchment or, simply, camp.

6. **Ahimelech** was a soldier of fortune serving now with David. The Hittites were a mighty nation whose principal cities were Carchemish on the Euphrates, Kadesh on the Orantes, and Pteria near the Halys, in Asia Minor. Mongolian, probably, by race, they have left monuments of their power, which lasted from 1600 to 500 *B.C.,* allover western Asia as far as Smyrna. Sections of this people established themselves in Palestine even before the age of the patriarchs. See further, vol. ii. p. 1 0 4.

Abishai, with his brother Joab and Asahel, the sons of David's sister Zeruiah, plays a conspicuous part in the subsequent narrative. (See Index, s.v.).

of Zeruiah, brother to Joab, saying, Who will go down with me to Saul to the camp? And Abishai said, I will go down with thee. 7. So David and Abishai came to the people by night: and, pehold, Saul lay sleeping within the trench, and his spear stuck in the ground at his bolster: but Abner and the people lay round about him. 8. Then said Abishai to David, God hath delivered thine enemy into thine hand this day: now therefore let me smite him, I pray thee, with the spear even to the earth at once, and I will not smite him the second time.

He spares Saul's life (for the second time?)—9. And David said to Abishai, Destroy him not: for who can stretch forth his hand against the LORD'S anointed, and be guiltless? 10. David said furthermore, As the LORD liveth, the LORD shall smite him; or his day shall come to die; or he shall descend into battle and perish. 11. The LORD forbid that I should stretch forth mine hand against the LORD'S anointed: but I pray thee, take thou now the spear that is at his bolster, and the cruse of water, and let us go. 12. So David took the spear and the cruse of water from Saul's bolster; and they gat them away, and no man saw it, nor knew it, neither awaked: for they were all asleep; because a deep sleep from the LORD was fallen upon them.

He chides Abner for his criminal negligence— 13. Then David went over to the other side and stood on the top of a hill afar off; a great space being between them: 14. and David cried to the people, and to Abner the son of Ner, saying, Answerest thou not, Abner? Then Abner answered and said, who art thou that criest to the king? 15. And David said to Abner, Art not thou a valiant man? and who is like to thee in Israel? wherefore then hast thou not kept thy Lord the king? for there came one of the people in to destroy the king thy Lord. 16. This thing is not good that thou hast done. As the LORD liveth, ye are worthy to die, because ye have not kept your master, the LORD'S anointed. And now see where the king's spear is, and the cruse of water that was at his bolster.

And pleads with Saul—17. And Saul knew David's voice, and said, Is this thy voice, my son David? And David said, It is my

---

7. The lance standing upright marks the chief's quarters, as with the Bedouin Arabs today.

III—6

voice, my Lord, O king. 18. And he said, wherefore doth my Lord thus pursue after his servant? for what have I done? or what evil is in mine hand? 19. Now therefore, I pray thee, let my Lord the king hear the words of his servant. If the LORD have stirred thee up against me, let him accept an offering: but if they be the children of men, cursed be they before the LORD; for they have driven me out this day from abiding in the inheritance of the LORD, saying, Go, serve other gods. 20. Now therefore, let not my blood fall to the earth *away from the presence* of the LORD: for the king of Israel is come out to seek a flea, as when one doth hunt a partridge in the mountains.

Saul blesses him—21. Then said Saul, I have sinned: return, my son David: for I will no more do thee harm, because my soul was precious in thine eyes this day: behold, I have played the fool, and have erred exceedingly. 22. And David answered and said, Behold the king's spear! and let one of the young men come over and fetch it. 23. The LORD render to every man his righteousness and his faithfulness: for the LORD delivered thee into my hand

19. David asks what is the cause of Saul's persistent enmity. (1) Is he impelled by Jehovah? If so, let Jehovah be appeased by "inhaling the smell of a sacrifice—an old anthropomorphic[1] religious idea: cf. Gen. 8: 21, "Jehovah smelled a sweet savor," and Homer, Iliad, *passim.* (2) Is he misled by some human slanderers of David? If so, may God's curse light on them and slay them.

Go, serve other gods gives expression to the idea, still prevalent at that time, that Jehovah was the local God of the Hebrews. He could only be served in His own territory. An exile must worship the heathen gods of the land of his banishment. This notion, too, was dispelled by the inspired teaching of the prophets. Compare the religious conceptions of this date, 1020 B.C., with those of (a) the patriarchs, (b) Israel after the Captivity, 5th cent. B.C.: and what is meant by God's *progressive* revelation of Himself becomes clear.

20. **Away . . . presence,** *i.e.* in a land outside Jehovah's territory.
The idea of dying in some heathen god's land was abhorrent to the pious Hebrew of that day.

21. **soul,** *i.e.,* life, as often.

23. "May God reward my righteousness, and save me, as I have saved thee.

[1]Anthropomorphic (Gk.), "in human form," *i.e.,* God, though a spiritual Being, is spoken of and thought of in language really applicable only to a man. It was not till after the teaching of the greater prophets that the conception of God as a universal Spirit became a real part of the religious ideas of the Hebrews. Even now it is hard, almost impossible, for us to conceive of God as a Spirit. We cannot help picturing Him with human attributes, *i.e.,* anthropomorphically.

today, but I would not stretch forth mine hand. against the LORD'S anointed. 24. And, behold, as thy life was much set by this day in mine eyes, so let my life be much set by in the eyes of the LORD, and let him deliver me out of all tribulation. 25. Then Saul said to David, Blessed be thou, my son David: thou shalt both do great things, and also shalt still prevail. So, David went on his way, and Saul returned to his place.

(d) Carmel: David's Marriage with Abigail

1 Samuel 25

1b. And David arose and went down to the wilderness of Maon. 2. And there was a man in Maon, whose possessions were in Carmel; and the man was very great, and he had three thousand sheep, and a thousand goats: and he was shearing his sheep in Carmel. 3. Now the name of the man was Nabal; and the name of his wife Abigail: and she was a woman of good understanding, and of a beautiful countenance: but the man was churlish and evil in his doings; and he was of the house of Caleb.

The outlaw chief demands gifts of food from Nabal—4. And David heard in the wilderness that Nabal did shear his sheep. 5. And David sent out ten young men, and David said unto the young men, Get you up to Carmel, and go to Nabal, and greet him in my name: 6. and thus shall ye say to him that liveth in prosperity, Peace be both to thee, and peace be to thine house, and peace be unto all that thou hast. 7. And now I have heard that thou hast shearers: now thy shepherds which were with us, we hurt them not, neither was there ought missing

1. **Maon**. Four miles south of Ziph, and one mile south of Carmel (xv. 12). For Maon the Heb. gives Paran, which is impossible.

This chapter, from our oldest source, is "a masterpiece of Hebrew narrative, the work of a literary artist" (Kenn.).

3. The Calebites, the clan of the famous son of Jephunneh, though appearing in history as a branch of the tribe of Judah, were originally an offshoot of the Kenizzites, an Edomite tribe. They were settled by Joshua in and around Hebron, at the north of the Negeb, and ultimately were absorbed in the tribe of Judah (see H. D.B., s.v.).

unto them, all the while they were in Carmel. 8. Ask thy young men, and they will shew thee. Wherefore let the young men find favor in thine eyes: for we come in a good day: give, I pray thee, whatsoever cometh to thine hand unto thy servants, and to thy son David. 9. And when David's young men came, they spake to Nabal according to all those words in the name of David and ceased.

On refusal, he prepares to relieve his necessities by force—10. And Nabal answered David's servants, and said, Who is David? and who is the son of Jesse? there be many servants now a days that break away every man from his master. 11. Shall I then take my bread, and my water, and my flesh that I have killed for my shearers, and give it unto men, whom I know not whence they be? 12. So David's young men turned their way, and went again, and came and told him all those sayings. 13. And David said unto his men, Gird ye on every man his sword. And they girded on every man his sword; and David also girded on his sword: and there went up after David about four hundred men; and two hundred abode by the stuff.

A shepherd lad begs Abigail to intervene—14. But one of the young men told Abigail, Nabal's wife, saying, Behold, David sent messengers out of the wilderness, to salute our master; and he railed on them. 15. But the men were very good unto us, and we were not hurt, neither missed we anything, as long as we were conversant with them, when we were in the fields: 16. they were a wall unto us both by night and day, all the while we were with them keeping the sheep. 17. Now therefore know and consider what thou wilt do; for evil is determined against our master, and against all his household: for he is such a son of Behal, that a man cannot speak to him.

Abigail acts as a conciliatory diplomat—18. Then Abigail made haste, and took two hundred loaves, and two bottles

---

8. A good day, *i.e.,* a time of feasting, which the sheep-shearing season always was in the East. David plays the Robin Hood in good earnest. "This species of blackmail is regularly levied at the present day by the Bedouin living on the borders of the desert. In return they guarantee the protection of life and property in these notoriously insecure districts" (Kenn.).

of wine, and five sheep ready dressed and five measures of parched corn, and an hundred clusters of raisins, and two hundred cakes of figs, and laid them on asses. 19. And she said unto her servants, Go on before me; behold, I come after you. But she told not her husband Nabal. And it was so, as she rode on the ass, that she came down by the covert of the hill, and behold, David and his men came down against her; and she met them. Now David had said, Surely in vain have I kept all that this fellow hath in the wilderness,   so that   nothing was missed of all that pertained unto him: and he hath requited me evil for good. 22. So and more also do God unto the enemies of David, if I leave of all that pertain to him by the m orning light so much as one man child.

*Dissociating herself front her husband's meanness—*23. And when Abigail saw David, she hasted, and lighted off the ass, and fell before David on her face, and bowed herself to the ground, 24. and fell at his feet, and said, Upon me, my Lord, upon me let this iniquity be: and let thine handmaid, I pray thee, speak in thine audience, and hear the words of thine handmaid. 25. Let not my Lord, I pray thee, regard this man of Belial, even Nabal: for as his name is, so is he; Nabal is his. name, and folly is with him: but I thine handmaid saw not the young men of my Lord, whom thou didst send. 26. Now therefore, my Lord, as the LORD liveth, and as thy soul liveth, seeing the LORD hath withholden thee from coming to shed blood, and from avenging thyself with thine own hand, now let thine enemies, and they that seek evil to my Lord, be as Nabal. 27. And now this blessing which thine handmaid hath brought unto my Lord, let it even be given unto the young men that follow my Lord.

And predicting glory for David and his house—28. Ipray thee, forgive the trespass of thine handmaid: for the LORD will certainly make my Lord a sure house; because my Lord fighteth the battles of the LORD, and evil hath not been found in thee all thy days. 29. Yet a man

20. **covert.** The verse means that the contour of the ground prevented David seeing her approach. They met suddenly, just when David was vowing vengeance. A dramatic moment.

20. **Nabal** = "Fool"–a reckless disregarder of God and man.

is risen to pursue thee, and to seek thy soul: but the soul of my Lord shall be bound in the bundle of life with the LORD thy God; and the souls of thine enemies, them shall he. sling out, as out of the middle of, a sling. 30. And it shall come to pass, when the LORD shall have done to my Lord according to all the good that he hath spoken concerning thee, and shall have appointed thee ruler over Israel; 31. that this shall be no grief unto thee, nor offence of heart unto my Lord, either that thou hast shed blood causeless, or that my lord hath avenged himself: but when the LORD shall have dealt well with my lord then remember thine handmaid.

David's anger is appeased—32. And David said to Abigail, Blessed be the LORD God of Israel, which sent thee this day to meet me: 33. and blessed be thy advice, and blessed be thou, which hast kept me this day from coming to shed blood, and from avenging myself with mine own hand. 34. For in very deed, as the LORD God of Israel liveth, which hath kept me back from hurting thee, except thou hadst hasted and come to meet me, surely there had not been left unto Nabal by the morning light so much as one man child. 35. So David received of her hand that which she had brought him, and said unto her, Go up in peace to thine house; see, I have hearkened to thy voice, and have accepted thy person

Sudden illness and death of Nabal—36. And Abigail came to Nabal; and, behold, he held a feast in his house, like the feast of a king; and Nabal's heart was merry within him, for he was very drunken: wherefore she told him nothing, less or more, until the morning light. 37. But it came to pass in the morning, when the wine was gone out of Nabal, and his wife had told him these things, that his heart died within him, and he became as a stone. 38. And

29. "May thy life be bound up in the bundle of the living in the care of God" –a metaphor from precious stones, carefully wrapped up and guarded. The prayer is for m a terial prosperity in this life, not beyond the grave, though the words are commonly applied in this latter sense nowadays, especially by the Jews. The exact converse occurs in the metaphor of the sling.

31. **offence of heart,** *i.e.,* remorse.

35. accepted thy person. Heb. "lifted up thy countenance," *i.e.,* relieved thy anxiety by granting thy request.

37. Nabal had a **paralytic stroke.**

it came to pass about ten days after, that the LORD smote Nabal, that he died.

Romantic finale to the story—39. And when David heard that Nabal was dead, he said, Blessed be the LORD, that hath pleaded the cause of my reproach from the hand of Nabal, and hath kept his servant from evil: for the LORD hath returned the wickedness of Nabal upon his own head. And David sent and communed with Abigail, to take her to him to wife. 40. And when the servants of David were come to Abigail to Carmel, they spake unto her, saying, David sent us unto thee, to take thee to him to wife. 41. And she arose, and bowed herself on her face to the earth, and said, Behold, let thine handmaid be a servant to wash the feet of the servants of my Lord. 42. And Abigail hasted, and arose, and rode upon an ass, with five damsels of her's that went after her; and she went after the messengers of David, and became his wife.

Two other incidents in David's domestic life—43. David also took Ahinoam of Jezreel; and they were also both of them his wives. 44. But Saul had given Michal his daughter, David's wife to Phalti the son of Laish, which was of Gallim.

6. TO THE PHILISTINES

(a) As a refugee at the court of Achish, King of Gath

1 Samuel 27:1-4

1. And David said in his heart, I shall now perish one day by the hand of Saul; there is nothing better for me than that I should speedily escape into the land of the

39. pleaded ... reproach, *i.e.,* has acted as arbitrator in the case of the insult I received from Nabal, and has given the award to my side.

43. Jezreel. A village between Ziph and Carmel, not the famous northern town.

Ahinoam became mother of David's first-born, Amnon.

44. "Saul regarded David's flight as desertion of his wife, which brought her back under her fathers power." (Smith). *Cf.* Samson's Philistine wife, Judg. 14:20.

27:1. In spite of his advantageous marriage, David, driven from pillar to post, found it hopeless any longer to try to maintain himself in his own country. His own fellow-countrymen had

Philistines; and Saul shall despair of me, to seek me any more in any coast of Israel: so shall I escape out of his hand. 2. And David arose, and he passed over with the six hundred men that were with him unto Achish, the son of Maoch, king of Gath. 3. And David dwelt with Achish at Gath, he and his men, every man with his household, even David with his two wives, Ahinoam the Jezreelitess, and Abigail the Carmelitess, Nabal's wife. 2. And it was told Saul that David was fled to Gath: and he sought no more again for him.

(b) As a feudal lord at Ziklag

1 Samuel 2 7 : 5 -12; 1 Chronicles 12:1-22

27:5. And David said unto Achish, If I have now found grace in thine eyes, let them give me a place in some town in the country, that I may dwell there: for why should thy servant dwell in the royal city with thee? Then Achish gave him Ziklag that day: (wherefore Ziklag pertaineth into the kings of Judah unto this day.) And the time that David dwelt in the country of the Philistines was a full year and four months.

8. And David and his men went up, and invaded the Geshurites, and the Gezrites, and the Amalekites: for

given him but scant assistance: occasionally, as we saw, they were active in betraying him. He therefore took the "desperate step" of placing his services and those of his followers at the disposal of the Philistines, who, as a brave, warlike people, possibly presented attractions to the eyes of a harried band of desperadoes.

The fragment (1 Sam. 21:11-16) which makes David come alone to Gath and subsequently feign imbecility has no historical context whatsoever: it is inconsistent with what precedes and what follows, at whatever period in David's wanderings we attempt to place it. Probably it was a late composition designed as a substitute for the older accounts with the object of excusing the seemingly unpatriotic action of the favorite hero of their national history in resorting to the side of their enemies. See, however, *H.D.B.*, p. 178.

5. At Ziklag, in the Negeb (verse 1 0), somewhere south-east of Gaza on the Philistine frontier, David was established as a feudal chief, *i.e.,* an independent prince bound only to render military service to his over-Lord. Why did he seek this change? (1) To be more independent. (2) The close proximity of himself and his followers may not have proved altogether congenial to Achish. (3) To have liberty to conform to the rites of his own religion.

8. **Geshurites, Gezrites**. Desert-tribes between Palestine and Egypt.

those nations were of old the inhabitants of the land, as thou goest to Shur, even unto the land of Egypt. 9 . And David smote the land, and left neither man nor woman alive, and took away the sheep, and the oxen, and the asses, and the camels, and the apparel, and returned, and came to Achish. 1 0 . And Achish said, Whither have ye made a road to day? And David said, Against the south of Judah, and against the south of the Jerahmeelites, and against the south of the Kenites. 11. And David saved neither man nor woman alive, to bring tidings to Gath, saying, Lest they should tell on us, saying, So did David, and so will be his manner all the while he dwelleth in the country of the Philistines. 12. And Achish believed David, saying, He hath made his people Israel utterly to abhor him; therefore, he shall be my servant forever.

Character of some of the warriors who j oined fortunes with David—1 Chron. 1 2 : 1 . Now these are they that came to David to Ziklag, while he yet kept himself close because of Saul the son of Kish: and they were among the mighty men, *his helpers in war.* 2. They were armed with bows; and could use both the right hand and the left in hurling stones and shooting arrows out of a bow; *they were* of Saul's brethren of Benjamin. *[Then follow their names.]*

8. And of the Gadites there separated themselves unto David into the hold to the wilderness,

> Men of might,
> And men of war fit for the battle,
> That could handle shield and buckler,
> Whose faces were like the faces of lions,
>
> And were as swift as the roes upon the mountains;
> 14.   One of the least was *equal to* an hundred,
> And the greatest *to* a thousand.

10. In order to retain the king's favor he pretended to have ravaged his own countrymen. Jerahmeel was Caleb's brother, and his descendants, like the Calebites, were absorbed in the outlying population of Judah.

The south,   *i.e.,* the Negeb, the "steep and haggard ridges" stretching from Hebron to many miles below Beer-sheba *(H.G.H.L.,* p. 278).

15. These are they that went over Jordan in the first month, when it had overflown all his banks; and they put to flight all them of the valleys, both toward the east, and toward the west.

16. And there camc of the children of Benjamin and Judah to the hold unto David. 17. And David went out to meet them, and answered and said unto them, If ye be come peaceably unto me to help me, mine heart shall be knit unto you: but if ye be come to betray me to mine enemies, seeing there is no wrong in mine hands, the God of our fathers look thereon, and rebuke it. 18. Then the spirit came upon Amasai, who was chief of the captain, and he said,

> Thine are we, David,
> And on thy side, thou son of Jesse:
> Peace, peace be unto thee,
> And peace be to thine helpers;
> For thy God helpeth thee.

Then David received them, and made them captains of the band.

19. And there fell some of Manasseh to David, when he came with the Philistines against Saul to battle: but they helped them not: for the Lords of the Philistines upon advisement sent him away, saying, He will fall away to his master Saul to the jeopardy of our heads. 21. And they helped David against the band of the rovers: for they were all mighty men of valour, and were captains in the host. 22. For *from day to day* there came to David to help him, until it was a great host, like the host of God.

(c) On the March against his Countrymen. Will he fight?

1 Samuel 28:1, 2, and 2 9

28:1. And it came to pass in those days, that the Philistines gathered their armies together for warfare, to

---

18. Amasai. We should perhaps read Abishai (1 Sam. 26:6, etc.); or possibly he is identical with Amasa (2 Sam. 27:25-seq.).

19. The allusion is to the events of section (c) below, on this page.
fell to = joined.
upon advisement, i.e., after deliberation.

21. rovers, i.e., the Amalekites, below, p. 92.

22. The earlier historian (Sl), however, still computes them more modestly at six hundred men (1 Sam. 30:9).

fight with Israel. And Achish said unto David, Know thou
assuredly, that thou shalt go out with me to battle, thou and thy
men. 2. And David said unto Achish, *Good and well: now*
thou shalt know what thy servant *will* do. And Achish said to David,
Therefore will I make thee keeper of mine head for ever.

The Philistine Tyrants mistrust David's loyalty—29:1. Now the
Philistines gathered together all their armies to Aphek: and
the Israelites pitched by a fountain which is in Jezreel. 2. And the
Lords of the Philistines passed on by hundreds, and by thousands:
but David and his men passed on in the rereward with Achish. 3.
Then said the princes of the Philistines, What do these Hebrews here?
And Achish said unto the princes of the Philistines, Is not this David,
the servant of Saul the king of Israel, which hath been with me these
days, or these years, and I have found no fault in him since he fell unto
me unto this day? 4. And the princes of the Philistines were wroth
with him; and the princes of the Philistines said unto him, Make this

1. This is one of the most dramatic moments in ancient history. Achish
orders his vassal to take the field against his own country. David is in a
quandary. To fight is treason; not to fight is probably death. which will he
do? Fortunately, the Philistine princes have the sagacity. to solve the difficulty
for him. The verdict of history upon David's character turns upon the crucial
question, What were his real intentions at the moment? His whole previous
and subsequent behavior, his ambiguous language in 28:2, his deception
of Achish in 27:7-12, combine to convince the reader that at the critical
hour he would have contrived an expedient to avoid his obligations to this
Philistine protector at such a price. What a situation for a tragedian to
treat

Events occur in rapid succession in these chapters:

(1) The Philistines march north to Aphek and subsequently against Saul's position
in the south-east corner of the valley of Jezreel, near Mount Gilboa.

But before the battle:

(2) At Aphek David is dismissed from service.

(3) He returns to Ziklag and starts on a punitive expedition against the
Amalekites.

(4) Saul consults a "witch."

(5) Next day Saul is defeated and slain in battle.

2. David's reply is intentionally ambiguous. Achish understands
him to promise great deeds on behalf of the Philistines, and promises, as a
reward, to make him captain of the royal bodyguard.

fellow return, that he may go again to his place which thou hast appointed him, and let him not go down with us to battle, lest in the battle he be an adversary to us: for wherewith should he reconcile himself unto his master? should it not be with the heads of these men? 5. Is not this David, of whom they sang one. to another in dances, saying,

> Saul hath slain his thousands,
> And David his ten thousands?

And force Achish, by unanswerable arguments, to dismiss him—6. Then Achish called David, and said unto him, Surely, as the LORD liveth, thou hast been upright, and thy going out and thy coming in with me in the host is good in my sight: for I have not found evil in thee since the day of thy coming unto me unto this day: nevertheless the Lords favor thee not. 7. Wherefore now return, and go in peace, that thou displease not the Lords of the Philistines.

David pretends to feel hurt—8. And David said unto Achish, But what have I done? and what hast thou found in thy servant so long as I have been with thee unto this day, that I may not go fight against the enemies of my Lord the king? 9. And Achish answered and said to David, I know that thou art good in my sight, as an angel of God: notwithstanding the princes of the Philistines have said, He shall not go up with us to the battle. 10. wherefore now rise up early in the morning with thy master's servants that are come with thee: and as soon as ye be up early in the morning, and have light, depart. 11. So David and his men rose up early to depart in the morning to return into the land of the Philistines. And the Philistines went up to Jezreel.

(d) David's Pursuit of the Amalekites

1 Samuel 30

1. And it came to pass, when David and his men were come   to Ziklag   on   the   third   day,   that   the Amalekites had

4. **these** men, *i.e.,* the Philistine soldiers, or whose side he was *supposed* to be going to fight.

place . . . appointed = Ziklag.

30:1. Amalekites, p. 51. They had seized the opportunity of revenging David's merciless treatment of them (27:8).

invaded the south, and Ziklag, and smitten Ziklag, and burned it with fire;
2. and had taken the women captives, that were therein: they slew not any,
either great or small, but carried them away, and went on their way.

David's band exhibit resentment against their leader—3. So David
and his men came to the city, and, behold, it was burned with fire;
and their wives, and their sons and their daughters, were taken
captives. 4. Then David and the people that were with him lifted
up their voice and wept, until they had no more power to weep. *5.* And
David's two wives were taken captives, Ahinoam the Jezreelitess,
and Abigail the wife of Nabal the Carmelite. And David was
greatly distressed; for the people spake of stoning him, because the
soul of all the people was grieved, every man for his sons and for
his daughters: but David encouraged himself in the LORD his God.
7. And David said to Abiathar the priest, Ahimelech's son,
I pray thee, bring me hither the ephod. And Abiathar brought
thither the ephod to David. 8. And David enquired at the LORD,
saying, Shall I pursue after this troop? shall I overtake them? And
he answered him, Pursue: for thou shalt surely overtake them, and
without fail recover all.

The pursuit—9. So David went, he and the six hundred men
that were with him, and came to the brook Besor, where those that
were left behind stayed. 10. For two hundred abode behind, which
were so faint that they could not go over the brook Besor. But David
pursued, he and four hundred men.

\ *On the scent: a lucky find*—11. And they found an Egyptian
in the field, and brought him to David, and gave him bread,
and he did eat; and they made him drink water; 12. and they
gave him a piece of a cake of f i gs, and two clusters of raisins:
and when he had eaten, his spirit came again to him: for he
had eaten no bread, nor drunk any water, three days and three
nights. 13. And David said unto him, To whom belongest thou?
and whence art thou? And he said, I am a young man of Egypt,
servant to an Amalekite; and my master left me, because three

---

1. **the south,** *i.e.,* the Negeb.
2. **carried them away—** to sell in the Egyptian slave-market.

days agone I fell sick. 14. We made an invasion upon the south of the Cherethites, and upon the coast which belongeth to Judah, and upon the south of Caleb; and we burned Ziklag with fire. 15. And David said to him, Canst thou bring me down to this company? And he said, Swear unto me by God, that thou wilt neither kill me nor deliver me into the hands of my master, and I will bring thee down to this company.

The attack and recovery of the plunder—16. And when he had brought him down, behold, they were spread abroad upon all the earth, eating and drinking, and dancing, because of all the great spoil that they had taken out of the land of the Philistines, and out of the land of Judah. 17. And David smote them from the twilight even unto the evening of the next day: and there escaped not a man of them, save four hundred young men, which rode upon camels, and fled. 18. And David recovered all that the Amalekites had carried away: and David rescued his two wives. 19. And there was nothing lacking to them, neither small nor great, neither sons nor daughters, neither spoil, nor any thing that they had taken to them: David recovered all. 20. And David took all the flocks and the herds, which they drave before those other cattle, and said, This is David's spoil.

A dispute as to the division of spoil—21. And David came to the two hundred men, which were so faint that they could not follow David, whom they had made also to abide at the brook Besor: and they went forth to meet David, and to meet the people that were with him: and when David came near to the people, he saluted them. 22. Then answered all the wicked men and men of Belial, of those that went with David, and said, Because they went not with us, we will not give them ought of the spoil that we have recovered, save to every man his wife and his children; that they may lead them away, and depart.

14. **the south or the Cherethites.** The Cherethite Negeb—that portion of the Negeb occupied by the Cherethites, a clan allied to the Philistines. Similarly, also "the Calebite Negeb."

20. Text corrupt. The meaning required is that, in addition to recovering the stolen booty, David and his men captured much spoil.

22. **wife and his children**—whom the four hundred had rescued for them from the Amalekites

From which originated a permanent Hebrew law—23. Then said David, Ye shall not do so, my brethren, with that which the LORD hath given us, who hath preserved us, and delivered the company that came against us into our hand. 24. For who will hearken unto you in this matter? but as his part is that goeth down to the battle so shall his part be that tarried by the stuff: they shall part alike. 25. And it was so from that day forward, that he made it a statute and an ordinance for Israel unto this day.

His politic and grateful disposal of his spoil—26. And when David came to Ziklag, he sent of the spoil unto the elders of Judah, even to his friends, saying, Behold a present for you of the spoil of the enemies of the LORD; 31. *even* to all the places where David himself and his men were wont *to* haunt.

THE "WITCH" OF EN-DOR

1 Samuel 28 : 3-25

Death of Samuel—3. Now Samuel was dead, and all Israel had lamented him, and buried him in Ramah, even in his own city.

Despair of Saul—And Saul had put away those that had familiar spirits, and the wizards, out of the land.

24. **part** = share. This law, like all the rest, was by a "legal fiction" subsequently assigned to Moses (Num. 31 : 27), as Athenian laws were to Solon. For the growth of the Hebrew codes of law, see vol. ii. pp. 21 *seq.*

28:3. The precise period, during the late events, at which Samuel had died is not recorded; but his death seems to have preceded David's flight to Philistia sixteen months back.

The strange scene described in this chapter on the night preceding the battle of Mount Gilboa no doubt rests on a true historical basis. Recourse to necromancy—that is, consultation of the dead—exercised a morbid fascination over the minds of many in ancient days, as it does still over the minds of some. Sorcery had been forbidden in Israel in one of their oldest laws, dating from the Mosaic age (Exod. 22:18, from the "Book of the Covenant"), and again in later legislation. Saul himself, too, had issued strict injunctions against it. A modern writer, in describing such a scene, would probably speak of it as a "spiritualistic seance," and call the woman a "medium."

4. And the Philistines gathered themselves together, ana came and pitched in Shunem: and Saul gathered all Israel together, and they pitched in Gilboa.   5. And when Saul saw the host of the Philistines, he was afraid, and his heart greatly trembled.   6. And when Saul enquired of the LORD, the LORD answered him not, neither by dreams, nor by Urim, nor by prophets.

Abandoned, as he thinks, by God, he resorts to the "black art"—7. Then said Saul unto his servants, Seek me a woman that hath a familiar spirit, that I may go to her, and enquire of her. And his servants said to him, Behold, there is a woman that hath a familiar spirit at En-dor. 8. And Saul disguised himself, and put on other raiment, and he went, and two men with him, and they came to the woman by night: and he said, I pray thee, divine unto me by the familiar spirit, and bring me him up, whom I shall name unto thee. 9 . And the woman said unto him, Behold, thou knowest what Saul hath done, how he hath cut off those that have familiar spirits, and the wizards, out of the land: wherefore then layest thou a snare for my life, to cause me to die? 1 0 . And Saul sware to her by the LORD. saying, As the LORD liveth, there shall no punishment happen to thee for this thing.

The midnight scene in the witch's hut—11. Then said the woman, whom shall I bring up unto thee? And he said, Bring me up Samuel. 12. And when the woman saw Samuel, she cried with a loud voice: and the woman spake to Saul, saying, Why hast thou deceived me? for thou

---

4. From Aphek in the plain of Sharon the Philistines, as we saw, had advanced to the valley of Jezreel. Here we find them at Shunem, on the north side of the valley; on the morrow they crossed to the south side and assailed Saul's position on the western slopes of Gilboa. Thus they took Saul on his left flank. They could not attack his front (north); the ground was too steep for them.

The aim of their invasion apparently was to make for the Jordan Valley, by way of Jezreel, and thus to occupy the eastern frontier of Ephraim and Benjamin and coop Israel up in the highlands. For a slightly different view of the campaign see the detailed description in *H.G.H.L.,* pp. 400 *seq.*

6. **Urim** = the sacred stone which, with its counterpart called Tummim, was used for casting lots vol. ii. p. 46.

7. **En-dor** = "the fountain of Dor"; close to the Philistine camp at Shunem.

12. If the text is right, the first effect of the appearance of Samuel's shade upon the woman was that she became conscious who her visitor really was.

art Saul. 13. And the king said unto her, Be not afraid: for what sawest thou? And the woman said unto Saul I saw gods ascending out of the earth. 14. And he said unto her, What form is he of? And she said, An old man cometh up: and he is covered with a mantle. And Saul perceived that it was Samuel, and he stooped with his face to the ground, and bowed himself.

Samuel's ghost pronounces Saul's doom—15. And Samuel said to Saul, why hast thou disquieted me, to bring me up? And Saul answered, I am sore distressed; for the Philistines make war against me, and God is departed from me, and answereth me no more, neither by prophets, nor by drearns: therefore I have called thee, that thou mayest make known unto me what I shall do. 16. Then said Samuel, Wherefore then dost thou ask of me, seeing the LORD is departed from thee, and is become thine enemy? 17. And the LORD hath done *for himself,* as he spake by me: for the LORD hath rent the kingdom out of thine hand, and given it to thy neighbor, even to David: 18. because thou obeyedst not the voice of the LORD, nor executedst his fierce wrath upon Amalek, therefore hath the LORD done this thing unto thee this day. 19. Moreover the LORD will also deliver Israel with thee into the hand of the Philistines: and tomorrow shalt thou and thy sons be with me: the LORD also shall deliver the host of Israel into the hand of the Philistines.

Saul faints at the utterance—20. Then Saul fell straightway all along on the earth, and was sore afraid, because of the words of Samuel: and there was no strength in him; for he had eaten no bread all the day, nor all the night. 21. And the woman came unto Saul, and saw that he was sore troubled, and said unto him, Behold, thine handmaid hath obeyed thy voice, and I have put my life in my hand, and I have hearkened unto thy words which thou spakest unto me. 22. Now therefore, I pray thee, hearken thou also unto the voice of thine handmaid, and let me set a morsel of bread before thee; and eat, that thou mayest have strength, when thou goest on thy way.

The woman restores him with food—23. But he refused, and said, I will not eat. But his servants, together with the woman, compelled him; and he hearkened unto their

III-7

voice. So he arose from the earth, and sat upon the bed. 24. And the woman had a fat calf in the house; and she hasted, and killed it, and took flour, and kneaded it, and did bake unleavened bread thereof: *25.* and she brought it before Saul, and before his servants; and they did eat. Then they rose up and went away that night.

THE BATTLE OF MOUNT GILBOA

1 Samuel 31

Defeat of Israel—1. Now the Philistines fought against Israel: and the men of Israel fled from before the Philistines, and fell down slain in mount Gilboa. 2. And the Philistines followed hard upon Saul and upon his sons; and the Philistines slew Jonathan, and Abinadab, and Melchishua, Saul's sons. 3. And the battle went sore against Saul, and the archers hit him; and he was sore wounded of the archers.

Suicide of Saul—4. Then said Saul unto his armorbearer, Draw thy sword, and thrust me through therewith; lest these uncircumcised come and thrust me through, and abuse me. But his armorbearer would not; for he was sore afraid. Therefore Saul took a sword, and fell upon it. 5. And when his armorbearer saw that Saul was dead, he fell likewise upon his sword, and died with him. 6. So Saul died, and his three sons, and his armorbearer, and all his men, that same day together.

Panic of the neighboring Israelites—7. And when the men of Israel that were *in the cities of* the valley, and *in the cities of* Jordan, saw that the men of Israel fled, and that Saul and his sons were dead, they forsook the cities, and fled; and the Philistines came and dwelt in them.

Mutilation of Saul's body—8. And it came to pass on the morrow, when the Philistines came to strip the slain, that they found Saul and his three sons fallen in Mount Gilboa. 9. And they cut off his head, and stripped off

2. Saul's other son Ishvi, or Ishbosheth, perhaps was not at the battle.

4. "Cases of suicide are remarkably rare in Scripture" (Kenn.). Ahithophel, Zimri, Judas Iscariot, are cited.

his armor, and sent into the land of the Philistines round about, to publish it in the house of their idols, and among the people. 10. And they put his armor in the house of Ashtaroth: and they fastened his body to the wall of Beth-shan.

Loyalty of the men of Jabesh—11. And when the inhabitants of Jabesh-gilead heard of that which the Philistines had done to Saul; 12. all the valiant men arose, and went all night, and took the body of Saul and the bodies of his sons from the wall of Beth-shan, and came to Jabesh, and burnt them there. 13. And they took their bones, and buried them under a tree at Jabesh, and fasted seven days.

DAVID'S RECEPTION OF THE NEWS: HIS DIRGE

2 Samuel 1

A messenger brings the tidings to David at Ziklag—1. Now it came to pass after the death of Saul, when David was r eturned from the slaughter of the Amalekites, and David had abode two days in Ziklag; 2. it came even to pass on the third day, that, behold, a man came out of the camp from Saul with his clothes rent, and earth upon his head: and so it was, when he came to David, that he fell to the earth, and did obeisance. 3. And David said unto him, From whence comest thou? And he said unto him, Out of the camp of Israel am I escaped. 4. And David

10. Astarte's temple at Ashkelon is probably meant.

Beth-shan. Four miles east of mount Gilboa, at the bottom of the valley of Jezreel.

11. This act was prompted by gratitude for Saul's deliverance of their town seventeen years before (chap. xi.).

12. **burnt.** We should probably accept a slight emendation of the Heb. and read "lamented for." Cremation—save for this instance—is entirely unknown to Hebrew custom, and abhorrent to their notions; they always buried their dead. The replica of this passage in 1 Chron. 10 makes no mention of burning the bodies. Later on the remains were brought home to the family tomb in Benjamin (2 Sam. 21).

13. The result of the battle of Gilboa was to replace the Philistines in the position of ascendancy over all the country west of Jordan which they had held at Saul's accession. The war of Independence must be fought over again.

Said unto him, How went the matter? I pray thee, tell me. And he answered, That the people are fled from the battle, and many of the people also are fallen and dead; and Saul and Jonathan his son are dead also.

The Amalekite's story—5. And David said unto the man that told him, How knowest thou that Saul and Jonathan his son be dead? 6. And the young man that told him said, As I happened by chance upon mount Gilboa, behold, Saul leaned upon his spear; and, lo, the chariots and horsemen followed hard after him. 7. And when he looked behind him, he saw me, and called unto me. And I answered, Here am I. 8. And he said unto me, Who art thou? and I answered him, I am an Amalekite. 9. He said unto me again, Stand, I pray thee, upon me, and slay me: for anguish is come upon me, because my life is yet whole in me. 1 0 . So I stood upon him, and slew him, because I was sure that he could not live after that he was fallen: and I took the crown that was upon his head, and the bracelet that was on his arm, and have brought them hither unto my Lord.

Grief of David. 11. Then David took hold on his clothes, and rent them; and likewise all the men that were with him. 12. And they mourned, and wept, and fasted until even, for Saul, and for Jonathan his son, and for the people of the LORD, and for the house of Israel; because they were fallen by the Sword.

He deals faithfully with the Amalekite—13. And David said unto the young man that told him, whence are thou?

6. The Amalekite gives quite a different account of the occurrence from that which we have already read in 1 Sam. 31. How is this to be explained? Either:

(1) That the Amalekite was a liar; he hoped to profit by falsely claiming credit for an act which he imagined Saul's life-long victim would applaud. There is, however, no suggestion in the text that the author wished to represent the man as romancing. On the other hand, critical deamination (see Kent or Kenn. *ad loc.)* discovers too many divergences, linguistic and historical, from the rest of the narrative to make this theory acceptable. Or:

(2) It is an independent account, representing a variant tradition as to the mode of Saul's end, worked into the text by a redactor. The author disliked and disbelieved the suicide story. If verses 5-10, 13-16 are cut out, the remainder presents a sequence consistent with what has preceded and what follows.

And he answered, I am the son of a stranger, an Amalekite. 14. And David said unto him, How wast thou not afraid to stretch forth thine hand to destroy the LORD'S anointed? 16. And David said unto him, Thy blood be upon thy head; for thy mouth hath testified against thee, saying, I have slain the LORD'S anointed. 15. And David called one of the young men, and said, Go near, and fall upon him. And he smote him that he died.

His elegy—17. And David lamented with this lamentation over Saul and over Jonathan his son: 18 *a.* (behold it is written in the book of Jasher) *and said:*

(a) The Greatness of the Calamit

18b.   *Weep, O Judah!*
       Grieve, O Israel!

19. The beauty of Israel is slain upon thy high places: how are the mighty fallen!

13. stranger. Heb. *ger* (cf. Byron's *The Giaour*), i.e., a resident alien admitted to a modified citizenship in the State, regulated by—law. David was a *ger* in the Philistine state when he abode at Ziklag.

17. This noble song is admitted by all, except the most extreme critics, to have been composed by David himself. It is the most ancient poem of any length in all Hebrew literature, except the Song of Deborah.

Together with other poetical pieces and fragments-such as Joshua's cry to the sun and moon at Ajalon—it was embodied in a collection of national poetry made about Solomon's time and known as the Book of Jasher, that is the Upright Ones, the heroes. Quotations are occasionally made in the Bible texts from other ancient poetical collections—e.g. The Song of the Well (Num. 20:17), The Song of the Country, from the Book of the Wars of the Lord (Num. 20:14), The Song of the Sword (Gen. 4:23). In these references we have a hint as to the character of the oldest literary records from which Hebrew poetry and history gradually developed.

On critical grounds upon which most modern commentators are agreed, the versions of verse 18 given both in A.V. and R.V. (Song of the Bow, etc.) are impossible. The translation of it printed here (from Smith) represents the text as now generally accepted; it only necessitates the emendation of one or two letters in the Heb. The headings to the stanzas have been adopted from Kent's version.

19. **The beauty.** Abstract for the concrete: "The beautiful, or glorious ones"; but the rendering is doubtful.

20. Tell it not in Gath, publish it not in the streets of Askelon;   lest the daughters of the   Philistines rejoice, lest the daughters of the uncircumcised triumph.

21. Ye mountains of Gilboa, let there be no dew, neither let there be rain, upon you, *O ye fields of death:* for there the shield of the mighty is vilely cast away, the shield of Saul, not anointed with oil.

(b) Bravery and Attractiveness of the Fallen

22. From the blood of the slain, from the fat of the mighty, the bow of Jonathan turned not back, and the sword of Saul returned not empty.

23. Saul and Jonathan were lovely and pleasant in their lives, and in their death they were not divided: they were swifter than eagles, they were stronger than lions.

(c) Saul's Services to Israel

24. Ye daughters of Israel, weep over Saul, who clothed you in scarlet, with other delights, who put on ornaments of gold upon your apparel.

25a. How are the mighty fallen in the midst of the battle!

(d) David's Love for Jonathan

25b. O Jonathan, *in thy death thou hast wounded me.*

26. I am distressed for thee, my brother Jonathan: very pleasant hast thou been unto me: thy love to me was wonderful, passing the love of women.

27. How are the mighty fallen, and the weapons of war perished!

---

21. **not anointed**, *i.e.,* left to rust and rot.

PART III

DAVID THE KING

INTRODUCTORY

THE reader will form his own estimate of David's character. He should not, however, overlook one consideration which m ay help to balance his judgment. David has suffered from excessive praise; he was rather too much "the darling of the songs of Israel." "His canonization," as Wellhausen says, "by the later Jewish tradition, which made a Levitical saint of him" is much to blame. For our modern ideas of saintliness can hardly harmonize with the actual record of David's deeds presented by the following chapters. Tradition has set a false standard to judge him by, and we feel that he does not come up to it. But "take him as we find him, an antique king in a barbarous age" and we shall not be disappointed. We shall find much to imitate, admire, and love.[1]

A word as to David's reputation as a psalmist may not be out of place. That he was a highly gifted poet is a certain fact (pp. 101, 103); but the reader m ust not be misled by the title "The Psalm of David," which was applied to the Psalter long after David's time, into imagining that he was the sole, or even the principal, author of the psalms constituting that collection. Just as in the case of the Hebrew laws it became customary to call every law a law of Moses, because Moses was the founder of their

---

[1] Carlyle's estimate is worth turning to: *Heroes,* Leet. ii. p. 5.

codes of law, so it became a convention to call the national collection of psalms "The Psalms of David," out of graceful compliment to the memory of their popular poet king. At the same time it is true that the authorship of many individual psalms was specifically attributed by the Hebrews to David himself. It is unlikely that in this they were altogether mistaken. David clearly had the faculty for composing psalms. When so many were assigned to him some, at any rate, may reasonably be held to have been his in fact. "Where there is much smoke, there must have been some fire" *(H.D.R., p. 773).* Which of them in particular can thus be attributed with confidence *to* David it is beyond our province here to inquire.

OUTLINE OF DAVID'S LIFE

I—Born about 1040 B.C.
    A shepherd boy.
    Anointed by Samuel.
    Slays the giant.
    Introduced to court.
    Friendship with Jonathan.
    Lives as an outlaw captain.

II—A. King at Hebron (aged 30), for 7 years.
    Death of his rival, Ish-bosheth.

   B. King of all Israel, for 33 years.

    1st Period: Consolidation of the Kingdom.
      Subjugation of the Philistines.
      Jerusalem made the capital.
      Organizes the army.
      Gains an extensive empire.

    2nd Period: Domestic History.
      Incident of Bath-sheba.
      Rebellion and death of Absalom.
      Revolt of Sheba.
      Attempted usurpation of Adonijah.
      Appoints Solomon as his successor.
      Dies, aged 70: about 970 B.C.

GENEALOGICAL TREE

Showing the relationship of those members of David's family mentioned in this volume.

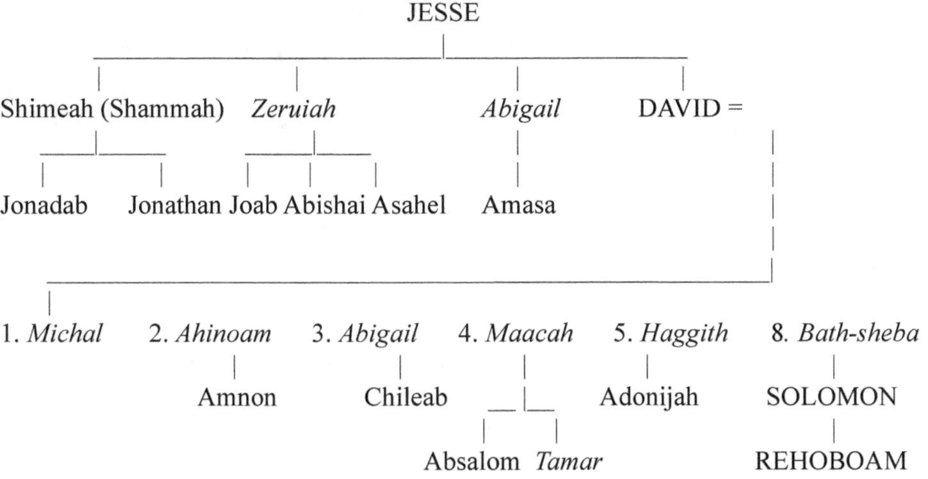

The names of women are printed in italics.

David had other wives, and more sons, besides those given above.

A. DAVID KING AT HEBRON

THE TWO KINGS: CIVIL WAR

2 Samuel 2-3:1

David anointed king at Hebron—2:1. And it came to pass after this, that David enquired of the LORD, saying, Shall I go up into any of the cities of Judah? And the LORD said unto him, Go up. And David said, whither shall I go up? And he said, Unto Hebron. 2. So David went up thither, and his two wives also, Ahinoam the Jezreelitess, and Abigail Nabal's wife the Carmelite.

1. On Saul's death civil war ensued. His surviving son, Ishbosheth, who was probably quite young and personally insignificant, was set up as his father's successor by Abner, on the east of Jordan. He had to dispute his title with both David and the Philistines. David at the same time established himself as tribal king over Judah, still as the vassal of the Philistines. As to the duration of this condition of affairs there are contradictory notices in our texts. That which assigns a period of seven and a half years is generally accepted.

3. And his men that were with him did David bring up, every man with his household: and they dwelt in the cities of Hebron. 4 *a*. And the men of Judah came, and there they anointed David king over the house of Judah.

His message of thanks to Jabesh-gilead—4 *b*. And they told. David, saying, That the men of Jabesh-gilead were they that buried Saul. 5. And David sent messengers unto the men of Jabesh-gilead, and said unto them, Blessed be ye of the LORD, that ye have shewed this kindness unto your Lord, even unto Saul, and have buried him. 6. And now the LORD shew kindness and truth unto you: and I also will requite you this kindness, because ye have done this thing. 7. Therefore now let your hands be strengthened and be ye valiant: for your master Saul is dead, and also the house of Judah have anointed me king over them.

Ish-bosheth appointed king of "all Israel" at Mahanaim—8. But Abner the son of Ner, captain of Saul's host, took Ish-bosheth the son of Saul, and brought him over to Mahanaim; 9. and made him king over Gilead, and over the Asherites, and over Jezreel, and over Ephraim, and over Benjamin, and over all Israel. 10. But the house of Judah followed David. 11. And the time that David was king in Hebron over the house of Judah was seven years and six months.

The battle of the Pool of Gibeon: triumph of David's party—12. And Abner the son of Ner, and the servants of Ish-bosheth the son of Saul, went out from Mahanaim to Gibeon. 13. And Joab the son of Zeruiah, and the servants of David, went out, and met together by the pool of Gibeon; and they sat down, the one on the one

7. David's diplomatic message implies that he claims to be Saul's legitimate successor and looks for the Gileadites' support.

8. **Mahanaim,** the scene of Jacob's vision (Gen. 3 2 ; 2), was the capital of Gilead, some fifteen miles north of the river Jabbok.

9. **Asherites,** the tribe of Asher. Owing to the Philistine occupation of the country west of Jordan Ish-bosheth was not king of "all Israel" in the sense which that title bore in later day. He was really only master of the tribes east of Jordan.

13. **Gibeon.** About three miles north-west of Saul's Gibeah in Benjamin.

Joab. David's nephew, the chief of the famous three, Joab, Abishai, and Asahel.

side of the pool, and the other on the other side of the pool. 14. And Abner said to Joab, Let the young men now arise, and play before us. And Joab said, Let them arise. 15. Then there arose and went over by number twelve of Benjamin, which pertained to Ishbosheth the son of Saul, and twelve of the servants of David. 16. And they caught everyone his fellow by the head, and thrust his sword in his fellow's side; so they fell down together: wherefore that place was called Helkath hazzurim, which is in Gibeon. 17. And there was a very sore battle that day; and Abner was beaten, and the men of Israel, before the servants of David.

Asahel's rashness and consequent death—18. And there were three sons of Zeruiah there, Joab, and Abishai, and Asahel: and Asahel was as light of foot as a wild roe. 19. And Asahel pursued after Abner; and in going he turned not to the right hand nor to the left from following Abner. 20. Then Abner looked behind him, and said, Art thou Asahel? And he answered, I am. 21. And Abner said to him, Turn thee aside to thy right hand or to thy left, and lay thee hold on one of the young men, and take thee his armor. But Asahel would not turn aside from following of him. 22. And Abner said again to Asahel, Turn thee aside from following me: wherefore should I smite thee to the ground? how then should I hold up my face to Joab thy brother? 23. Howbeit he refused to turn aside: wherefore Abner with the hinder end of the spear smote him under the fifth rib, that the spear came out behind him; and he fell down there and died in the same place: and it came to pass, that as many as came to the place where Asahel fell down and died stood still.

Abner appeals to Joab to stop further bloodshed—24. But Joab and Abishai pursued after Abner: and the sun

14. The generals propose a tournament (*cf.* the Horatii of Roman legend). Such tournaments in olden days often proved the preliminary to a general engagement.

16. **Helkath-hazzurim.** The name means "Field of the Enemies," or else "of the Sword Edges."

20. **Abner,** conscious of his own superiority, counsels the young man to content his ambition with a lesser antagonist.

23. **with the hinder end.** Was it sharp enough? Better translation "with a backward stroke."

went down when they were come to the hill of Ammah, that lieth before Giah by the way of the wilderness of Gibeon. 25. And the children of Benjamin gathered themselves together after Abner, and became one troop, and stood on the top of an hill. 26. Then Abner called to Joab, and said, Shall the sword devour forever? knowest thou not that it will be bitterness in the latter end? how long shall it be then, ere thou bid the people return from following their brethren? 27. And Joab said, As God liveth, unless thou hadst spoken, surely then in the morning the people had gone up every one from following his brother. 28. So Joab blew a trumpet, and all the people stood still, and pursued after Israel no more, neither fought they anymore.

Result of the battle—29. And Abner and his men walked all that night through the plain, and passed over Jordan, and went through all Bithron, and they came to Mahanaim. 30. And Joab returned from following Abner: and when he had gathered an the people together, there lacked of David's servants nineteen men and Asahel. 31. But the servants of David had smitten of Benjamin, and of Abner's men, so that three hundred and threescore men died. 32. And they took up Asahel, and buried him in the sepulchre of his father, which was in Bethlehem. And Joab and his men went all night, and they came to Hebron at break of day.

General trend of the civil war—3:1. Now there was long war between the house of Saul and the house of David: but David waxed stronger and stronger, and the house of Saul waxed weaker and weaker.

ABNER'S QUARREL WITH THE PUPPET-KING: HIS MURDER

2 Samuel 3 : 6-39

Abner's presumption rebuked—6. And it came to pass, while there was war between the house of Saul and the

---

25. **an hlll.** Rather, "the hill of Ammah," where Joab was.

27. **in the morning,** *i.e.,* not until tomorrow morning: the pursuit would have continued all night.

29. **the plain.** The Arabah of which the Jordan Valley formed part (Appendix II.). **Bithron.** "The Ravine," leading up to Mahanaim.

house of David, that Abner made himself strong *in* the house of Saul.
7. And Saul had a concubine, whose name was Rizpah, the daughter
of Mah: and Ish-bosheth said to Abner, Wherefore hast thou taken
to thyself my father's concubine? 8. Then was Abner very wroth for
the words of Ish-bosheth, and said, Am I a dog's head, which against
Judah do shew kindness this day unto the house of Saul thy father,
to his brethren, and to his friends, and have not delivered thee
into the hand of David, that thou chargest me today with a fault
concerning *a* woman? 9. So do God to Abner, and more also,
if, as the LORD hath sworn to David, *I do not* even so *to* him; 1 0.
to translate the kingdom from the house of Saul, and to set up the
throne of David over Israel and over Judah, from Dan even to Beer-
sheba. 11. And he could not answer Abner a word again, because
he feared him.

Thereupon Abner makes overtures to David—12. And Abner sent
messengers to David, saying, Whose is the land? saying also, Make
thy league with me, and, behold, my hand shall be with thee, to
bring about all Israel unto thee. 13. And he said, well; I will
make a league with thee: but one thing I require of thee, that
is, Thou shalt not see my face, except thou first bring Michal
Saul's daughter, when thou comest to see my face. 14. And David sent
messengers to Ish-bosheth Saul's son, saying, Deliver me my wife
Michal, which I espoused to me. 15. And Ish-bosheth sent, and took her
from her husband, even from Phaltiel the son of Laish. 16. And
her husband went with her along weeping behind her to Bahurim. Then
said Abner unto him, Go, return. And he returned.

And persuades Ish-bosheth' s partisans to transfer their

6. Abner was the real master and presumed upon his position. To take the late king's
concubine was reasonably interpreted by Ish-bosheth, according to the ideas of the day,
as equivalent to claiming the succession and inheritance. Absalom (16:21) and Adonijah
(1 Kings 2:17) got into trouble on the same grounds.
    7. **Rizpah.** " The heroine of the tragedy" of chap. 1 1, below, p. 130.
    8. Abner affects to make light of the affair.
    12. **Whose . . . land?**—*i.e.,* "I am master here."
    16. **Bahurim.** In Benjamin, on the frontier of Judah.

allegiance to David—17. And Abner had communication with the elders of Israel, saying, Ye sought for David in times past to be king over you: 18. now then do it: for the LORD hath spoken of David, saying, By the hand of my servant David I will save my people Israel out of the hand of the Philistines, and out of the hand of all their enemies. 19. And Abner also spake in the ears of Benjamin: and Abner went also to speak in the ears of David in Hebron all that seemed good to Israel, and that seemed good to the whole house of Benjamin. 20. So Abner came to David to Hebron, and twenty men with him. And David made Abner and the men that were with him a feast. 21. And Abner said unto David, I will arise and go, and will gather all Israel unto my Lord the king, that they may make a league with thee, and that thou mayest reign over all that thine heart desireth. And David sent Ahner away; and he went in peace.

His assassination by Joab—22. And behold, the servants of David and Joab came from pursuing a troop, and brought in a great spoil with them: but Abner was not with David in Hebron; for he had sent him away, and he was gone in peace. 23. When Joab and all the host that was with him were come, they told Joab, saying, Abner the son of Ner came to the king, and he hath sent him away, and he is gone in peace. 24. Then Joab came to the king, and said, what hast thou done? behold, Abner came unto thee; why is it that thou hast sent hirn away, and he is quite gone? 25. Thou knowest Abner the son of Ner, that he came to deceive thee, and to know thy going out and thy coming in, and to know all that thou doest. 26. And when Joab was come out from David, he sent messengers after Abner, which brought him again from the well of Sirah: but David knew it not. 27. And when Abner was returned to Hebron, Joab took him aside in the gate to speak with him quietly, and smote him there under the fifth rib, that he died, for the blood of Asahel his brother.

David disowns and condemns the act—28. And afterward when David heard it, he said, I and my kingdom are guiltless before the LORD forever from the blood of Abner

26. **Sirah.** Three miles north of Hebron.

the son of Ner: 29. let it rest on the head of Joab, and on all his father's house; and let there not fail from the house of Joab one that hath disease or that is a leper, or that leaneth on a staff, or that falleth *by* the sword, or that lacketh bread.

His lament for Abner—31. And David said to Joab, and to all the people that were with him, Rend your clothes, and gird you with sackcloth, and mourn before Abner. And king David himself followed the bier. 32. And they buried Abner in Hebron: and the king lifted up his voice, and wept at the grave of Abner; and all the people wept. 33. And the king lamented over Abner, and said,

> *Must Abner die* as a fool dieth?
> Thy hands were not bound,
> Nor thy feet put into fetters:
> As a man falleth before wicked men, so fellest thou.

34. And all the people wept again over him. 35. And when all the people came to cause David to eat meat while it was yet day, David sware, saying, So do God to me, and more also, if I taste bread, or ought else, till the sun be down. 36. And all the people took notice of it, and it pleased them: as whatsoever the king did pleased all the people. 37. For all the people and all Israel understood that day that it was not of the king to slay Abner the son of Ner. 38. And the king said unto his servants, l(now ye not that there is a prince and a great man fallen this day in Israel? 39. And I am this day weak, though anointed king; and these men the sons of Zeruiah be too hard for me: the LORD shall reward... the doer of evil according to his wickcdness.

29. **leaneth on a staff**. Heb. "holdeth the pindle," like a woman, *i.e.,* is effeminate.

33. This is another unquestionable example of David's own compositions; *cf.* the Dirge above. Paraphrase: " Alas! that Abner had to die like a fool, who brings premature death on himself by his folly (Prov 7 : 22 *seq.);* not honorably, as a warrior deserved. Without one blow in self-defense! The shame of it! Had he been bound hand and foot, like a prisoner of war, the shame would have had excuse. He fell, helpless, under villainous treachery."

III-8

ASSASSINATION OF ISH-BOSHETH: END OF THE CIVIL WAR

2 Samuel 4

1. And when Saul's son heard that Abner was dead in Hebron, his hands were feeble, and all the Israelites were troubled. 2. And Saul's son had hvo men that were captains of bands: the name of the one was Baanah, and the name of the other Rechab, the sons of Rimmon a Beerothite, of the children of Benjamin: 5. and they went and came about the heat of the day to the house of Ish-bosheth, who lay on a bed at noon. 6. And they came thither into the midst of the house, as though they would have fetched wheat; and they smote him under the fifth rib: and Rechab and Baanah his brother escaped. 7. For when they came into the house, he lay on his bed in his bedchamber, and they smote him, and slew him, and beheaded him, and took his head, and gat them away through the plain all night. 8. And they brought the head of Ish-bosheth unto David to Hebron, and said to the king, Behold the head of Ish-bosheth the son of Saul thine enemy, which sought thy life; and the LORD hath avenged my Lord the king this day of Saul, and of his seed.

David executes the murderers—9. And David answered Rechab and Baanah his brother, the sons of Rimmon the Beerothite, and said unto them, As the LORD liveth, who hath redeemed my soul out of all adversity, 10. When one told me, saying, Behold, Saul is dead, thinking to have brought good tidings, I took hold of him, and slew him in Ziklag, who thought that I would have given him a reward for his tidings: 11. How much more, when wicked

2. **Beeroth,** nine miles north of Jerusalem. The motive to the murder was either (1) hope to ingratiate themselves with David by giving the *coup de grace* to an already lost cause; or (2) to take vengeance for Saul's ill-treatment of their kin. The Beerothites were really native Canaanites, members of the Gibeonite league, which Saul had persecuted (below, chap. 21).

It is to be regretted that our records preserve only such scant information of the history of these seven-and-a-half years as is contained in the foregoing chapters.

9. **who hath redeemed.** An early note, in this the oldest Biblical narrative, of that profound religious conviction which afterwards found such rich expression in the Psalms.

men have slain a righteous person in his own house upon his bed? Shall I not therefore now require his blood of your hand, and take you away from the earth? 12. And David commanded his young men, and they slew them, and cut off their hands and their feet, and hanged them up over the pool in Hebron. But they took the head of Ish-bosheth, and buried it in the sepulchre of Abner in Hebron.

B. DAVID KING OF ALL ISRAEL

I. FIRST PERIOD. CONSOLIDATION OF THE KINGDOM

His "CORONATION"

2 Samuel 5:1-5; 1 Chronicles 12:38-40

1. Then came all the tribes of Israel to David unto Hebron, and spake, saying, Behold, we are thy bone and thy flesh. 2. Also in time past, when Saul was king over us, thou wast he that leddest out and broughtest in Israel: and the LORD said to thee, Thou shalt feed my people Israel, and thou shalt be a captain over Israel. 3. So all the elders of Israel came to the king to Hebron; and king David made a league with them in Hebron before the LORD: and they anointed David king over Israel.

The same event idealized by the ecclesiastical chronicler of a later age—1 Chron. 12:38. And [many thousands] of warriors united by a single purpose, came to Hebron, to make David king over all Israel: and all the rest also of Israel were of one heart to make David king. 39. And there they were with David three days, eating and drinking: for their brethren had prepared for them. 40. Moreover they that were nigh them, even unto Issachar and Zebulun and Naphtali, brought bread on asses, and on camels, and on mules, and on oxen, and meat, meal, cakes of fig.3, and hunches of raisins, and wine, and oil, and oxen, and sheep abundantly: for there was joy in Israel.

2 Sam. 5:4. David was thirty years old when he began to reign, and he reigned forty years. 5. In Hebron he reigned over Judah seven years and six months: and in

Jerusalem he reigned thirty and three years over all Israel and Judah.

SUBJUGATION OF THE PHILISTINES: END OF THE WAR OF INDEPENDENCE

2 Samuel 5 : 17-25, 8 : 1, 2 1 : 15-22, 2 3 : 9-17

5:17. Now when the Philistines heard that they had anointed   David king over Israel, all the Philistines went up to seek David;   and David heard of it, and   went down to the hold.

Devotion of three nameless heroes to their king—23:13. And three of the thirty chiefs went down, and came to David in the harvest time unto the *hold* of Adullam: and the troop of the Philistines pitched in the valley of Rephaim. 14.   And   David   was   then in an hold, and   the   garrison   of the Philistines was then in Bethlehem. 15. And David longed, and   said, Oh, that one would give me *to* drink of the water of the   well of Bethlehem, which is by the gate! 1 6.   And the three mighty men brake through the host of the Philistines, and drew water out of the well of Bethlehem, that was by the gate, and took it and brought it to David: nevertheless, he would not drink thereof, but poured it out unto the LORD.   17.   And he said, Be it far from me, O LORD, that I should do this: is not this the blood of the men that went in jeopardy of their lives? therefore   he would not drink it.

17. On succeeding to the undivided throne, David realised that, in order to retain the allegiance of his subjects, his first indispensable duty was to throw off the Philistine over-lordship to which he had bowed throughout his career at Hebron. In this object he was eventually successful. This was "undoubtedly the greatest achievement of his   reign." Unfortunately, our texts supply only meager details of these events, which must have lasted long and yet must have preceded the capture of Jerusalem and the organization of the kingdom. W e possess only a disordered reference or two to the campaigns and some traditional legends of individual exploits. These are here collected and printed together.

the hold, *i.e.,* to Adullam, formerly his fortress against Saul.

23:13. **the thirty.** See note below, p. 1 4 0 .

Rephaim. Just north-west of Bethlehem which is ten miles from Adullam.

1 4. garrison. Heb.= " Resident," or "Governor."

First victory at Rephaim—5:18. Now the Philistines had come and spread themselves in the valley of Rephaim. 19. And David enquired of the LORD, saying, Shall I go up to the Philistines? wilt thou deliver them into mine hand? And the LORD said unto David, Go up: for I will doubtless deliver the Philistines into thine hand. 20. And David came to Baal-perazim, and David smote them there, and said, The LORD hath broken forth upon mine enemies before me, as the breach of waters. Therefore he called the name of that place Baal-perazim. 21. And there they left their images, and David and his men *took them away.*

Second victory at Rephaim—22. And the Philistines came up yet again, and spread themselves in the valley of Rephaim. 23. And when David enquired of the LORD, he said, Thou shalt not go up; but fetch a compass behind them, and come upon them over against the mulberry trees. 24. And let it be, when thou hearest the sound of a going in the tops of the mulberry trees, that then thou shalt bestir thyself: for then shall the LORD go out before thee, to smite the host of the Philistines. 25. And David did so, as the LORD had commanded him; and smote the Philistines from Geba until thou come to Gazer.

Anecdotes of Various Heroes—21:15. Moreover the Philistines had yet war again with Israel; and David went down, and his servants with him, and fought against the Philistines: and David waxed faint. 16. And Ishbibenob, which was of the sons of the giant, the weight of whose spear weighed three hundred shekels of brass in weight, he being girded with a new sword, thought to have

20. **Baal-perazim** = "Lord of breaches."

21. **images,** *i.e.,* their idols, which they had brought down to the battle to fight for them.

23. **fetch a compass**, means "make a detour," as in Acts. 28:13 (A.V.)..

24. For the omen, see above, p. 2 r *n.*

25. **Geba.** One of the many places of that name, obviously near Bethlehem and the valley of Rephaim. **Gazer** (Gezer) is twenty miles north-west of Bethlehem, towards Joppa; a hill town famous in the history of warfare in Palestine (see *H.G.H.L.,* p. 215 *seq.),* "a remarkable bastion which the Shephelah flings out to the west—the most prominent object in view of the traveller from Jaffa towards Jerusalem."

21:16. **of the giant**. Rather, "of the giants."

slain David. 17. But Abishai the son of Zeruiah succored him, and smote the Philistine, and killed him. Then the men of David sware unto him, saying; Thou shalt go no more out with us to battle, that thou quench not the light of Israel. 18. And it came to pass after this, that there was again a battle with the Philistines at Gob: then Sibbechai the Hushathite slew Saph, which was of the sons of the giant. 19. And there was again a battle in Gob with the Philistines, where Elhanan the son of Jaareoregim, a Bethlehemite, slew Goliath the Gittite, the staff of whose spear was like a weaver's beam. 20. And there was yet a battle in Gath, where was a man of great stature, that had on every hand six fingers, and on every foot six toes, four and twenty in number; and he also was born to the giant. 21. And when he defied Israel, Jonathan the son of Shimeah the brother of David slew him. 22. These four were born to the giant in Gath, and fell by the hand of David, and by the hand of his servants.

23:9. And *there* was Eleazar the son of Dodo the Ahohite, one of the three mighty men with David, when they defied the Philistines that were there gathered together to battle, and the men of Israel were gone away: 10. He arose, and smote the Philistines until his hand was weary, and his hand clave unto the sword: and the LORD wrought a great victory that day; and the people returned after him only to spoil. 11. And *there* was Shammah the son of Agee the Hararite. And the Philistines were gathered together into a troop, where was a piece of ground full of lentiles: and the people fled from the Philistines. 12. But he stood in the midst of the ground, and defended it, and slew the Philistines: and the LORD wrought a great victory.

The summary: Complete overthrow of the Philistine power—8:1. And after this it came to pass, that David smote the Philistines, and subdued them: and

19. Elhanan. See 1 Sam. 17:4 *n.,* p. 58. Yet a possible solution of the difficulty there discussed is that there were two Goliaths, father and son: David slew the father, and Elhanam the son.

8:1. **the bridle,** *i.e.,* the possession of the Philistine capital, Gath; but the text is corrupt and the meaning, therefore, quite uncertain.

David took *the bridle of the mother city* out of the hand of the Philistines.

JERUSALEM CAPTURED AND ESTABLISHED AS THE CAPITAL

2 Samuel 5 : 6-12

6. And the king and his men went *to* Jerusalem unto the Jebusites, the inhabitants of the land: which spake unto David, saying, thou shalt not come in hither, *but the blind and the lame shall turn thee away:* thinking, David cannot come in hither. 7. Nevertheless David took the strong hold of Zion (the same is the city of David). 8. And David said on that day, whosoever *smiteth the Jebusites, let him get up through the watercourse and smite* the lame and the blind, that are hated of David's soul. wherefore they said, The blind and the lame shall not come into the house. 9. So David dwelt in the fort, and called it the city of David. And David built round about from Millo and inward. 10. And David went on, and grew great, and the LORD God of hosts was with him.

6. The capture of Jerusalem has a threefold importance. (1) The last remnant of independent Canaanite and Amorite power is overthrown. (2) An almost impregnable and central capital is acquired. (3) A center for worship is established. This capture "opened what later proved to be one of the most important chapters in the religious history of mankind" (Kent).

Jebusites were a clan of the Amorites, pre-Israelite natives, who had occupied this fortress. From them the Biblical writers sometimes call Jerusalem Jebus. Jebus, however, was not the ancient name of Jerusalem. The city was called Jerusalem from earliest times, as is proved by the Tel-el-Amarna tablets, letters written from Babylonia and Palestine to the kings of Egypt, Amenhotep III and IV, *c.* 1400 B.C.

7. **Zion** was the eastern of the two hills of Jerusalem, not the hill at the south-west corner of the modern city, as was formerly supposed. Subsequently Zion became the favorite name for the whole city. It is not known whether *the watercourse* alludes to the Virgin's Fount, which was not far from the south end of the fortress of Zion, or to an open sewer in that vicinity, or to something which we cannot identify.

8. **Wherefore,** etc., is a late note connecting with this incident the subsequent law forbidding the lame and blind to enter the Temple (Lev. 10, 11 : 18).

The Chronicler states that Joab accepted this challenge, with success (1 Chron. 11:6).

9. **Millo,** an unidentified part of the hill which David now fortified.

11. And Hiram king of Tyre sent messengers to David, and cedar trees, and carpenters, and masons: and they built David an house. 12. And David perceived that the LORD had established him king over Israel, and that he had exalted his kingdom for his people Israel's sake.

TRANSFERENCE OF THE ARK TO THE NEW CAPITAL

2 Samuel 6

1. Again, David gathered together all the chosen men of Israel, thirty thousand. 2. And David arose, and went with all the people that were with him *to* Baale of Judah, to bring up from thence the ark of God, whose name is called by the name of the. LORD of hosts that dwelleth between the cherubims. 3. And they set the ark of God upon a new cart, and brought it out of the house of Abinadab that was *on the hill,* and Uzzah and Ahio, the sons of Abinadab, drave the new cart. 4. And they brought it out of the house of Abinadab which was *on the hill, with* the ark of God: and Ahio went before the ark. 5. And David and all the house of Israel played before the LORD on all manner of instruments made of fir wood, even on harps, and on psalteries, and on timbrels, and on cornets, and on cymbals.

An untoward incident—6. And when they came to Nachon's threshing floor, Uzzah put forth his hand to the ark of God and took hold of

11. **Hiram.** Probably a mistake for Abi-baal, Hiram's father. For Hiram only came to his throne, at the earliest computation, at the *end* of David's reign.

1. **Baale.** Identified in I Chron. 13:6 with Kirjath-jearim, where we last heard of the Ark (1 Sam. 7:1).

2. **cherubims.** This phrase has been added by a later hand, by one who knew the idealized representation of the Ark drawn by the Priestly writers. On the top of this idealized Ark, we are told, there was a slab of gold called the Mercy-seat, upon which stood the cherubim-creatures with outstretched wings symbolizing the strength. and swiftness of the Divine Power. Their mystic shape is described in Ezek. 1:5 *seq.; cf. 22:11.* 11 below, and Victor Hugo, *The Toilers of the Sea,* Book iii. Chap. 1: "Something terrible. It is the wind. The wind; or rather, that populace of Titans which we call the gale. The unseen multitude. India knew them as the Maroubs, Judea as the Cherubims, Greece as the Aquilones. They are the invisible winged creatures of the Infinite. Their blasts sweep over the earth."

5. **timbrels** were the same as tabrets, small hand-drum.

it; for the oxen *stumbled.* 7. And the anger of the LORD was kindled against Uzzah; and God smote him there for his error; and there he died by the ark of God.   8. And David was displeased, because the LORD had made a breach upon Uzzah: and he called the name of the place Perez-uzzah to this day. 9. And David was afraid of the LORD that day, and said, How shall the ark of the LORD come to me? 10. So David would not remove the ark of the LORD unto him into the city of David: but David carried it aside into the house of Obed-edom the Gittite.   11. And the ark of the LORD continued in the house of Obed-edom the Gittite three months: and the LORD blessed Obed-edom, and all his household.

The Ark welcomed to the city of David—12. And it was told king David, saying, The LORD hath blessed the house of Obed-edom and all that pertaineth unto him, because of the ark of God. So David went and brought up the ark of God from the house of Obed-edom into the city of David with gladness. 13. And it was so, that when they that bare the ark of the LORD had gone six paces, he sacrificed oxen and fatlings.   14. And David danced. before the LORD with all his might; and David was girded with a linen ephod.   15. So David and all the house of Israel brought up the ark of the LORD with shouting, and with

8. **made a breach**= "broken forth upon." **Perez-uzzah**="breach of Uzzah." In his attempt to save the Ark from falling Uzzah probably stumbled and was run over and killed. But the Ark was so sacred-only to be touched by the ceremonially "sanctified"– that the pious historian, and his contemporaries perhaps too, regarded his accident as a "judgment" on him for daring to lay hand on it.   His intentions were excellent; but the act was sacrilege.   Many, perhaps most, persons would pass a similar verdict on a man who met his death in rifling a church. It would be regarded as a judgment on him.   Uzzah's act was of this kind, though prompted by a superior motive. The value of the story lies in the light it throws on the deep-seated religious scruples of the time, and on the reverence with which the Ark was very properly regarded.

11. **the Gittite.** He must have been an alien (p. 1 0 1 *n.)* resident somewhere near Jerusalem.

14. David, ever an impulsive nature, did not stop to consider whether his hilarious dancing suited the dignity of a king at such a moment.

the sound of the trumpet. 16. And as the ark of the LORD came into the city of David, Michal Saul's daughter looked through a window, and saw king David leaping and dancing before the LORD; and she despised him in her heart.

David's largesse to the populace—17. And they brought in the ark of the LORD, and set it in its place, in the midst of the tabernacle that David had pitched for it: and David offered burnt offerings and peace offerings before the LORD. 18. And as soon as David had made an end of offering burnt offerings and peace offerings, he blessed the people in the name of the LORD of hosts. 19. And he dealt anlong all the people, even among the whole multitude of Israel, as well to the women as men, to everyone a cake of bread, and a good piece of flesh, and a flagon of wine. So all the people departed every one to his house.

Michal's sarcasm—20. Then David returned to bless his household. And Michal the daughter of saul came out to meet David, and said, How glorious was the king of Israel to day, who uncovered himself today in the eyes of the handmaids of his servants, as one of the vain fellows shamelessly uncovereth himself! 21. And David said unto Michal, It was before the LORD, which chose me before thy father, and before all his house, to appoint me ruler over the people of the LORD, over Israel: therefore will I play before the LORD. 22. And I will yet be more vile than thus, and will be base in mine own sight: and of the maidservants which thou hast spoken of, of them shall I be had in honor. 23. Therefore Michal the daughter of Saul had no child unto the day of her death.

GOD PROMISES THE PERMANENCE OF DAVID'S DYNASTY

2 Samuel 7

David's anxiety to build a temple—1. And it came to pass when the king sat in his house, and the LORD had given him rest round about from all his enemies; 2. that

---

18. **he blessed the people.** A royal prerogative afterwards transferred exclusively to the priests, p. 28, above. The Chronicler (1 Chron. 13) gives a *resume* of this chapter with characteristic enlargements.

the king said unto Nathan the prophet, See now, I dwell in an house of cedar, but the ark of God dwelleth within curtains. 3. And Nathan said *to* the king, Go, do all that is in thine heart; for the LORD is with thee.

His plan disapproved by God—4. And it came to pass that night, that the word of the LORD came unto Nathan, saying, 5. Go and tell my servant David, Thus said the LORD, Shalt thou build me an house for me *to* dwell in? 6. Whereas I have not dwelt in any house since the time that I brought up the children of Israel out of Egypt, even *to* this day, but have walked in a tent and in a tabernacle. 7. In all the places wherein I have walked with all the children of Israel spake I a word with any of the tribes of Israel, whom I commanded *to* feed my people Israel, saying, Why build ye not me an house of cedar?

God's mercy in the past—8. Now therefore so shalt thou say unto my servant David, thus saith the LORD of hosts, I took thee from the sheepcote, from following the sheep, to *be* ruler over my people, over Israel: 9. And I was with thee whithersoever thou wentest, and have cut off thine enemies out of thy sight, and have made thee a great name, like unto the name of the great men that arc in the earth.

His promise for the future—10. Moreover I will appoint a place for my people Israel, and will plant them, that they may dwell in a place of their own, and move no more; neither shall the children of wickedness afflict them any more, as beforetime, 11. *even* since the time that I commanded judges *to* be over my people Israel. *And I will cause* thee *to* rest from all thine enemies.

And assurance of the succession to David's family—Also the LORD telleth thee that he will make thee an house. And when thy days be fulfilled, and thou shalt sleep with thy fathers, I will set up thy seed after thee, which shall proceed out of thy bowels, and I will establish his kingdom. 14. I will be his father, and he shall be my

6. The temporary "temple" of 1 Sam. 1 : 9 is not reckoned as a temple strictly.

11. **house,** *i.e.,* family. "God will securely establish thy dynasty."

This whole chapter is "fundamentally important for the study of the growth of the Messianic hope in Israel" (Kenn.). Psalms 132 and 8 9 should be read in connection with these passages.

son. If he commit iniquity, I will chasten him with the rod of men, and with the stripes of the children of men: 15. But my mercy shall not depart away from him, as I took it from Saul, whom I put away before thee. 16. And thine house and thy kingdom shall be established for ever before thee: thy throne shall be established forever.

17. According to all these words, and according to all this vision, so did Nathan speak unto David.

David's prayer of thanksgiving—18. Then went king David in, and sat before the LORD, and he said, Who am I, O Lord God? and what is my house, that thou hast brought me hitherto? 19. And this was yet a small thing in thy sight, O Lord God; but thou hast spoken also of thy servant's house for a great while to come, and hast shewn me the generations of men for evermore. 20. And what can David say more unto thee? for thou, Lord God, knowest thy servant. 21. For thy word's sake, and according to thine own heart, hast thou done all these great things, to make thy servant know them. 22. Wherefore art thou great, O LORD GOD: for there is none like thee, neither is there any God beside thee, according to all that we have heard with our ears.

What nation has a God such as Jehovah is to Israel?—23. And what one nation in the earth is like thy people, even like Israel, whom a god went to redeem for a people to himself, and to make him a name, and to do for them great things and terrible, in driving a people and its god before his people? 24. For thou hast confirmed to thyself thy people Israel to be a people unto thee forever: and thou, LORD, art become their God. 25. And now, O LORD God, the word that thou hast spoken concerning thy servant, and concerning his house, establish it forever, and do as thou hast said. 26. And let thy name be magnified forever, saying, The LORD of hosts is the God over Israel: and let the house of thy servant David be established before thee. 27. For thou, O LORD of hosts, God of Israel, hast revealed to thy servant, saying,

18. **sat**. Probably upon his heels; in the tabernacle before the Ark.
23. The antecedent of "whom" is "nation," not Israel.

I will build the an house: therefore hath thy servant found in his heart to pray this prayer unto thee. 28. And now, O Lord GOD, thou art God, and thy words be true, and thou hast promised this goodness unto thy servant: 29. therefore now let it please thee to bless the house of thy servant, that it may continue for ever before thee: for thou, O Lord GOD, hast spoken it: and with thy blessing let the house of thy servant be blessed forever.

DAVID'S PSALM OF THANKSGIVING

2 Samuel 22

1. And David spake unto the LORD the words **of** this song in the day that the LORD had delivered him out of the hand of all his enemies, and out of the hand of Saul:
Prelude—2. And he said,
The LORD is my rock, and my fortress, and my deliverer;
3. The God of my rock; in him will I trust: he is my shield, and the horn of my salvation, my high *tower,* and my refuge, my savior; thou savest me from violence.
4. I will call on the LORD, who is worthy to be praised: so shall I be saved from mine enemies.

Jehovah has been my Savior—5. When the waves of death compassed me, the floods of ungodly men made me afraid; 6. The sorrows of hell compassed me about; the snares of death prevented me; 7. In my distress I called upon the LORD and cried to my God: and he did hear my voice out of his temple, and my cry did enter into his ears.

2 7. **build thee an house.** As in verse 11.

22:1. This Song of Triumph, which was thought worthy of inclusion in the collections of Psalms, where it stands as Ps. 18, is found in the Appendix to the Books of Samuel (2 Sam. 2 1 - 2 4). That it comes from David's own pen is maintained by perhaps the majority of critics. The preamble (verse 1) suggests that this is the appropriate place to introduce the song. David's troubles with Saul and Philistia were over, his career assured. The accompanying notes are based on Kirkpatrick's commentary on Ps. 1 8 .

5. **floods** = "torrents of ungodliness": a forcible metaphor.

6. **prevented** = "went before"; so "confronted me," "encountered me."

"Nature, in awe to Him" signalled His advent as the Fighter of my battles—8. Then the earth shook and trembled; the foundations of heaven moved and shook, because he was wroth.

9. There went up a smoke out of his nostrils, and fire out of his mouth devoured: coals were kindled by it.

10. He bowed the heavens also and came down; and darkness was under his feet.

11. And he rode upon a cherub and did fly: and he was seen upon the wings of the wind.

12. And he made darkness pavilions round about him, dark waters, and thick clouds of the skies.

13. Through the brightness before him were coals of fire kindled.

14. The LORD thundered from heaven, and the most High uttered his voice.

15. And he sent out arrows, and scattered them; lightning, and discomfited them.

16. And the channels of the sea appeared, the foundations of the world were discovered, at the rebuking of the LORD, at the blast of the breath of his nostrils.

And as my deliverer from Saul—17. He sent from above, he took me; he drew me out of many waters;

18. He delivered me from my strong enemy, and from them that hated me: for they were too strong for me.

19. They prevented me in the day of my calamity but the LORD was my stay.

20. He brought me forth also into a large place: he delivered me, because he delighted in me.

For I had a "princely heart of innocence."—21. The LORD rewarded me according to my righteousness: according to the cleanness of my hands hath he recompensed me.

22. For I have kept the ways of the LORD and have not wickedly departed from my God.

23. For all his judgments were before me: and as for his statutes, I did not depart from them.

8 ff. The usual poetic imagery expressing the terrible power of God. The details of the metaphors must not be pressed.

11. **cherub.** See above, p. 120 *n.*

12. **pavilions,** *i.e.,* tents, to shroud His majesty.

20. **large place** = freedom and safety.

24. I was also upright before him and have kept myself from mine iniquity.

25. Therefore the LORD hath recompensed me according to my righteousness; according to my cleanness in his eye sight.

God's methods of moral government—26. With the merciful thou wilt shew thyself merciful, and with the upright man thou wilt shew thyself upright.

27. With the pure thou wilt show thyself pure; and with the froward thou wilt shew thyself unsavoury.

28. And the afflicted people thou wilt save: but thine eyes are upon the haughty, that thou mayest bring them down.

David's own experience—29. For thou art my lamp, O LORD: and the LORD will lighten my darkness.

30. For by thee I have run through a troop: by my God have I leaped over a wall.

31. As for God, his way is perfect; the word of the LORD is tried: he is a buckler to all them that trust in him.

32. For who is God, save the LORD? and who is a rock, save our God?

33. God is my strength and power: and he maketh my way perfect.

34. He maketh my feet like hinds' feet: and setteth me upon my high places.

35. He teacheth my hands to war; so that a bow of steel is broken by mine arms.

36. Thou hast also given me the shield of thy salvation: and thy gentleness hath made me great.

37. Thou hast enlarged my steps under me; so that my feet did not slip.

38. I have pursued mine enemies and destroyed them; and turned not again until I had consumed them.

---

26. **thou,** i.e., God. "His attitude towards them is conditioned by their attitude towards Him" (Kirkpatrick).

27. **unsavory.** Rather, "froward," " perverse."

30. "I have been successful both in pursuit and siege-work."

37. **enlarged my steps**, i.e., " given me free space and power to move."

39. And I have consumed them, and wounded them, that they could not arise: yea, they are fallen under my feet.

40. For thou hast girded me with strength to battle: them that rose up against me hast thou subdued under me.

41. Thou hast also given me the necks of mine enemies, that I might destroy them that hate me.

42. They looked, but there was none to save; even unto the LORD, but he answered them not.

43. Then did I beat them as small as the dust of the earth, I did stamp them as the mire of the street and did spread them abroad.

My dominion has been established by Thee—44. Thou also hast delivered me from the strivings of my people, thou hast kept me to be head of the heathen: a people which I knew not *did* serve me.

45. Strangers shall submit themselves unto me: as soon as they hear, they shall be obedient unto me.

46. Strangers shall fade away, and they shall be afraid out of their close places.

Doxology—47. The LORD liveth; and blessed be my rock; and exalted be the God of the rock of my salvation.

48. It is God that avengeth me, and that bringeth down the people under me,

49. And that bringeth me forth from mine enemies: thou also hast lifted me up on high above them that rose up against me: thou hast delivered me from the violent man.

50. Therefore I will give thanks unto thee, O LORD, among the heathen, and I will sing praises unto thy name.

51. He is the tower of salvation for his king: and showeth mercy to his anointed, unto David, and to his seed for evermore.

44. **heathen** simply = "other nations."

45. **shall**. Read *did* and *were* throughout these two verses: the reference is to past events.

46. **close places** = strongholds.

THE FORTUNES OF SAUL'S HOUSE

(a) Public Execution of his Sons; (b) Royal Provision for Jonathan's Son

2 Samuel 21:1-14, 4:4, 9

(a) Saul's sons are delivered up to the Gibeonites to be hanged—21:1. Then there was a famine in the days of David three years, year after year; and David enquired of the LORD. And the LORD answered, It is for Saul, and for his bloody house, because he slew the Gibeonites. *2.* And the king called the Gibeonites and said unto them; (now the Gibeonites were not of the children of Israel, but of the remnant of the Amorites; and the children of Israel had sworn unto them: and Saul sought *to* slay them in his zeal *to* the children of Israel and Judah.) 3. Wherefore David said unto the Gibeonites, What shall I do for you? and wherewith shall I make the atonement, that ye may bless the inheritance of the LORD? 4. And the Gibeonites said unto him, We will have no silver nor gold of Saul, nor of his house; neither *is it for us to put any man to death* in Israel. And he said, What ye shall say, that will I do for you. 5. And they answered the king, The man that consumed us, and that devised against us that we should be destroyed from remaining in any of the coasts of Israel, 6. let seven men of his sons be delivered unto us, and we shall hang them up unto the LORD in Gibeah of Saul, whom the LORD did choose. And the king said, I will give them. 8. *And* the king took

1. "Few sections of the O.T. show more clearly the religious ideas of the time. We see how Yahweh, as the avenger of a broken covenant, requires from the children of the offender the blood that has been shed" (Smith, 374).

2. The circumstances under which they had contrived to exact from Joshua this covenant which Saul had broken are described in Josh. 9.

4. *(a)* They will not accept blood-money—the *weregeld* of mediaeval history—as a satisfaction; (b) it was not in *their* power to condemn the guilty to death by law; therefore they hint (c) that David, as supreme justician, should do so. Modern sensibilities must not be shocked that their bloodthirsty petition was granted by " an antique king in a barbarous age."

the two sons of Rizpah the daughter of Aiah, whom she bare unto Saul, Armoni and Mephibosheth; and the five sons of *Merab* the daughter of Saul, whom she brought up for Adriel the son of Barzillai the Meholathite: 9. and he delivered them into the hands of the Gibeonites, and they hanged them in the hill before the LORD: and they fell all seven together, and were put to death in the days of harvest, in the first days, in the beginning of barley harvest.

A mother's devotion to her dead—10. And Rizpah the daughter of Aiah took sackcloth, and spread it for her upon the rock, from the beginning of harvest until water dropped upon them out of heaven, and suffered neither the birds of the air to rest on them by day, nor the beasts of the field by night. 11. And it was told David what Rizpah the daughter of Mah, the concubine of Saul, had done.
12. And David went and took the bones of Saul and the bones of Jonathan his son from the men of Jabesh gilead, which had stolen them from the street of Beth shan, where the Philistines had hanged them, when the Philistines had slain Saul in Gilboa: 13. and he brought up from thence the bones of Saul and the bones of Jonathan his son; and they gathered the bones of them that were hanged. 14. And the bones of Saul and Jonathan his son buried they in the country of Benjamin in Zelah, in the sepulchre of Kish his father: and they performed all that the king commanded. And after that God was intreated for the land.

(b) Mephibosheth: his lameness—4:4. Now Jonathan, Saul's son, had a son that was lame of his feet. He was five years old when tidings came of Saul and Jonathan out of Jezreel, and his nurse took him up, and fled: and it came to pass, as she made haste to flee, that he fell, and became lame. And his name was Mephibosheth.

10. **until water dropped** probably means that she watched them for six months, from April until the autumn rains of October. She would not leave them until pity induced the monarch to bury them. The scene has been painted by Briton Riviere.

12. p. 99, above.

14. **Zelah.** The locality of the family tomb is unknown. **was intreated,** *i.e.,* God accepted the offering and was appeased.

4:4. **Mephibosheth.** His original name was Merib-baal: for the change see p. 24, note to Baalim.

David seeks him out—9:1. And David said, Is there yet any that is left of the house of Saul, that I may shew him kindness for Jonathan's sake? 2. And there was in the house of Saul a servant whose name was Ziba. And when they had called him unto David, the king said unto him, Art thou Ziba? And he said, Thy servant is he. And the king said, Is there not yet any of the house of Saul, that I may shew the kindness of God unto him? And Ziba said unto the king, Jonathan hath yet a son, which is lame on his feet. 4. And the king said unto him, where is he? And Ziba said unto the king, Behold, he is in the house of Machir, the son of Ammiel, in Lo-debar.

And welcomes him kindly—5. Then king David sent, and fetched him out of the house of Machir, the son of Ammiel, from Lo-debar. 6. Now when Mephibosheth, the son of Jonathan, the son of Saul, was come unto David, he fell on his face, and did reverence. And David said, Mephibosheth. And he answered, Behold thy servant! And David said unto him, Fear not: for I will surely shew thee kindness for Jonathan thy father's sake, and will restore thee all the land of Saul thy father; and thou shalt eat bread at my table continually. 8. And he bowed himself, and said, what is thy servant, that thou shouldest look upon such a dead dog as I am?

His lands and royal status are restored to him—9. Then the king called *to* Ziba, Saul's servant, and said unto him, I have given unto thy master's son all that pertained to Saul and to all his house. 10. Thou therefore, and thy sons, and thy servants, shall till the land for him, and thou shalt bring in the fruits, that thy master's son may have food *to* eat: butMephibosheth thy master's son shall eat bread always at my table. Now Ziba had fifteen sons and twenty servants. 11. Then said Ziba unto the king, According to all that my Lord the king hath commanded his servant, so shall thy servant do. As for Mephibosheth, said the king, he shall eat at my table, as one of the king's sons. 12. And all that dwelt in the house of Ziba were servants unto Mephibosheth. 13. So Mephibosheth dwelt in Jerusalem: for he did eat continually at the king's table; and was lame on both his feet.

4. **Lo-debar**. Beyond Jordan, near Mahanaim.

THE CENSUS: AND THE CONSECRATION
OF THE SITE OF THE FUTURE TEMPLE

2 Samuel 24

The king orders the people to be numbered—1. And again the anger of the LORD was kindled against Israel, and he moved David against them to say, Go, number Israel and Judah. 2. For the king said to Joab the captain of the host, which was with him, Go now through all the tribes of Israel, from Dan even *to* Beer-sheba, and number ye the people, that I may know the number of the people. 3. And Joab said unto the king, Now the LORD thy God add unto the people, how many soever they be, an hundred-fold, and may the eyes of my Lord the king see it: but why doth my Lord the king delight in this thing? 4. Notwithstanding the king's word prevailed against Joab, and against the captains of the host. And Joab and the captains of the host went out from the presence of the king, to number the people of Israel.

8. So when they had gone through all the land, they came to Jerusalem at the end of nine months and twenty clays. 9. And Joab gave up the sum of the number of the people unto the king: and there were in Israel eight hundred thousand valiant men that drew the sword; and the men of Judah were five hundred thousand men.

His conscience smites him—10. And David's heart smote

1. This chapter has been well described as "the charter of the most famous of the world's holy places." It recounts the consecration of the spot where soon stood the altar of Solomon's Temple and today stands the great Mosque which is one of the most sacred of Mohammedan shrines (Kenn.).

The Lord moved David to an undertaking which He intended to punish heavily. The later Chronicler (1 Chron. 21 : 1) will not allow this. He says *Satan* moved David. Mark the progress in the conception of God as between the two authors. why the taking of a census should have been accounted offensive to the Deity we do not know. Perhaps it denoted in the monarch a reprehensible pride in the extent of his dominions, like that of the miser gloating over his guineas. Perhaps it was intended as the preliminary to some unpopular social measure—an income tax or a more onerous form of conscription. The incident, which is related without any note as to the date in the Appendix to *Samuel* (2 Sam. 21 - 24), is referred by scholars to these early years of David's reign, with some reason.

him after that he had numbered the people. And David said unto the LORD, I have sinned greatly in that I have done: and now, I beseech thee, O LORD, take away the iniquity of thy servant; for I have done very foolishly. 11. For when David was up in the morning, the word of the LORD came unto the prophet Gad, David's seer, saying, 12. Go and say unto David, Thus saith the LORD, I offer thee three things; choose thee one of them, that I may do it unto thee. 13. So Gad came to David, and told him, and said unto him, Shall seven years of famine come unto thee in thy land? or wilt thou flee three months before thine enemies, while they pursue thee? or that there be three days' pestilence in thy land? now advise, and see what answer I shall return to him that sent me. 14. And David said unto Gad, I am in a great strait: let us fall now into the hand of the LORD; for his mercies are great: and let me not fall into the hand of man.

The pestilence—15. So the LORD sent a pestilence upon Israel from the morning even to the time appointed: and there died of the people from Dan even to Beer-sheba seventy thousand men. 16. And when the angel stretched out his hand upon Jerusalem to destroy it, the LORD repented him of the evil, and said to the angel that destroyed the people, It is enough: stay now thine hand. And the angel of the LORD was by the threshing-place of Araunah the Jebusite. 17. And David spake unto the LORD when he saw the angel that smote the people, and said, Lo, I have sinned, and I have done wickedly: but these sheep, what have they done? let thine hand, I pray thee, be against me, and against my father's house.

An altar built on the propitious site—18. And Gad came that day to David, and said unto him, Go up, rear an altar, unto the LORD in the threshing-floor of Araunah the Jebusite. 19. And David, according to the saying of Gad, went up as the LORD commanded. 20. And Araunah looked and saw the king and his servants coming on toward him: and Araunah went out, and bowed himself before the king on his face upon the ground. 21. And Araunah said, Wherefore is my Lord the king come to his servant? And David said, To buy the threshing-floor of thee, to build an altar unto the LORD, that the plague may be stayed from the people. 22. And Araunah said unto David, Let my Lord the king take and offer up what seemeth good unto him: behold, here be oxen for burnt sacrifice, and threshing instruments and other instruments of the oxen for wood. 23. All these things *doth the servant of my Lord the king* give unto the king. And Araunah said unto the king, The LORD thy God accept thee. 24. And the king said unto Araunah, Nay; but I will surely buy it of thee at a price: neither will I offer burnt offerings unto the LORD my God of that which doth cost me nothing. So David bought *the* threshing-floor and the oxen for fifty shekels of silver. 25. And David built there an altar unto the LORD and offered burnt offerings and peace offerings. So, the LORD was intreated for the land, and the plague was stayed from Israel.

EXTENSION OF THE EMPIRE: THE WARS OF CONQUEST

2 Samuel 8 : 2-14, 1 0 , 11 : 1, 1 2 : 26-31

Moab—8:2. And he smote Moab, and measured them with a line, casting them down to the ground; even with two lines measured he to put to death, and one full line to keep alive. And *so* the Moabites became David's servants, and brought gifts.

Ammon: cause of the war—10:1. And it came to pass after this, that the king of the children of Ammon died, and Hanun his son reigned in his stead. 2. Then said David, I will shew kindness unto Hanun the son of Nahash,

22. with Araunah's professions of readiness to give his property gratis *cf.* the scene between Abraham and Ephron over the cave of Machpelah (Gen. 2 3).

24. fifty shekels = about £7.

25. In the parallel version of the ecclesiastical Chronicler David proceeds to make vast preparations for the erection of the Temple on this site (1 Chron. 2 2).

8:2. Relations with Moab had changed since David's exile days (1 Sam. 2 2); why, we are not told. He put to death two rows out of every three.

gifts is the usual euphemism for "tribute." Two-thirds of the male population were put to the ban, *i.e.,* devoted to death, a severity which was deemed one of the religious duties of the age. *Cf.* Saul's slaughter of Amalek above, pp. 52, 55 *n.*

10:1. For the former international relations with Ammon refer back top. 37.

as his father shewed kindness unto me. And David sent to comfort him by the hand of his servants for his father. And David's servants came into the land of the children of Ammon. *3:* And the princes of the children of Ammon said unto Hanun their Lord, thinkest thou that David doth honour thy father, that he hath sent comforters unto thee? hath not David rather sent his servants unto thee, to search the city, and to spy it out, and *to* overthrow it?   4. Wherefore Hanun took David's servants, and shaved off the one half of their beards, and cut off their garments in the middle, even to their hips, and sent them away. 5. when they told it unto David, he sent to meet them, because the men were greatly ashamed: and the king said, Tarry at Jericho until your beards be grown, and then return.

1st campaign—6. And when the children of Ammon saw that they stank before David, the children of Ammon sent and hired the Syrians of Beth-rehob, and the Syrians of Zoba, twenty thousand footmen, and of king Maacah a thousand men, and of Ish-tob twelve thousand men. 7. And when David heard of it, he sent Joab, and all the host of the mighty men. 8. And the children of Ammon came out, and put the battle in array at the entering in of the gate: and the Syrians of Zob, and of Rehob, and Ish-tob, and Maacah, were by themselves in the field. 9. When Joab saw that the front of the battle was against him before and behind, he chose of the choice men of Israel, and put them in array against the Syrians: 10. and the rest of the people he delivered into the hand of Abishai his brother, that he might put them in array against the children of Ammon. 11. And he said, If the Syrians be too strong for me, then thou shalt help me: but if the children of Ammon be too strong for thee, then I will come and help thee. 12. Be of good

6. **stank.** As we say, "were in bad odor with."

Beth-rehob. In the north, just west of Dan; the other three principalities lay to the north and east of this.

8. **the gate,** *i.e.,* of their capital, Rabbah, twenty-three miles east of Jordan in the latitude of Jericho. Joab's force lay between two fires: that of the Ammonites on the city side, and that of their allies in the open country. He directed Abishai against the former, and himself confronted the latter.

courage, and let us play the men for our people, and for the cities of our God: and the LORD do that which seemeth him good. 13. And Joab drew nigh, and the people that were with him, unto the battle against the Syrians: and they fled before him. 14. And when the children of Ammon saw that the Syrians were fled, then fled they also before Abishai, and entered into the city. So, Joab returned from the children of Ammon, and came to Jerusalem.

1st victory over Syria, the allies of Ammon—15. And when the Syrians saw that they were smitten before Israel, they gathered themselves together. 16. And Hadadezer sent, and brought out the Syrians that were beyond the river: and they came to Helam; and Shobach the captain of the host of Hadadezer went before them. 17. And when it was told David, he gathered all Israel together, and passed over Jordan, and came to Helam. And the Syrians set themselves in array against David and fought with him. 18. And the Syrians fled before Israel; and David slew the men of seven hundred chariots of the Syrians, and forty thousand horsemen, and smote Shobach the captain of their host, who died there. 19. And when all the kings that were servants to Hadadezer saw that they were smitten before Israel, they made peace with Israel, and served them. So, the Syrians feared to help the children of Ammon any more.

2nd victory—8:3. David smote also Hadadezer, the son of Rebob, king of Zobah, as he went to recover his border at the river Euphrates. 4. And David took from him a thousand chariots, and seven hundred horsemen, and twenty thousand footmen: and David houghed all the chariot horses, *and* reserved of them *only an hundred,* 5. And when the Syrians of Damascus came to succor Hadadezer king of Zobah, David slew of the Syrians two

16. **the river,** *i.e.,* the Euphrates. **Helam** is not identified.

18. The corrupt text has not made even a pretense of preserving the right numbers or equipment. Probably we should read "seven hundred horse and forty thousand foot."

19. **And served them.** This curtly informs us that David became suzerain of all nearer Syria from Hermon to the Ammonite border. In the next paragraph we learn that Damascus also became tributary to him.

3. **Zobah,** site **unknown:** somewhere to the north-east **towards** Damascus.

4. **houghed** (pronounce "hocked"): to cut the sinews of the legs.

and twenty thousand men. 6. Then David put garrisons in Syria
of Damascus; and the Syrians became servants *to* David, and
brought gifts. And the LORD preserved David whithersoever he
went. 7. And David took the shields of gold that were on the
servants of Hadadezer, and brought them to Jerusalem. 8. And
from Betah, and from Berothai, cities of Hadadezer, king David
took exceeding much brass.

Hamath—9. When Toi king of Hamath heard that David had
smitten all the host of Hadadezer, 10. then Toi sent Joram his son
unto king David, to salute him, and to bless him, because he
had fought against Hadadezer, and smitten him: for Hadadezer had
wars with Toi. And Joram brought with him vessels of silver, and
vessels of gold, and vessels of brass: 11. which also king David
did dedicate unto the LORD, with the silver and gold that he
had dedicated of all nations which he subdued; 12. of Syria, and of
Moab, and of the children of Ammon, and of the Philistines, and of
Amalek, and of the spoil of Hadadezer, son of Rehob, king of Zobah.

Edom—13. And David gat him a name. *And* when he returned
from smiting of the Syrians *he smote Edom* in the valley of
Salt, eighteen thousand men. 14. And he put garrisons in Edom;
throughout all Edom put he garrisons, and all they of Edom became
David's servants. And the LORD preserved David whithersoever
he went.

*Ammon: 2nd campaign—*11:1. And it came to pass, *at the return
of the year,* at the time when kings go forth to battle, that David
sent Joab, and his servants with him, and all Israel; and they destroyed
the children of Ammon, and besieged Rabbah. But David tarried
still at Jerusalem. 12:26. And Joab fought against Rabbah of the
children of Ammon and took the city *of waters.*

6. **garrisons.** See on 1 Sam. 10:5 above, p. 32.
8, 9.   **Hamath.** In the far north, on the Orontes, probably a Hittite center (p. 80).
13. **valley of Salt.** At the southern end of the Dead Sea.
11:1 **tarried at Jerusalem.** For the sequel, his sin with Bathsheba, sec next section.
12:26. **city of waters,** *i.e.,* the Water Fort outside the capital commanding the
water supply, on the retention of which the lives of the besieged depended.

27. And Joab sent messengers to David, and said, I have fought against Rabbah, and have taken the city of waters. 28. Now therefore gather the rest of the people together, and encamp against the city, and take it: lest I take the city, and it be called after my name. 29. And David gathered all the people together, and went to Rabbah, and fought against it, and took it. 30. And he took their king's crown from off his head, the weight whereof was a talent of gold with the precious stones; and it was set on David's head. And he brought forth the spoil of the city in great abundance. 31. And he brought forth the people that were therein, and put them *at the* saws, and *at the* harrows of iron, and *at the* axes of iron, and made them *labor at* the brick-kiln: and thus did he unto all the cities of the children of Ammon. So David and all the people returned unto Jerusalem.

MILITARY ORGANIZATION UNDER DAVID

The instrument by which David achieved his conquests must have been an efficient army. Our texts supply us only with scattered indications of the character of the military organization. From these it can be gathered that it was only with the establishment of the monarchy that anything in the nature of a national army came into being. Its composition was roughly as follows:

(1) **The Militia.** Every able-bodied man between the ages of twenty and fifty was liable to be called out. This force was composed solely of infantry. War-chariots, after the manner of the surrounding nations, were not introduced until Solomon's time. The general term for this corps used by Biblical writers is "the people." It

---

31. The A.V. and R.V. rendering of this verse, which makes David subject his captives to abominable torture, is grammatically unsound. Furthermore, why should David go to the trouble of carrying them all away ("brought forth") if he merely meant to torture and execute them?

was organized upon a territorial basis. Each tribe was divided into a number of local clans, or "thousands," and each of these thousands supplied a battalion (a "thousand") to the army. Each battalion was subdivided into ten companies ("hundreds"), and so on into half-companies ("fifties") and squads ("tens").

War was a religious duty. Before and during operations each man was obliged to be strictly "sanctified"; that is, he had to keep in training by abstention from any practice which would impair his efficiency or distract his attention.

(2) Besides his Territorial Force, David possessed the nucleus of a **professional army** in (a) the bodyguard, (b) the remainder of his outlaw band, (c) other mercenaries. (a) The bodyguard was called the Krethi and the Plethi—Cherethites and Pelethites. They were foreign mercenaries, the Plethi being possibly Philistines, under the command of Benaiah, one of the m ost distinguished Hebrew officers. Of him it is related that " he went down and slew a lion in the midst of a pit in time of snow: and he slew an Egyptian, a goodly man: and the Egyptian had a spear in his hand: but he went down to him with a staff, and plucked the spear out of the Egyptian's hand, and slew him with his own spear" (2 Sam. 23) . (b) These are called "the mighty men": they supplied many *of* the officers of the battalions. (c) Of these the largest and most noted body was a corps of six hundred Gittites led by Ittai.

(3) The Officers. The king was *ex-officio* head of the army; but he appointed Joab to represent him as Commander-in-Chief of the forces. The subordinate officers were either members of the "mighty men," of whom some were foreigners, or else heads of clans and families.

Among his officers David instituted two **Military Orders of Knighthood,** admission to which was gained by conspicuous personal bravery.

(a) The Order of the Three. This was the most coveted distinction. It appears to have been held by Ish-baal, Eleazar, and Shammah (p. 118, and Index *s.v.* Ish-baal).

(b) The Order of the Thirty. The knight-commander of this order was Abishai, and Benaiah one of its most distinguished members. Eliam, Ittai, and Uriah are also members of the order, of whose personality we know something.

The " rude literary form" of the lists of these braves (2 Sam. 23) "suggests great antiquity . . . Their deeds reveal a spirit of chivalry which was very like that which inspired the knights of Arthur's round table" (Kent).

II. SECOND PERIOD. DOMESTIC HISTORY

BATH-SHEBA

2 Samuel 11:2-12:25

David's crime—11:2. And it came to pass [*while Joab was besieging Rabbath-Ammon*] in an evening-tide, that David arose from off his bed, and walked upon the roof of the king's house: and from the roof he saw a woman washing herself; and the woman was very beautiful to look upon. 3. And David sent and enquired after the woman. And one said, Is not this Bathsheba, the daughter of Eliam, the wife of Uriah the Hittite? 4. And David sent messengers, and took her; and she came unto him;

Uriah, being a Hittite, was a *ger-a* resident foreigner-in Jerusalem. He was included in the list of David's more famous warriors (chap. 23). **Eliam** was son of Ahithophel (chap. 15. *seq.*). So Ahithophel's subsequent antagonism to David can be explained partly on the ground of this injury inflicted by the king on his grand-daughter.

and afterward she returned unto her house. 5. And the woman conceived, and sent and told David, and said, I am with child.

His unsuccessful attempts to conceal it—6. And David sent *to* Joab, saying, Send me Uriah the Hittite. And Joab sent Uriah *to* David. 7. And when Uriah was come unto him, David demanded of him how Joab did, and how the people did, and how the war prospered. 8. And David said to Uriah, Go down *to* thy house, and wash thy feet. And Uriah departed out of the king's house, and there followed him a mess of meat from the king. 9. But Uriah slept at the door of the king's house with all the servants of his Lord and went not down *to* his house. 10. And when they had told David, saying, Uriah went not down unto his house, David said unto Uriah, Camest thou not from thy journey? why then didst thou not go down unto thine house? 11. And Uriah said unto David, The ark, and Israel, and Judah, abide in tents; and my Lord Joab, and the servants of my Lord, are encamped in the open fields; shall I then go into mine house, to eat and *to* drink, and *to* be with my wife? as thou livest, and as thy soul liveth, I will not do this thing. 12. And David said *to* Uriah, Tarry here *to* day also, and tomorrow I will let thee depart. So Uriah abode in Jerusalem that day, and the morrow. 13. And when David had called him, he did. eat and drink before him; and he made him drunk: and at even he went out to lie on his bed with the servants of his Lord, but went not down to his house.

"It must be by his death": one crime leads to another—14. And it came to pass in the morning, that David wrote a letter to Joab, and sent it by the hand of Uriah. 15. And he wrote in the letter, saying, Set ye Uriah in the forefront of the hottest battle, and retire ye from him, that he may be smitten, and die. 16. And it came to pass, when Joab observed the city, that he assigned Uriah unto a place where he knew that valiant men were.

11. The Ark, the visible symbol of Jehovah's presence and aid, was taken down to battle, as at Aphek, and apparently as a general practice.

15. Cf. Saul's designs on David himself, p. 64.

17. And the men of the city went out and fought with Joab: and there fell some of the people of the servants of David; and Uriah the Hittite died also.

Joab's field-report—18. Then Joab sent and told David all the things concerning the war; 19. and charged the messenger, saying, when thou hast made an end of telling the matters of the war unto the king, 20. and if so be that the king's wrath arise, and he say unto thee, wherefore approached ye so nigh unto the city when ye did fight? knew ye not that they would shoot from the wall? 21. who smote Abimelech the son of Jerubbesheth? Did not a woman cast a piece of a millstone upon him from the wall, that he died in Thebez? why went ye nigh the wall? then say thou, Thy servant Uriah the Hittite is dead also.

And the reply to it—22. So the messenger went, and came and shewed David all that Joab had sent him for. 23. And the messenger said unto David, Surely the men prevailed against us, and came out unto us into the field, and we were upon them even unto the entering of the gate. 24. And the shooters shot from off the wall upon thy servants; and some of the king's servants be dead, and thy servant Uriah the Hittite is dead also. 25. Then David said unto the messenger, Thou shalt say unto Joab, Let not this thing displease thee, for the sword devoured one as well as another: make thy battle more strong against the city, and overthrow it. And encourage thou him.

Marriage of Bath-sheba with the king—26. And when the wife of Uriah heard that Uriah her husband was dead, she mourned for her husband. 27. And when the mourning was past, David sent and fetched her to his house, and she became his wife, and. bare him a son. But the thing that David had done displeased the LORD.
  Nathan's parable—12:1. And the Lord sent Nathan unto David. And he came unto him, and said unto him, There were two men in one city; the one rich, and the other

---

21. **Abimelech.** See Judg. 9. Jerubbesheth is the euphemistic emendation of Jerubbaal (p. 24).

12:1. There are four other examples of the parable in the O.T.:(1) Joab and the blood-feud, below, p. 147; (2) The prophet and Ahab's lenience to Benhadad (1 Kings 20:39);(3) Isaiah and Jerusalem's wild grapes (Isa. 5 : 1); (4) Isaiah and the ploughman (Isa. 28:24 *seq.).* A parable is not to be confused with a fable

poor. 2. The rich man had exceeding many flocks and herds: 3. but the poor man had nothing, save one little ewe lamb, which he had bought and nourished up: and it grew up together with him, and with his children; it did eat of his own meat, and drank of his own cup, and lay in his bosom, and was unto her as a daughter. 4. And there came a traveler unto the rich man, and he spared *to* take of his own flock and of his own herd, to dress for the wayfaring man that was come unto him; but took the poor man's lamb and dressed it for the man that was come to him.

5. And David's anger was greatly kindled against the man; and he said to Nathan, As the LORD liveth, the man that hath done this thing shall surely die: 6. and he shall restore the lamb fourfold, because he did this thing, and because he had no pity.

Its application—7. And Nathan said to David, Thou art the man. Thus saith the LORD God of Israel, I anointed thee king over Israel and I delivered thee out of the hand of Saul; 8. and I gave thee thy master's house, and thy master's wives into thy bosom, and gave thee the house of Israel and of Judah; and if that had been too little, I would moreover have given unto thee such and such things. 9. Wherefore hast thou despised the commandment of the LORD, to do evil in his sight? thou hast killed Uriah the Hittite with the sword, and hast taken his wife to be thy wife, and hast slain him with the sword of the children of Ammon. 10. Now therefore the sword shall never depart from thine house; because thou hast despised me, and hast taken the wife of Uriah the Hittite to be thy wife. 11. Thus saith the LORD, Behold, I will raise up evil against thee out of thine own house, and I will take thy wives before thine eyes, and give them unto thy neighbor, and he shall ravish thy wives in the sight of this sun. 12. For thou didst it secretly: but I will do this thing before all Israel, and before the sun.

David's compunction—13. And David said unto Nathan, I have sinned against the LORD.   And Nathan said unto

(e.g. Jotham and the King of the Trees, Judg. 9), which introduces the unnatural: it is a higher artistic device, and bears a deeper meaning. See *H.D.B.,* p. 679.

David, the LORD also hath put away thy sin; thou shalt not die. 14. Howbeit, because by this deed thou hast given great occasion to the enemies of the LORD to blaspheme, the child also that is born unto thee shall surely die.

For seven days he intercedes with God to spare his child—15. And Nathan departed unto his house, and the LORD struck the child that Uriah's wife bare unto David, and it was very sick. 16. David therefore besought God for the child; and David fasted, and went in, and lay all night upon the earth. 17. And the elders of his house arose, and went to him, to raise him up from the earth: but he would not, neither did he eat bread with them.

His resignation to God's will—18. And it came to pass on the seventh day, that the child died. And the servants of David feared to tell him that the child was dead: for they said, Behold, while the child was yet alive, we spake unto him, and he would not hearken unto our voice: how will he then vex himself, if we tell him that the child is dead? 1 9. But when David saw that his servants whispered, David perceived that the child was dead: therefore, David said unto his servants, Is the child dead? And they said, He is dead. 20. Then David arose from the earth, and washed, and anointed himself, and changed his apparel, and came into the house of the LORD, and worshipped: then he came to hjs own house; and when he required, they set bread before him, and he did eat. 21. Then said hjs servants unto him, What thing is this that thou hast done? thou didst fast and weep for the child, while it was alive; but when the child was dead, thou didst rise and eat bread. 22. And he said, while the child was yet alive, I fasted and wept: for I said, who can tell whether GOD will be gracious to me, that the child may live? *23.* But now he is dead, wherefore should I fast? C an I bring him back again? I shall go to him, but he shall not return to me.

23. Some anticipation of a continued existence in the after-world, the shadowy *Sheol,* is exhibited in the O.T. from earliest times; as in Greek and all other ancient literature. But no clear hope of a resurrection from the dead was reached until post-Exilic days.

Subsequent birth of Solomon—24. And David comforted Bath-Sheba his wife, and she bare a son, and he called his name Solomon: and the LORD loved him. 25. And he sent by the hand of Nathan the prophet, and called his name Jedidiah, *the Beloved of the* LORD.

AMNON AND ABSALOM

2 Samuel 13, 14

Prologue—Amnon, the king's eldest son, had done grievous wrong to Tamar, Absalom's beautiful sister, his own half-sister. By the Hebrew law of that time, though it was illegal afterwards (Lev. 18:9), he might have married her. But his love for her turned to bitter hate, and he refused.

Absalom nurses his revenge against his half-brother—21. But when king David heard of all these things, he was very wroth. 22. And Absalom spake unto his brother Amnon neither good nor bad: for Absalom hated Amnon because he had wronged his sister Tamar.

His plot to get Amnon to his farm—23. And it came to pass after two full years, that Absalom had sheepshearers in Baal-hazor, which is beside Ephraim: and Absalom invited all the king's sons. 24. And Absalom came to the king, and said, Behold now, thy servant hath sheepshearers; let the king, I beseech thee, and his servants go with thy servant. 25. And the king said to Absalom, Nay, my son, let us not all now go, lest we be chargeable unto thee. And he pressed him: howbeit he would not go but blessed him. 26. Then said Absalom, If not, I pray

21. LXX adds the important detail: "Yet he did not discipline Amnon his son, for he loved him, because he was his eldest" a weakness in David's character which led to disastrous consequences.

23. **Baal-hazor**. About five miles north of Bethel.

25. **chargeable**. "It would be too much expense and burden to Absalom to entertain so many guests."

thee, let my brother Amnon go with us. And the king said unto him, Why should he go with thee? 27. But Absalom pressed him, that he let Amnon and all the king's sons go with him.

Murder of Amnon (c. 983 B.C.)—28. Now Absalom had commanded his servants, saying, Mark ye now when Amnon's heart is merry with wine, and when I say unto you, Smite Amnon; then kill him, fear not: have not I commanded you? be courageous, and be valiant. 29. And the servants of Absalom did unto Amnon as Absalom had commanded. Then all the king's sons arose, and every man gat him up upon his mule, and fled.

The news flies—"*Viresqite adquirit eundo*"—30. And it came *to* pass, while they were in the way, that tidings came to David, saying, Absalom hath slain all the king's sons, and there is not one of them left. 31. Then the king arose, and tare his garments, and lay on the earth; and all his. servants stood by with their clothes rent. 32. And Jonadab, the son of Shimeah David's brother, answered and said, Let not my Lord suppose that they have slain all the young men the king's sons; for Amnon only is dead: for by the appointment of Absalom this hath been determined from the day that he wronged his sister Tamar. 33. Now therefore let not my Lord the king take the thing to his heart, to think that all the king's sons are dead: for Amnon only is dead. 34. And the young man that kept the watch lifted up his eyes, and looked, and, behold, there came much people by the way of *Beth-horon on* the hill side. 35. And Jonadab said unto the king, Behold, the king's sons come: as thy servant said, so it is. 36. And it came to pass, as soon as he had made an end of speaking, that, behold, the king's sons came, and lifted up their voice and wept: and the king also and all his servant wept very sore.

Flight of Absalom—37. But Absalom fled, and went to Talmai, the son of Ammihud, king of Geshur. And David mourned for his son every day. 38. So Absalom fled, and went to Geshur, and was there three years. 39. And

37. **Talmai** was Absalom's maternal grandfather. **Geshur** was north-east of the Sea of Galilee, in Syria.

the soul of king David longed to go forth unto Absalom: for he was comforted concerning Amnon, seeing he was dead.

Joab's ruse to secure Absalom's recall—14:1. Now Joab the son of Zeruiah perceived that the king's heart was toward Absalom. 2. And Joab sent *to* Tekoah, and fetched thence a wise woman, and said unto her, I pray thee, feign thyself to be a mourner, and put on now mourning apparel, and anoint not thyself with oil, but be as a woman that had a long time mourned for the dead: 3. and come to the king, and speak on this manner unto him. So Joab put the words in her mouth.

The wise woman's parable of the blood-feud—4. And when the woman of Tekoah spake to the king, she fell on her face to the ground, and did obeisance, and said, Help, O king. 5. And the king said unto her, What aileth thee? And she answered, I am indeed a widow woman, and mine husband is dead. 6. And thy handmaid had two sons, and they two strove together in the field, and there was none to part them, but the one smote the other, and slew him. 7. And, behold, the whole family is risen against thine handmaid, and they said, Deliver him that smot his brother, that we may kill him, for the life of his brother whom he slew; and we will destroy the heir also. And so they shall quench my coal which is left, and shall not leave to my husband neither name nor remainder upon the earth.

The king vows that he will stop this (fictitious) vendetta—8. And the king said unto the woman, Go to thine house, and I will give charge concerning thee: 9. And the woman of Tekoah said unto the king, My Lord, O king, the iniquity be on me, and on my father's house: and the king and his throne be guiltless. 10. And the king said, whosoever saith ought unto thee, bring him to me, and he shall not touch thee anymore. 11. Then said she, I pray thee, let the king remember the LORD thy God, that thou wouldest not suffer the revengers of blood to destroy any more, lest they destroy my son. And he said, As the

2. **Tekoah.** Six miles south of Bethlehem: the birthplace of the prophet Amos.

LORD liveth, there shall not one hair of thy son fall to the earth.

Application of the parable—12. Then the woman said, Let thine handmaid, I pray thee, speak one word unto my Lord the king. And he said, Say on. 13. And the woman said, wherefore then hast thou thought such a thing against the people of God (for the king doth speak this thing as one which is faulty) in that the king doth not fetch home again his banished? 14. For we must needs die, and are as water spilt on the ground, which cannot be gathered up again; neither *will God take away the life of him who deviseth means whereby he that is banished may not re-main banished from him.* 15. Now therefore that I am come to speak of this thing unto my Lord the king, it is because the people have made me afraid: and thy handmaid said, I will now speak unto the king; it may be that the king will perform the request of his handmaid. 16. For the king will hear, to deliver his handmaid out of the hand of the man that would destroy me and my son together out of the inheritance of God. 17. Then thine handmaid said, The word of my Lord the king shall now be comfortable: for as an angel of God, so is m y Lord the king to discern good and bad: therefore the LORD thy God will be with thee.

David shrewdly surmises who prompted her appeal—18. Then the king answered and said unto the woman, Hide not from me, I pray thee, the thing that I shall ask thee. And the woman said, Let my Lord the king now speak. 19. And the king said, Is not the hand of Joab with thee in all this? And the woman answered and said, As thy soul liveth, my Lord the king, none can turn to the right hand or to the left from ought that my Lord the king hath spoken: for thy servant Joab he bade me, and he put all these words in the mouth of thine handmaid: 20. to *change the face of the matter* hath thy servant Joab done this thing: and my Lord is wise, according to the wisdom of an angel of God, to know all things that are in the earth.

14. "All must die: no harshness to Absalom can recall your dead Amnon to life. God will grant you long life if you restore your banished son to His land."

Absalom (a) is allowed to return to his own house—21: And the king said unto Joab, Behold now, I have done this thing: go therefore, bring the young man Absalom again. 22. And Joab fell to the ground on his face, and bowed himself, and thanked the king: and Joab said, Today thy servant knoweth that I have found grace in thy sight, my Lord, O king, in that the king hath fulfilled the request of his servant. 23. So Joab arose and went *to* Geshur, and 'brought Absalom to Jerusalem. 24. And the king said, Let him turn to his own house, and let him not see my face. So Absalom returned to his own house, and saw not the king's face.

Absalom's personal beauty—25. But in all Israel there was none to be so much praised as Absalom for his beauty: from the sole of his foot even to the crown of his head there was no blemish in him. 26. And when he polled his head, (for it was at every year's end that he polled it: because the hair was heavy on him, therefore he polled it:) he weighed the hair of his head at two hundred shekels after the king's weight.

(b) Finally he is readmitted to court (c. 978 B.C.)—28. So Absalom dwelt two full years in Jerusalem, and saw not the king's face. 29. Therefore Absalom sent for Joab, to have sent him to the king; but he would not come to him: and when he sent again the second time, he would not come. 30. Therefore he said unto his servants, See, Joab's field is near mine, and he hath barley there; go and set it on fire. And Absalom's servants set the field on fire. 31. Then Joab arose, and came to Absalom unto his house, and said unto him; Wherefore have thy servants set my field on fire? 32. And Absalom answered Joab, Behold I sent unto thee, saying, Come hither, that I may send thee to the king, to say, Wherefore am I come from Geshur? it had been good for me *to* have been there still: now therefore let me see the king's face; and if there be any iniquity in me, let him kill me. 33. So Joab came *to* the king, and told him: and when he had called for Absalom he came to the king, and bowed himself on his face to the ground before the king: and the king kissed Absalom.

21. **done this thing.** " I forthwith grant the request you have made by the woman's mouth."

26. **polled** = cut his hair. It weighed nearly 4 lbs,

THE REBELLION OF ABSALOM

2 Samuel 15-19

(a) Outbreak of the Revolt

Absalom assumes the status of heir-apparent—15:1. And it came to pass after this, that Absalom prepared him chariots and horses, and fifty men to run before him.

And plays the demagogue—2. And Absalom rose up early, and stood beside the way of the gate: and it was so, that when any man that had a controversy came to the king for judgment, then Absalom called unto him, and said, Of what city art thou? And he said, Thy servant is of one of the tribes of Israel. 3. And Absalom said unto him, See, thy matters are good and right; but there is no man deputed of the king to hear thee. 4. Absalom said moreover, Oh that I were made judge in the land, that every man which hath any suit or cause might come unto me, and I would do him justice! 5. And it was so, that when any man came nigh to him to do him obeisance, he put forth his hand, and took him, and kissed him. 6. And on this manner did Absalom to all Israel that came to the king for judgment: so Absalom stole the hearts of the men of Israel.

He raises the standard of revolt at Hebron—7. And it came to pass after *four* years, that Absalom said unto the king, I pray thee, let me go and pay my vow, which I have vowed unto the LORD, in Hebron. 8. For thy servant vowed a vow while I abode at Geshur in Syria, saying, If the LORD shall bring me again indeed to Jerusalem,

---

33. The kiss signified full reconciliation and pardon. Absalom, however, had been embittered by this long estrangement from his fatber, as the sequel shows.

15:1. After Amnon's death Absalom still had an elder brother, Chileab; but " primogeniture has never been the rule in the East," as we see indeed by David's subsequent bequest of the throne to a younger son, Solomon.

7. **four years.** After his former restoration, that is. This dates the REBELLION at *c.* 974 B.C.

then I will serve the LORD. 9 . And the king said unto him, Go in peace. So he arose, and went to Hebron.

The conspiracy swells—10. But Absalom sent spies throughout all the tribes of Israel, saying, As soon as ye hear the sound of the trumpet, then ye shall say, Absalom reigneth in Hebron. 11. And with Absalom went two hundred men out of Jerusalem, that were called; and they went in their simplicity, and they knew not any thing. 12. And Absalom sent for Ahithophel the Gilonite, David's counsellor, from his city, even from Giloh, while he offered sacrifices. And the conspiracy was strong; for the people increased continually with Absalom.

(b) Retreat of David across Jordan

David abandons his capital—13. And there came a messenger *to* David, saying, The hearts of the men of Israel are after Absalom. 14. And David said unto all his servants that were with him at Jerusalem, Arise, and let us flee; for we shall not else escape from Absalom; make speed *to* depart, lest he overtake us suddenly, and bring evil upon us, and smite the city with the edge of the sword. 15. And the king's servants said unto the king, Behold, thy servants are ready *to* do whatsoever my Lord the king shall appoint. 16. And the king went forth, and all his household after him. And the king left ten women, which were concubines, to keep the house.

11. **called,** *i.e.,* invited to the feast in fulfilment of his simulated vow.

knew not anyt hing. " Ignorant as yet of his intentions."

12. **Giloh.** Seven miles north-west of Hebron. For Ahithophel's motives, see p. 140 *n.*

The causes of the popularity of Absalom's attack on the throne suggested in these chapters, besides his own artifices, are: (1) Jealousy of the Judahites at the transference of the seat of government from Hebron, their tribal capital, to Jerusalem. (2) Resentment of Benjamin against a king who had supplanted the house of their tribesman, Saul. (3) The influence of Ahithophel.

14. Why this pusillanimous retreat? (1) David was taken by surprise: he was not sure if his capital would prove loyal to him. (2) Tender-hearted refusal to chastise a son of his own-exhibited on several other occasions. He hoped that the cloud would blow over without raising a storm. But Joab, as before, " was too hard for him," and put a sterner soul into the defense of the throne.

17. And the king went forth, and all the people after him, and tarried in *Beth Merhak.* 18. And all his servants passed on beside him; and all the Cherethites, and all the Pelethites, and all the Gittites, six hundred men which came after him from Gath, passed on before the king.

Loyalty of a mercenary officer—19. Then said the king to Ittai the Gittite, Wherefore goest thou also with us? return to thy place, and abide with the king: for thou art a stranger, and also an exile. 20. Whereas thou earnest but yesterday, should I this day make thee go up and down with us? seeing I go whither I may, return thou, and take back thy brethren: mercy and truth be with thee. 2I. And Ittai answered the king, and said, As the LORD liveth, and as my Lord the king liveth, surely in what place my Lord the king shall be, whether in death or life, even there also will thy servant be. 22. And David said to Ittai, Go and pass over. And Ittai the Gittite passed over, and all his men, and all the little ones that were with him. 23. And all the country wept with a loud voice, and all the people passed over: the king also himself passed over the brook Kidron, and all the people passed over, toward the way of the wilderness.

He sends the Ark back—24. And lo Zadok also *and Abiathar* (and all the Levites) were with him, bearing the ark of the covenant of God: and they set down the ark of God until all the people had done passing out of the city. 25. And the king said unto Zadok, Carry back the ark of God into the city: if I shall find favor in the eyes of the LORD, he will bring me again, and shew me both it, and his habitation: 26. but if he thus say, I have no delight in thee; behold, here am I, let him do to me as seemeth good unto him. 27. The king said also unto Zadok the priest, *See now:* return into the city in peace, and your two sons with you, Ahimaaz thy son, and Jonathan the son of Abiathar. 28. See, I will tarry in the plain of the

17. **Beth Merhak,** "The Far House," obviously was in the Kedron Valley between the city and the Mount of Olives.

18. **Cherethites and Pelethites** formed the royal bodyguard; they were foreign mercenaries, see p. 139.

19. the king. Half scornfully, David alludes to Absalom.

23. wilderness, the uncultivated land north-east of Jerusalem towards Jordan.

wilderness, until there come word from you to certify me. 29. Zadok therefore and Abiathar carried the ark of God again to Jerusalem: and they tarried there.

On the Mount of Olives—30. And David went up by the ascent of mount Olivet, and wept as he went up, and had his head covered, and he went barefoot: and all the people that was with him covered every man his head, and they went up, weeping as they went up. 31. And one told David, saying, Ahithophel is among the conspirators with Absalom. And David said, O LORD I pray thee, turn the counsel of Ahithophel into foolishness.

Hushai, "the King's Friend," is directed to act as his spy—32. And it came to pass, that when David was come to the top of the mount, where he worshipped God, behold, Hushai the Archite came to meet him with his coat rent, and earth upon his head: 33. unto whom David said, If thou passest on with me, then thou shalt be a burden unto me: 34. but if thou return to the city, and say unto Absalom, I will be thy servant, O king; as I have been thy father's servant hitherto, so will I now also be thy servant: then mayest thou for me defeat the counsel of Ahithophel. 35. And hast thou not there with thee Zadok and Abiathar the priests? therefore it shall be, that what thing soever thou shalt hear out of the king's house, thou shalt tell it to Zadok and Abiatha the priests. 36. Behold, they have there with them their two sons, Ahimaaz Zadok's son, and Jonathan Abiathar's son; and by them ye shall send unto me everything that ye can hear. 37. So Hushai David's friend came unto the city, and Absalom came into Jerusalem.

Ziba slanders Mephibosheth—16:1. And when David was a little past the top of the hill, behold, Ziba the servant of Mephibosheth met him, with a couple of asses saddled, and upon them two hundred loaves of bread, and an hundred bunches of raisins, and an hundred of summer fruits, and a bottle of wine. 2. And the king said unto Ziba, What meanest thou by these? And Ziba said, The asses be for the king's household to ride on; and the bread and summer fruit for the young men to eat; and the wine, that such as be faint in the wilderness may

32. **Archite** = native of a town just to the west of Bethel.

drink. 3. And the king said, And where is thy master's son? And Ziba said unto the king, Behold, he abideth at Jerusalem: for he said, To day shall the house of Israel restore me the kingdom of my father. 4. Then said the king to Ziba, Behold, thine are all that pertained unto Mephibosheth. And Ziba said, I humbly beseech thee that I may find grace in thy sight, my Lord, O king.

Shimei reviles the king—5. And when king David came to Bahurim, behold, thence came out a man of the family of the house of Saul, whose name was Shimei, the son of Gera: he came forth, and cursed still as he came. 6. And he cast stones at David, and at all the servants of king David: and all the people and all the mighty men were on his right hand and on his left. 7. And thus said Shimei when he cursed, Come out, come out, thou bloody man, and thou man of Belial: 8. the LORD hath returned upon thee all the blood of the house of Saul, in whose stead thou hast reigned; and the LORD hath delivered the kingdom into the hand of Absalom thy son: and, behold, thou art taken in thy mischief, because thou art a bloody man.

Abishai's natural impulse restrained—9. Then said Abishai the son of Zeruiah unto the king, why should this dead dog curse my Lord the king? let me go over, I pray thee, and take off his head. 10. And the king said, What have I to do with you, ye sons of Zeruiah? so let him curse, because the LORD hath said unto him, Curse David. Who shall then say, wherefore hast thou done so? 11. And David said to Abishai, and to all his servants, Behold, my son, which came forth of my bowels, seeketh my life: how much more now may this Benjamite do it? Let him alone and let him curse; for the LORD hath hidden him. 12. It may be that the LORD will look on mine affliction, and that the LORD will requite me good for his cursing this day. 13. And as David and his men went by the way, Shimei went along on the hill's side over against him, and cursed as he went, and threw stones

3. **Ziba** (p. 131), by a baseless accusation against his master, prevails on David to assign all the latter's possessions to him. He subsequently had to disgorge half of them (29:25-9).

5. **Bahurim**, See p. 111n.

at him, and cast dust. 14. And the king, and all the people that were with him, came weary *to Jordan* and refreshed themselves there.

(c) The Usurper in the Capital

Hushai proves himself a consummate actor—15. And Absalom, and all the people the men of Israel, came to Jerusalem, and Ahithopriel with him. 16. And it came to pass, when Hushai the Archite, David's friend, was come unto Absalom, that Hushai said unto Absalom, Goel save the king, God save the king. 17. Absalom said to Hushai, Is this thy kindness to thy friend? why wentest thou not with thy friend? 18. And Hushai said unto Absalom, Nay; but whom the LORD, and this people, and all the men of Israel, choose, his will I be, and wi th him will I abide. 19. And again, whom should I serve? should I not serve in the presence of his son? as I have served in thy father's presence, so will I be in thy presence.

Sage advice from Ahithophel—20. Then said Absalom to Ahithophel, Give counsel among you what we shall do. 21. And Ahithophel said unto Absalom, Take to thyself thy father's c oncubines, which h e hath left to keep the house; and all Israel shall hear that thou art abhorred of thy father: then shall the hands of all that are with thee be strong. 22. So they spread Absalom a tent upon the top of the house; and Absalom took to himself his father's concubines in the sight of all Israel. 23. And the counsel of Ahithophel, which he counselled in those days, was as if a man had enquired at the oracle of God: so was all the counsel of Ahithophel both with David and with Absalom.

Further sage advice from Ahithophel—17:1. Moreover Ahithophel said unto Absalom, Let me now choose out twelve thousand men, and I will arise and pursue after David this night: 2. and I will come upon him while

17. **thy friend.** Absalom sarcastically alludes to Hushai's unofficial title, "the King's Friend."

21. The taking possession of the king's concubines rendered the breach between the usurper and his father irreparable. It was equivalent to declaring that he had definitely succeeded to all "the late king's" estates (p. 1 1 1).

he is weary and weak handed, and will make him afraid: and all the people that are with him shall flee; and I will smite the king only: 3. and I will bring back all the people unto thee *as a bride returns to her husband: thou seekest only the life of one man, and* all the people shall be in peace. 4. And the saying pleased Absalom well, and all the elders of Israel. 5. Then said Absalom, Call now Hushai the Archite also, and let us hear likewise what he saith. 6. And when Hushai was come to Absalom, Absalom spake unto him, saying, Ahithophel hath spoken after this manner: shall we do after his saying? if not; speak thou.

Counteracted by the King's Friend—7. And Hushai said unto Absalom, The counsel that Ahithophel hath given is not good at this time. 8. For, said Hushai, thou knowest thy father and his men, that they be mighty men, and they be chafed in their minds, as a bear robbed of her whelps in the field: and thy father is a man of war, and will not lodge with the people. 9. Behold, he is hid now in some pit, or in some other place: and it will come to pass, when some of them be overthrown at the first, that whosoever heareth it will say, There is a slaughter among the people that follow Absalom. 10. And he also that is valiant, whose heart is as the heart of a lion, shall utterly melt: for all Israel knoweth that thy father is a mighty man, and they which be with him are valiant men. 11. Therefore I counsel that all Israel be generally gathered unto thee, from Dan even to Beer-sheba, as the sand that is by the sea for multitude; and that thou go to battle in thine own person. 12. So shall we come upon him in some place where he shall be found, and we will light upon him as the dew falleth on the ground: and of him and of all the men that are with him there shall not be left so much as one. 13. Moreover, if he be gotten into a city, then shall all Israel bring ropes to that city, and we will draw it into the river, until there be not one small stone

7. Hushai realised that delay would be favorable to David.

8. **will not lodge,** etc. "David, whose person only Ahithophel intends to attack, is too shrewd to be surprised: he will not be found bivouacking with his force but will be in some secret retreat and undiscoverable. Thence he will deliver (verse 9) a sudden onslaught and cause a general panic in your army."

found there. 14. And Absalom and all the men of Israel said, The counsel of Hushai the Archite is better than the counsel of Ahithophel. For the LORD had appointed to defeat the good counsel of Ahithophel, to the intent that the LORD might bring evil upon Absalom.

Hushai communicates with David—15. Then said Hushai unto Zadok and to Abiathar the priests, Thus and thus did Ahithophel counsel Absalom and the elders of Israel; and thus and thus have I counseled. 16. Now therefore send quickly, and tell David, saying, Lodge not this night in the plains of the wilderness, but speedily pass over; lest the king be swallowed up, and all the people that are with him. 17. Now Jonathan and Ahimaaz stayed by En-rogel; for they might not be seen to come into the city: and a wench went and told them; and they went and told king David.

Adventures of the secret service messengers—18. Nevertheless, a lad saw them, and told Absalom: but they went both of them away quickly, and came to a man's house in Bahurim, which had a well in his court; whither they went down. 19. And the woman took and spread a covering over the well's mouth and spread ground corn thereon; and the thing was not known. 20. And when Absalom's servants came to the woman to the house, they said, where is Ahiinaaz and Jonathan? And the woman said unto them, They be gone over the brook of water. And when they had sought and could *not* find them, they returned to Jerusalem. 21. And it came to pass, after they were departed, that they came up out of the well, and went and told king David, and said unto David, Arise, and pass quickly over the water: for thus hath Ahithophel counselled against you. 22. Then David arose, and all the people that were with him, and they passed over Jordan: by the morning light there lacked not one of them that was not gone over Jordan.

Suicide   of   Ahithophel—23.   And   when Ahithophel saw that his counsel was not followed, he saddled his ass, and arose, and gat him home to his house, to his city, and put

17. **En-rogel,** "The Fullers' Spring," was at the junction of the valleys of Hinnom and Kedron, just outside Jerusalem, to the south-east.

his household in order, and hanged himself, and died, and was buried in the sepulchre of his father.

Movements of the forces—24. Then David came to Mahanaim. And Absalom passed over Jordan, he and all the men of Israel with him. 25. And Absalom made Amasa captain of the host instead of Joab: which Amasa *was son of Abigail,* sister to Zeruiah Joab's mother. 26. So Israel and Absalom pitched in the land of Gilead. 27. And it came to pass, when David was come *to* Mahanaim, that Shobi the son of Nahash of Rabbah of the children of Ammon, and Machir the son of Ammiel of Lodebar, and Barzillai the Gileadite of Rogelim, 28. brought beds, and basons; and earthen vessels, and wheat, and barley, and flour, and parched corn, and beans, and lentiles, and parched pulse, 29. and honey, and butter, and sheep, and cheese of kine, for David, and for the people that were with him, to eat: for they said, The people is hungry, and weary, and thirsty, in the wilderness.

(d) The Battle of Ephraim Forest

Attack orders issued to the troops—18:1. And David numbered the people that were with him and set captains of thousands and captains of hundreds over them. 2. And David sent forth a third part of the people under the hand of Joab, and a third part under the hand of Abishai the son of Zeruiah, Joab's brother, and a third part under the hand of Ittai the Gittite. And the king said unto the people, I will surely go forth with you myself also. 3. But the people answered, Thou shalt not go forth: for if we flee away, they will not care for us; neither if half of us die, will they care for us: but now thou art worth ten thousand of us: therefore now it is better that thou succor us out of the city. 4. And the king said unto them, What seemeth you best I will do. And the king stood by the gate side, and all the people came out by hundreds and by thousands. 5. And the king commanded

17:1. If Ahithophel's advice had been followed David would have been surprised before he had taken these measures to organize his supporters.

Joab and Abishai and Ittai, saying, Deal gently for my sake with the young man, even with Absalom. And all the people heard when the king gave all the captains charge concerning Absalom.

Defeat of the insurgents—6. So the people went out into the field against Israel: and the battle was in the wood of Ephraim; 7. where the people of Israel were slain before the servants of David, and there was there a great slaughter that day of twenty thousand men. 8. For the battle was there scattered over the face of all the country: and the wood devoured more people that day than the sword devoured.

Absalom's fate—9. And Absalom met the servants of David. And Absalom rode upon a mule, and the mule went under the thick boughs of a great oak, and his head caught hold of the oak, and he was taken up between the heaven and the earth; and the mule that was under him went away. 1 0 . And a certain man saw it, and told Joab, and said, Behold I saw Absalom hanged in an oak. 11. And Joab said unto the man that told him, And behold, thou sawest him, and why didst thou not smite him there to the ground? and I would have given thee ten shekels of silver, and a girdle. 12. And the man said unto Joab, Though I should receive a thousand shekels of silver in mine hand, yet would I not put forth mine hand against the king's son: for in our hearing the king charged thee and Abishai and Ittai, saying, Beware that none touch the young man Absalom. 13. Otherwise I should have wrought falsehood against mine own life: for there is no matter hid from the king, and thou thyself wouldest have set thyself against me. 14. Then said Joab, I may not tarry thus with thee. And he took three darts in his hand, and thrust them through the heart of Absalom, while he was yet alive in the midst of the oak. 15. And ten young men that bare Joab's armor compassed about and smote Absalom and slew him. 16. And Joab blew the trumpet,

---

6. The exact site in Gilead of the forest or jungle of Ephraim is unknown. It was clearly on the Jordan side of Mahanaim (see verse 23). For a general description of the locality see *H.G.H.L.*, pp. 335 *n.*, 522, 580.

3. **the wood devoured**. The "sea of rocks" and jungle presented death-traps to the fugitives on every side.

and the people returned from pursuing after Israel: for Joab held back the people. 17. And they took Absalom and cast him into a great pit in the wood, and laid a very great heap of stones upon h im: and all Israel fled everyone *to* his tent.

His memorial stone—18. Now Absalom in his l ifetime had taken and reared up for himself a pillar, which is in the king's dale: for he said, I have no son *to* keep my name remembrance: and he called the pillar after his own name: and it is called unto this day, Absalom's *monument.*

How the news was brought to David at Mahanaim—19. Then said Ahimaaz the son of Zadok, Let me now run, and bear the king tidings, how that the LORD hath avenged him of his enemies. 20. And Joab said unto him, Thou shalt not bear tidings this day, but thou shalt bear tidings another day: but this day thou shalt bear no tidings, because the king's son is dead. 21. Then said Joab *to a Cushite,* Go tell the king what thou hast seen. And *the Cushite* bowed himself unto Joab, and ran. 21. Then said Ahimaaz the son of Zadok yet again *to* Joab, But howsoever, let me, I pray thee, also run after *the Cushite.* And Joab said, Wherefore wilt thou run, my son, seeing that thou hast no tidings ready? 23. But howsoever, said he, let me run. And he said unto him, Run. Then Ahimaaz ran by the way of the plain and overran *the Cushite.* 24. And David sat between the two gates: and the watchman went up *to* the roof over the gate unto the wall, and lifted up his eyes, and looked, and behold a man running alone. 25. And the watchman cried, and told the king. And the king said, If he be alone, there is tidings in his mouth. And he came apace and drew near. 26. And the watchman saw another man running: and the watchman called unto the porter, and said, Behold another man running alone. And the king said, He also bringeth tidings. 27. And the watchman

18. **the king's dale** was somewhere near Jerusalem.

20. Joab was unwilling to allow Ahimaaz to be the bearer of disastrous tidings: precedent in the cases of Saul's and Abner's deaths warned him of the risk such a messenger ran. So he despatched a negro slave, the Cushite, whose life was regarded as of less value.

23. Ahmimaaz took the longer but easier course *via* the Jordan valley; the slave ran across country.

said, Me thinketh the running of the foremost is like the running of Ahimaaz the son of Zadok. And the king said, He is a good man, and cometh with good tidings. 28. And Ahimaaz called, and said unto the king, *Peace I* And he fell down to the earth upon his face before the king, and said, Blessed be the LORD thy God, which hath delivered up the men that lifted up their hand against my Lord the king. 29. And the king said, Is the young man Absalom safe? And Ahimaaz answered, When Joab sent the king's servant, and me thy servant, I saw a great tumult, but I knew not what it was. 30. And the king said unto him, Turn aside, and stand here. And he turned aside, and stood still. 31. And, behold, *the Cushite* came; and *the Cushite* said, Tidings, my Lord the king: for the LORD hath avenged thee this day of all them that rose up against thee. 32. And the king said unto *the Cushite,* Is the young man Absalom safe? And *the Cushite* answered, The enemies of my Lord the king, and all that rise against thee to do thee hurt, be as that young man is.

The king is broken-hearted—33. And the king was much moved, and went up to the chamber over the gate, and wept: and as he went, thus he said, O my son Absalom, my son, my son, Absalom! would God I had died for thee, O Absalom, my son, my son!

Joab's rough rebuke recalls him to a sense of his duty—19:1 And it was told Joab, Behold, the king weepeth and mourneth for Absalom. 2. And the victory that day was turned into mourning unto all the people: for the people heard say that day how the king was grieved for his son. 3. And the people gat them by stealth that day into the city, as people being ashamed steal away when they flee in battle. 4. But the king covered his face, and the king cried with a loud voice, Only son Absalom, O Absalom, my son, my son! 5. And Joab came into the house to the king, and said, Thou hast shamed this day the faces of all thy servants, which this day have saved thy life, and the lives of thy sons and of thy daughters and the lives of thy wives, and the lives of thy concubines;

5. Joab's masculine common sense and his genuine loyalty to the throne—in spite of a certain brutality in his methods—were conspicuous on this as on other occasions.

III-II

6. in that thou lovest thine enemies, and hatest thy friends. For thou hast declared this day, that thou regardest neither princes nor servants: for this day I perceive, that if Absalom had lived, and all we had died this day, then it had pleased thee well. 7. Now therefore arise, go forth, and speak comfortably unto thy servants: for I swear by the LORD, if thou go not forth, there will not tarry one with thee this night: and that will be worse unto thee than all the evil that befell thee from thy youth until now. 8a. Then the king arose and sat in the gate. And they told unto all the people, saying, Behold, the king doth sit in the gate. And all the people came before the king.

(e) The King's Return to His Capital

Revulsion of feeling in the North—8b. *Now* Israel had fled every man to his tent. 9. And all the people were at strife throughout all the tribes of Israel, saying, The king saved us out of the hand of our enemies, and he delivered us out of the hand of the Philistines; and now he is fled out of the land for Absalom. 10. And Absalom, whom we anointed over us, is dead in battle. Now therefore why speak ye not a word of bringing the king back?

David's liberal overtures to the South—11. And king David sent to Zadok and to Abiathar the priests, saying, Speak unto the elders of Judah, saying, Why are ye the last to bring the king back to his house? seeing the speech of all Israel is come to the king, even to his house. 12. Ye are my brethren, ye are my bones and my flesh: wherefore then are ye the last to bring back the king? 13. And say ye to Amasa, Art thou not of my bone, and of my flesh? God do so to me, and more also, if thou be not captain of the host before me continually in the room of Joab. 14. And he bowed the heart of all the men of Judah, even as the heart of one man; so that they sent this word unto the king, Return thou, and all thy servants. 15. So the king returned and came to Jordan. And Judah came

11. **all Israel,** *i.e.,* the northern tribes, as opposed to the "irreconcilables" of Judah.

to Gilgal, to go to meet the king, to conduct the king over Jordan.

The cringing and officious fear of two apprehensive rascals—16. And Shimei the son of Gera, a Benjamite, which was of Bahurim, hasted and came down with the men of Judah to meet king David. 17. And there were a thousand men of Benjamin with him, and Ziba the servant of the house of Saul, and his fifteen sons and his twenty servants with him; and they *dashed into* Jordan *in the presence of* the king. 18. And *they kept crossing the ford* to carry over the king's household, and to do what he thought good. And Shimei the son of Gera fell down before the king, as he was come over Jordan; 19. and said unto the king, Let not my Lord impute iniquity unto me, neither do thou remember that which thy servant did perversely the day that my Lord the king went qut of Jerusalem, that the king should take it to his heart. 20. For thy servant doth know that I have sinned: therefore, behold, I am come the first this day of all the house of Joseph to go down to meet my Lord the king. 21. But Abishai the son of Zeruiah answered and said, Shall not Shimei be put to death for this, because he cursed the LORD's anointed? 22. And David said, what have I to do with you, ye sons of Zeruiah, that ye should this day be adversaries unto me? shall there any man be put to death this day in Israel? for do not I know that I am this day king over Israel? 23. Therefore the king said unto Shimei, Thou shalt not die. And the king sware unto him.

Mephibosheth disposes of Ziba's calumny against him—24. And Mephibosheth the son of Saul came down to meet the king, and had neither dressed his feet, nor trimmed his beard, nor washed his clothes, from the day the king departed until the day he came again in peace. 25. And it came *to* pass, when he was come from Jerusalem to meet

20. **house of Joseph.** Shimei was a Benjamite, a tribe always associated with Judah and the South. Here the crafty villain tries to curry favor by pretending that the Benjamites were northerners and he the first of them to felicitate the triumphant king. There was some justice in his subsequent execution by Solomon (1 Kings 2). Another view, however, is that Shimei's conduct was excusable since David had shed the blood of his kinsfolk. (see pp. 129 and 154, verse 5).

the king, that the king said unto him, Wherefore wentest not thou with me, Mephibosheth? 26. And he answered, My Lord, O king, my servant deceived me: for thy servant said, Saddle me an ass, that I may ride thereon, and go to the king; because thy servant is lame. 27. And he hath slandered thy servant unto my Lord the king; but my Lord the king is as an angel of God: do therefore what is good in thine eyes. 28. For all of my father's house were but dead men before my Lord the king: yet didst thou set thy servant among them that did eat at thine own table. What right therefore have I yet to cry any more unto the king? 29. And the king said unto him, why speakest thou any more of thy matters? I have said, Thou and Ziba divide the land. 30. And Mephibosheth said unto the king, Yea, let him take all, forasmuch as my Lord the king is come again in peace unto his own house.

David's affectionate farewell to Barzillai—31. And Barzillai the Gileadite came down from Rogelim, and went with the king, to conduct him over Jordan. 32. Now Barzillai was a very aged man, even fourscore years old: and he had provided the king of sustenance while he lay at Mahanaim; for: he was a very great man. 33. And the king said unto Barzillai, Come thou over with me, and I will feed thee with me in Jerusalem. 34. And Barzillai said unto the king, How long have I to live, that I should go up with the king unto Jerusalem? 35. I am this day fourscore years old: and can I discern between good and evil? can thy servant taste what I eat or what I drink? can I hear any more the voice of singing men and singing women? wherefore then should thy servant be yet a burden unto my Lord the king? 36. Thy servant will go a little way over Jordan with the king: and why should the king recompense it me with such a reward? 37. Let thy servant, I pray thee, turn back again, that I may die in mine own city, and be buried by the grave of my father and of my mother. But behold thy servant Chimham; let him go over with my Lord the king; and do to him

26. *sc.* "But Ziba went off without fulfilling my orders."

29. "Say no more about it. I quite understand." Was David's compromise just? If Mephibosheth was found innocent should not David have restored *all* his land to him?

37. **Chimham** was Barzillai's son.

what shall seem good unto thee. 38. And the king answered, Chimham shall go over with me, and I will do to him that which shall seem good unto thee: and whatsoever thou shalt require of me, that will I do for thee. 39. And all the people went over Jordan. And when the king was come over, the king kissed Barzillai, and blessed him; and he returned unto his own place.

Jealousy between the North and the South—40. Then the king went on to Gilgal, and Chimham went on with him: and all the people of Judah conducted the king, and also half the people of Israel. 41. And, behold, all the men of Israel came to the king, and said unto the king, Why have our brethren the men of Judah stolen thee away, and have brought the king, and his household, and all David's men with him, over Jordan? 42. And all the men of Judah answered the men of Israel, Because the king is near of kin to us: wherefore then be ye angry for this matter? have we eaten at all of the king's cost? or hath he given us any gift? 43. And the men of Israel answered the men of Judah, and said, We have ten parts in the king, and we have also more right in David than ye: why then did ye despise us? *Were not we the first to speak of bringing back our king?* And the words of the men of Judah were fiercer than the words of the men of Israel.

SHEBA'S REVOLT

2 Samuel 20: 1-22

Sheba shows his colors—1. And there happened *to* be there a man of Belial, whose name was Sheba, the son of Bichri, a Benjamite: and he blew a trumpet, and said, we have no part in David, neither have we inheritance in

41. David's finesse (verses 11 *seq.* above) by which he had brought Judah to his feet produced a result which he little anticipated. Instead of consolidating the two provinces in a loyal adherence to the throne, he only succeeded in accentuating the rivalry between them, which led almost immediately to Sheba's revolt.

42. **have we eaten,** etc. "Our fidelity to the king is purely disinterested; we do not gain anything by it financially."

20:1. Sheba takes advantage of the growing animosity recorded in the last chapter to reopen the wound in the breast of Benjamin caused by the displacement of Saul's dynasty. His party catchword means "Down with the monarchy; revert to tribal institutions."

the son of Jesse: every man to his tents, O Israel. 2. So every man of Israel went up from after David and followed Sheba the son of Bichri: but the men of Judah clave unto their king, from Jordan even to Jerusalem.

Punishment of the women who had consented to Absalom's usurpation—3. And David came to his house at Jerusalem; and the king took the ten women his concubines, whom he had left to keep the house, and put them in ward, and fed them. So they were shut up unto the day of their death, living in widowhood.

Murder of Amasa—4. Then said the king to Amasa, Assemble me the men of Judah within three days, and be thou here present. 5. So Amasa went to assemble the men of Judah: but he tarried longer than the set time which he had appointed him. 6.And David said to Abishai, Now shall Sheba the son of Bichri do us more harm than did Absalom: take thou thy Lord's servants, and pursue after him, lest he get him fenced cities, and escape us. 7. And there went out after him Joab, and the Cherethites, and the Pelethites, and all the mighty men: and they went out of Jerusalem to pursue after Sheba the son of Bichri. 8. When they were at the great stone which is in Gibeon, Amasa *came to meet* them. And Joab's garment that he had put on was girded unto him, and upon it a girdle with a sword fastened upon his loins in the sheath thereof; and as he went forth it fell out. 9. And Joab said to Amasa, Art thou in health, my brother? And Joab took Amasa by the beard with the right hand to kiss him. 10. But Amasa took no heed to the sword that was in Joab's hand: so he smote him therewith in the fifth rib, and shed out his bowels to the ground, and struck him not again; and he died. So Joab and

4. **Amasa,** still, it would seem at heart disloyal, had been appointed *generalissimo* in place of Joab in accordance with David's threat that he would punish Joab's disobedience in killing Absalom.

6. By commissioning Abishai David was virtually re-employing Joab, the stronger partner, as the sequel proved.

8. The corrupt text conceals some such statement as this: Underneath his garment Joab held a hidden rapier in his left hand as he approached Amasa. His military sword, which was plain to view, slipped from its sheath, probably by its wearer's design, to prevent suspicion of his intentions.

Abishai his brother pursued after Sheba the son of Bichri. 11. And one of Joab's men stood by him, and said, He that favoreth Joab, and he that is for David, let him go after Joab. 12; And Amasa wallowed in blood in the midst of the highway. And when the man saw that all the people stood still, he removed Amasa out of the highway into the field, and cast a cloth upon him, when he saw that every one that came by him stood still. 13. When he was removed out of the highway, all the people went on after Joab, to pursue after Sheba the son of Bichri.

Siege of Sheba in Abel-beth-maachah—14. And *Sheba* went through all the tribes of Israel unto *Abel-bethmaachah,* and all the *Bichrites* were gathered together, and went also after him. 15. And they came and besieged him in Abel of Beth-maachah, and they cast up a bank against the city, and it stood *against the rampart:* and all the people that were with Joab battered the wall, to throw it down.

The city itself is saved—16. Then cried a wise woman out of the city, Hear, hear; say, I pray you, unto Joab, Come near hither, that I may speak with thee. 17. And when he was come near unto her, the woman said, Art thou Joab? And he answered, I am he. Then she said unto him, Hear the words of thine handmaid. And he answered, I do hear. 18. Then she spake, saying, They were wont to speak in old time, saying, *Let them ask in Abel and in Dan whether what the faithful in Israel established has come to an end. 19.* Thou seekest to destroy a city and a mother in Israel: why wilt thou Swallow up the inheritance of the LORD? 20. And Joab answered and said, Far be it, far be it from me, that I should swallow up or destroy. 21. The matter is not so: but a man of mount Ephraim, Sheba the son of Bichri by name, hath lifted up his hand against the king, even against David:

11. Joab stationed a "connecting file" at the spot, who should direct the supporting column to follow on after their new, selfappointed general.

14. Sheba's own clan, the Bichrites, seem to represent his only supporters. They concentrated in a town in the extreme north, just west of Dan.

18. "Abel has become a proverb for its loyalty to national institutions. Why do you seek to batter it down?"

deliver him only, and I will depart from the city. And the woman said unto Joab, Behold, his head shall be thrown to thee *over* the wall.

But the traitor's head delivered to the royal forces—22. Then the woman went unto all the people in her wisdom. And they cut off the head of Sheba the son of Bichri and cast it out to Joab. And he blew a trumpet, and they retired from the city, every man to his tent. And Joab returned to Jerusalem unto the king.

ATTEMPTED USURPATION OF ADONIJAH

1 Kings 1

The ministrations of Abishag—1. Now king David was old and stricken in years; and they covered him with clothes, but he gat no heat. 2. Wherefore his servants said unto him, Let there be sought for my Lord the king a young virgin: and let her stand before the king, and let her cherish him, and let her lie in thy bosom, that my Lord the king may get heat. 3. So they sought for a fair damsel throughout all the coasts of Israel, and found Abishag a Shunammite, and brought her to the king. 4. And the damsel was very fair, and cherished the king, and ministered to him.

Adonijah imitates the bad example of Absalom—5. Then Adonijah the son of Haggith exalted himself, saying, I will be king: and he prepared him chariots and horsemen, and fifty men to run before him. 6. And his father had not displeased him at any time in saying, Why hast thou done so? and he also was a very goodly man; and *he was born* after Absalom. 7. And he conferred with Joab the son of Zeruiah, and with Abiathar the priest: and they following Adonijah helped him. 8. But Zadok the priest, and Benaiah the son of Jehoiada, and Nathan the prophet, and Shimei, and Rei, and the mighty men which

3. Abishag came from Shunem, the town (p. 96) on the north side of the valley of Jezreel.

6. **Adonijah** was Absalom's half-brother, and next to him in order of seniority.

8. **Shimei and Rei** were court officials, and friends of Solomon. Shimei is not to be confused wit, his ill-favored namesake above.

belonged to David, were not with Adonijah. 9. And Adonijah slew sheep and oxen and fat cattle by the stone of Zoheleth, which is by En-rogel, and called all his brethren the king's sons; and all the men of Judah the king's servants: 10. but Nathan the prophet, and Benaiah, and the mighty men, and Solomon his brother, he called not.

Nathan's plan to ensure Solomon's succession—11. Wherefore Nathan spake unto Bath-sheba the mother of Solomon, saying, Hast thou not heard that Adonijah the son of Haggith doth reign, and David our Lord knoweth it not? 12. Now therefore *come,* let me, I pray thee, give thee counsel, that thou mayest save thine own life, and the life of thy son Solomon. 13. Go and get thee in unto king David, and say unto him, Didst not thou, my Lord, O king, swear unto thine handmaid, saying, Assuredly Solomon thy son shall reign after me, and he shall sit upon my throne? why then doth Adonijah reign? 14. Behold, while thou yet talkest there with the king, I also will come in after thee, and confirm thy words.

Bathsheba urges the claims of Solomon—15. And Bathsheba went in unto the king into the chamber: and the king was very old; and Abishag the Shunammite ministered unto the king. 16. And Bathsheba bowed and did obeisance unto the king. And the king said, What wouldest thou? 17. And she said unto him, My Lord, thou swarest by the LORD thy God unto thine handmaid, saying, Assuredly Solomon thy son shall reign after me, and he shall sit upon my throne. 18. And now, behold, Adonijah reigneth; and now, my Lord the king, thou knowest it not: 19. and he hath slain oxen and fat cattle

9. **Zoheleth** = "the serpent's stone," by En-rogel (p. 157).
slew, sacrificed.
10. **the mighty men** = the warriors of the standing army (see p. 139).

13. The suggestion of the context perhaps is that this previous promise of the throne to Solomon was invented by Nathan and Bathsheba for the occasion. They relied on David's failing memory— he was seventy and worn out— not to detect that they were imposing on him. In speaking to the king about Solomon, the two pretended to be acting quite independently of each other. Was their conduct altogether creditable? On the other hand the promise may have been a genuine one, of which we have no other record,

and sheep in abundance, and hath called all the sons of the king, and Abiathar the priest, and Joab the captain of the host: but Solomon thy servant hath he not called. 20. And thou, my Lord, O king, the eyes of all Israel are upon thee, that thou shouldest tell them who shall sit on the throne of my Lord the king after him. 21. Otherwise it shall come to pass, when my Lord the king shall sleep with his fathers, that I and my son Solomon shall be counted offenders.

She is seconded by Nathan—22. And, lo, while she yet talked with the king, Nathan the prophet also came in. 23. And they told the king, saying, Behold Nathan the prophet. And when he was come in before the king, he bowed himself before the king with his face to the ground. 24. And Nathan said, My Lord, O king, hast thou said, Adonijah shall reign after me, and he shall sit upon my throne? 25. For he is gone down this day, and hath slain oxen and fat cattle and sheep in abundance, and hath called all the king's sons, and the captains of the host, and Abiathar the priest; and, behold, they eat and drink before him, and say, God save king Adonijah. 26. But me, even me thy servant, and Zadok the priest, and Benaiah the son of Jehoiada, and thy servant Solomon, hath he not called. 27. Is this thing done by my Lord the king, and thou hast not shewed it unto thy servant, who should sit on the throne of my Lord the king after him?

David confirms the succession to Solomon—28. Then king David answered and said, Call me Bath-sheba. And she came into the king's presence and stood before the king. 29. And the king sware, and said, As the LORD liveth, that hath redeemed my soul out of all distress, 30. even as I sware unto thee by the LORD God of Israel, saying, Assuredly Solomon thy son shall reign after me, and he shall sit upon my throne in my stead; even so will I certainly do this day. 31. Then Bath-sheba bowed with her face to the earth, and did reverence to the king, and said, Let my Lord king David live forver.

28. Either Bathsheba had retired, or the aged king, who seems now to have been bedridden (verse 47), was too blind to see her still in the room.

His command that Solomon should be proclaimed king forthwith—32. And king David said, Call me Zadok the priest, and Nathan the prophet, and Benaiah the son of Jehoiada. And they came before the king. 33. The king also said unto them, Take with you the servants of your Lord, and cause Solomon my son to ride upon mine Own mule, and bring him down to Gihon: 34. and let Zadok the priest and Nathan the prophet anoint him there king over Israel: and blow ye with the trumpet, and say, God save king Solomon. 35. Then ye shall come up after him, that he may come and sit upon my throne; for he shall be king in my stead: and I have appointed him to be ruler over Israel and over Judah. 36. And Benaiah the son of Jehoiada answered the king, and said, Amen: the LORD God of my Lord the king say so too. 37. As the LORD hath been with my Lord the king, even so be he with Solomon, and make his throne greater than the throne of my Lord king David.

"Coronation" of Solomon—38. So Zadok the priest, and Nathan the prophet, and Benaiah the son of Jehoiada, and the Cherethites, and the Pelethites, went down, and caused Solomon to ride upon king David's mule, and brought him to Gihon. 39. And Zadok the priest took an horn of oil out of the tabernacle, and anointed Solomon. And they blew the trumpet; and all the people said, God save king Solomon. 40. And all the people came up after him, and the people piped with pipes, and rejoiced with great joy, so that the earth rent with the sound of them.

Announcement of this to the conspirators—41. And Adonijah and all the guests that were with him heard it as they had made an end of eating. And when Joab heard the sound of the trumpet, he said, Wherefore is this noise of the city being in an uproar? 42. And while he yet spake, behold, Jonathan the son of Abiathar the priest came: and Adonijah said unto him, Come in; for

---

33. **Gihon.** One of the fountains of that name close to the city, either (a) that on the west side beyond the Valley of Hinnom, or (b) that on the south-east, now called The Virgin's Fount, close to En-rogel. The former is preferable, since Adonijah's party already in the vicinity of En-rogel (see verses 9 and 41).

thou art a valiant man, and bringest good tidings. 43. And Jonathan answered and said to Adonijah, Verily our Lord king David hath made Solomon king. 44. And the king hath sent with him Zadok the priest, and Nathan the prophet, and Benaiah the son of Jehoiada, and the Cherethites, and the Pelethites, and they have caused him to ride upon the king's mule: 45. and Zadok the priest and Nathan the prophet have anointed him king in Gihon: and they are come up from thence rejoicing, so that the city rang again. This is the noise that ye have heard. 46. And also Solomon sitteth on the throne of the kingdom. 47. And moreover the king's servants came to bless our Lord king David, saying, God make the name of Solomon better than thy name, and make his throne greater than thy throne. And the king bowed himself upon the bed. 48. And also thus said the king, Blessed be the LORD God of Israel, which hath given one to sit on my throne this day, mine eyes even seeing it. 49. And all the guests that were with Adonijah were afraid, arid rose up, and went every man his way.

Adonijah is pardoned—*50.* And Adonijah feared because of Solomon, and arose, and went, and caught hold on the horns of the altar. 51. And it was told Solomon, saying, Behold, Adonijah feareth king Solomon: for, lo, he hath caught hold on the horns of the altar, saying, Let king Solomon swear unto me today that he will not slay his servant with the sword. 52. And Solomon said, If he will shew himself a worthy man, there shall not an hair of him fall to the earth: but if wickedness shall be found in him, he shall die. 53. So king Solomon sent, and they brought him down from the altar. And he came and bowed himself to king Solomon: and Solomon said unto him, Go to thine house.

50. To cling to the altar was generally accounted a security from pursuit in ancient times. The altar was an asylum, and it was sacrilege to drag a fugitive away or to slay him there.

Biblical history, perhaps, has hardly done justice to Adonijah. Court intrigues to secure the succession to the decrepit monarch's throne were rife. Adonijah had, as the elder, at least as much right to his expectations as Solomon; and, as the text shows, he had a strong and highly reputable party on his side. For an examination of the historical difficulties presented by the Bible text see *H.D.B.,* p. 13.

THE CLOSING SCENES OF DAVID'S LIFE

1 Kings 2 : 1-4, 10 ; 1 Chron. 28:1-10, 29:10-19; 2 Samuel 23 : 1-7

His charge to Solomon—2:1. Now the days of David drew nigh that he should die; and he charged Solomon his son, saying, 2. I go the way of all the earth: be thou strong therefore, and shew thyself a man; 3. and keep the charge of the LORD thy God, to walk in his ways, to keep his statutes, and his commandments, and his judgements, and his testimonies, as it is written in the law of Moses, that thou mayest prosper in all that thou doest, and whithersoever thou turnest thyself: 4. that the LORD may continue his word which he spake concerning me, saying, If thy children take heed to their way, to walk before me in truth with all their heart and with all their soul, there shall not fail thee (said he) a man on the throne of Israel.

*The account of the Ecclesiastical Chronicler of a later age—*1 Chron. 28:1. And David assembled all the princes of Israel, the princes of the tribes, and the captains of the companies that ministered to the king by course, and the captains over the thousands, and captains over the hundreds, and the stewards over all the substance and possession of the king, and of his sons, with the officers, and with the mighty men, and with all the valiant men, unto Jerusalem.

His forethought for the Temple—2. Then David the king stood up upon his feet, and said, Hear me, my brethren, and my people: As for me, I had in mine heart to build an house of rest for the ark of the covenant of the LORD, and for the footstool of our God, and had made ready for the building: 3. but God said unto me, Thou shalt not build an house for my name, because thou hast been a man of war, and hast shed blood. 4. Howbeit the LORD

4. In the judgment of the present editors it would be an error to mar the historical portrait of David presented in *Samuel* by introducing here the unworthy testament attributed to him in 1 Kings 2 : 5-9. That passage stands condemned as "the libel of a later hand seeking to invest him with a fictitious glory" (Well.), on evidence both literary and historical. (See Kent *ad loc.)* Those who retain the passage explain its harshness by assuming that David at this time was too decrepit intellectually to be responsible for his actions.

God of Israel chose me before all the house of my father to be king over Israel for ever: for he hath chosen Judah to be the ruler; and of the house of Judah, the house of my father; and among the sons of my father he liked me to make me king over all Israel: 5. and of all my sons (for the LORD hath given me many sons), he hath chosen Solomon my son to sit upon the throne of the kingdom of the LORD over Israel. 6. And he said unto me, Solomon thy son, he shall build my house and my courts: for I have chosen him to be my son, and I will be his father. 7. Moreover I will establish his kingdom fore ver, if he be constant to do my commandments and my judgments, as at this day. 8. Now therefore in the sight of all Israel the congregation of the LORD, and in the audience of our God; keep and seek for all the commandments of the LORD your God: that ye may possess this good land and leave it for an inheritance for your children after you fore ver.

Exhortation to Solomon—9. And thou, Solomon my son, know thou the God of thy father, and serve him with a perfect heart and with a willing mind: for the LORD searcheth all hearts, and understandeth all the imaginations of the thoughts: if thou seek him, he will be found of thee; but if thou forsake him, he will cast thee off fore ver. 1 0. Take heed now; for the LORD hath chosen thee to build an house for the sanctuary: be strong, and do it. *[Then follow David's instructions as to the manner of building and equipping the Temple, and the people's promises of gifts for that purpose.]*

His prayer and thanksgiving—29:1 0. Wherefore David blessed the LORD before all the congregation: and David said, Blessed be thou, LORD God of Israel our father, for ever and ever. 11. Thine, O LORD, is the greatness, and the power and the glory, and the victory, and the majesty: for all that is in the heaven and in the earth is thine; thine is the kingdom, O LORD, and thou art exalted as head above all. 12. Both riches and honor come of thee, and thou reignest over all; and in thine hand is power and light; and in thine hand it is to make great, and *to* give strength unto all. 13. Now therefore, our God, we thank thee, and praise thy glorious name.

14. But who am I, and what is my people, that we should be able to offer so willingly after this sort? for all things come of thee, and of thine own have we given thee. 15. For we are strangers before thee, and sojourners, as were all our fathers: our days on the earth are as a shadow, and there is none abiding. 16. O LORD our God, all this store that we have prepared to build thee an house for thine holy name cometh of thine hand, and is all thine own. 17. I know also, my God, that thou triest the heart, and hast pleasure in uprightness. As for me, in the uprightness of mine heart I have willingly offered all these things: and now have I seen with joy thy people, which are present here, *to* offer willingly unto thee. 18. O LORD God of Abraham, Isaac, and of Israel, our fathers, keep this fore ver in the imagination of the thoughts of the heart of thy people, and prepare their heart unto thee: 19. and give unto Solomon my son a perfect heart, *to* keep thy commandments, thy testimonies, and thy statutes, and to do all these things, and to build the palace, for the which I have made provision.

His "LAST WORDS"

2 Samuel 2 3 : 1

Now these be the last words of David:
1.   David the son of Jesse said,
       And the man who was raised up on high said,
       The anointed of the God of Jacob
       And the sweet psalmist of Israel:
2.   The Spirit of the LORD spake by me
       And his word was in my tongue.

1. **the last words.** This poem—the text of which is corrupt and difficult—is of comparatively late date. Like the blessings of Jacob (Gen. 49) and Moses (Deut. 33), it is a melodious farewell such as the poets of all times "love to put into the mouth of the dying heroes of the past."
raised up on high = exalted by God.
sweet psalmist of Israel. Rather, "the darling of the songs of Israel." David is their theme, not, in the present passage, their composer.

3.   The God of Israel said,
   The Rock of Israel spake to me:
   "He that ruleth over men righteously,
   Ruling in the fear of God,
4.   Like the light of morning shall he rise,
   The sun of a cloudless morn,
   Making the green earth brilliant after rain."
5.   Established is my house with God,
   For he hath made me an everlasting covenant,
   Ordered in all things, and sure:
   For all my salvation and all my delight are in him.
6.   But the sons of Belial shall not flourish,
   They are like thorns of the desert, all of them,
   Which are not harvested by the hand,
   Nor doth a man labour for them.
7.   Though armed with iron and spear
   They shall be utterly consumed with fire.

His DEATH

1 Kings 2:10

So David slept with his fathers, and was buried in the city of David.

3, 4. Contain the real theme of the poem—a eulogy of the ideal ruler.

5. Refers to chap. 7, God's assurance of the permanence of David's dynasty.

7. they in the last line = the sons of Belial. The translation given above is almost throughout the poem that of H.P. Smith. The A.V. version is, in the latter part, unintelligible.

APPENDIX

THE FORMATION OF THE OLD TESTAMENT
CANON

1. Canon primarily means the "standard" to which a book, or portion of a book, must attain in respect of its historical, moral, and religious value, in order to be ranked among the authoritative sacred Scriptures. Hence the term, from being used of the standard by which a book was judged, has come to be applied to the body of books themselves, which have satisfied the requirements of this standard. Thus the "Old Testament Canon" means those sacred books of Hebrew literature which were judged by the Hebrews to satisfy these requirements, just as the "New Testament Canon" means that body of sacred books which were judged by the early Christian Church to satisfy the requirements of the Christian standard. These two bodies of sacred literature, the one translated from the original Hebrew and Aramaic, the other translated from the original Greek, together form our Bible.

Besides those books which are included in the Old Testament and the New Testament, there existed many, and exist some, which, though valuable in their religious and moral teaching, were yet not considered sufficiently valuable to be admitted respectively into the Old Testament and New Testament Canons Such books are called

Apocryphal; that is, obscure, unrecognized, or spurious. Some of these are comprised in the "Apocrypha," which is often bound up with our modern Bibles, being placed after the end of the Old Testament. Parts of this are read in the English Church services, since they afford a good "example of life and instruction of manners."

There is, derived from the other two, yet a third meaning of the term "Canon." Since the sacred writings which are admitted into the Bible conform to a given standard, so in their turn they form the standard by which religious doctrines are judged. A doctrine, or belief, is canonical if it can be justified by the authority of the canonical books of the Bible; it is uncanonical, though not necessarily wrong, if it cannot thus be proved.

2. How and when was it decided which of the books of Hebrew sacred literature were worthy to be accounted canonical, and which should be relegated to the lower sphere of uncanonical works? In other words, when did the Hebrews decide what was, and what was not, part of their "Bible"? The answer is this. The Canon was not suddenly fixed by any one body of men, by any council, nor at any one time. It was the gradual result of criticism, appreciation, use, and experience. If any part of their sacred writings. was felt by the Jews to be valuable and useful and helpful and true, and was therefore continuously used by them as a source of their knowledge of God, and recognized as being part of His message by which He gradually, and more and more clearly as time went on, revealed Himself to them and showed them what He would have them be, and what His purpose, was towards them, then this part would be accepted by them as authoritative or canonical. Thus, part of the

Canon would have become fixed. Later on, another part would, by a similar critical process, be added to their Canon; and eventually, by about the time of our Lord, the entire Canon of the Old Testament, as we have it, would have been completed. We can, as a matter of fact, trace, though not with perfect clearness, this process. In quite early days the Decalogue was accepted in this way. It had been delivered to the Israelites by Moses, of whose personality only the most extreme critics of the Bible have ever had any doubt. To this were added in course of time the other different and more highly developed injunctions of the Hebrew law; until, after the specific promulgation of the Deuteronomic law by King Josiah in 621 B.C., and the careful collection of all their legislative documents by the scholars of the Exile, the first great part of the Canon, the Law (Torah), which we call the Pentateuch, was completed (445 B.C.).

By degrees, and by the same tests—the value, truth, and inspiration of the books—there was added to the Canon its second great volume, the Prophets (Nebhiim), as the Jews called it. This volume consisted of the following books: Joshua, Judges, Samuel, Kings, Isaiah, Jeremiah, Ezekiel, and the Twelve Minor Prophets, from Hosea to Malachi. This part of the Canon was defined before the end of the third century B.C.

The third volume of the Canon, which was called the Sacred Writings (Kethubhim, or in Greek, Hagiographa), embraced the Psalms, the Song of Solomon, Lamentations, Ruth, Chronicles, Ezra, Nehemiah, Esther, the prophet Daniel, and the Sapiential Literature, i.e., Proverbs, Job, and Ecclesiastes. It was probably accepted into the Canon by about the Christian era, though the date is not certain. Daniel, which was the last book of the Old Testament to be composed (165 B.C.), is quoted by our Lord, who refers by name, too, to the other two volumes, the Law and the Prophets; but some books in this last volume are not mentioned by our Lord or the apostles, and it is therefore argued by some that this volume was not entirely complete in their day. But this negative argument from silence is not conclusive evidence; and it is certain that the Jewish Bible in our Lord's time was practically, if not completely, identical with the Old Testament Canon as we have it. Thus the Old Testament Canon rests upon the highest possible authority, no less than that of Christ Himself. [1]

3. A word remains to be said upon the earliest version of the Hebrew Bible in a foreign language—that called the Septuagint, in Greek. This translation was rendered necessary owing to the spread of the Greek tongue as a familiar vehicle of speech, side by side with the vernacular Aramaic, throughout Syria and Palestine in the third and second centuries before Christ. Tradition has it that the work of translation was begun in the third century B.C., at Alexandria, under the auspices of Ptolemy Philadelphus, King of Egypt from 285 to 247 B.C. Of this we cannot be certain. But it is known with certainty that the work was only achieved slowly. The "Law" was the first part to be translated, and then the work was continued at different times and by different hands. Some portions of the version are far inferior to others, both in accuracy and style. At some date before the end of the pre- Christian era the translation of the whole Canon was

[1] See G. Adam Smith, Modern Criticism and the Preaching of the Old Testament, Lecture I.

eventually completed; and the result was, and is, most valuable as an assistance to the correction and interpretation of the Hebrew text as it has come down to us.

NOTE II
THE GEOGRAPHY OF PALESTINE

It is advisable, when we read the history recorded in the books of the Old Testament, that we should constantly bear in mind certain points about the geography of the Holy Land.

1. POSITION—It is at the extreme east of the Mediterranean, and forms a link between east and west, north and south, lying as it does on the main land route between Egypt, Assyria, and Asia Minor. Indeed, it is practically almost an isthmus, with the desert on one side and the sea on the other. So, in the history of the world, Hebrew and Jewish ideas have proved a connecting link between east and west, between the Semite and the Aryan.

2. SIZE—The country was tiny, the distance from "Dan to Beer-sheba," the phrase which was used to sum up the whole of Israel, being roughly 150 miles. The population was proportionately small; and the Hebrews themselves at no time occupied anything like the whole of it. In the reign of Hezekiah, after the fall of Samaria, "Judah"

The word "Hebrew" is used of the people of Israel throughout all their history. "Jew," properly applicable only to the Southern Kingdom after the fall of Samaria, came to have a wider significance until finally it denoted the whole race, as opposed to "the Gentiles," or heathen nations.

means the comparatively few towns on the highlands round Jerusalem.

3. FEATURES—The country of Palestine is as peculiar and distinctive in its features as the people who occupied it. Passing eastward from the seacoast we may mention the following divisions into which it naturally falls:

(a) The Maritime Plain, containing (in order from south to north) Philistia, the Plain of Sharon, and Phoenicia. The Plain is broken by the range of Carmel, which juts out into the sea, and stretches inland in a south-easterly direction.

(b) The Shephelah, or lowlands, sloping up to the highlands, and intersected by many streams and their valleys, the chief of which is the Plain of Dothan.

(c) The hill-country of Judah and Ephraim, to which the Hebrew population was in the main confined.

(d) The great rift, called the Arabah, leading from Dan and the Waters of Merom, continuing the Sea of Galilee, the River Jordan, and the Dead Sea, and issuing at last in the Gulf of Akaba, the north-east branch of the Red Sea. Much of this is considerably below sea-level; the Dead Sea, which is very salt, is 1,292 feet below the Mediterranean.

(e) East of the Jordan the land rises again very quickly, and only a very narrow strip intervenes before the desert is reached.

INDEX

INDEX